The Bender Gestalt Test for Young Children
Volume II, Research and Application, 1963 – 1973

The Bender Gestalt Test for Young Children

Volume II
Research and Application, 1963 – 1973

Elizabeth Munsterberg Koppitz, Ph.D.
Board of Cooperative Educational Services
Yorktown Heights, New York.

GRUNE & STRATTON
A Subsidiary of Harcourt Brace Jovanovich, Publishers
New York San Francisco London

Library of Congress Cataloging in Publication Data (Revised)

Koppitz, Elizabeth Munsterberg.
    The Bender gestalt test for young children.

Research and application, 1963-1973.
        Bibliography: p.
        Includes index.
        1. Bender gestalt test. I. Title. [DNLM:
1. Bender-Gestalt Test—in infancy & childhood.
WM145 K83b]
BF698.8.B4K66   Suppl.   155.2'84   63-19130
ISBN 0-8089-0873-1

Grune & Stratton, Inc.
111 Fifth Avenue
New York, New York 10003

Distributed in the United Kindom by
Academic Press, Inc. (London) Ltd.
24/48 Oval Road, London NW 1

Library of Congress Catalog Card Number 63-19130
International Standard Book Number 0-8089-0873-1

Printed in the United States of America

To Hugo and Peggy
who share my pleasure in
research and writing

Table of Contents

List of Tables and Figures

Preface

My first book, *The Bender Gestalt Test for Young Children,* was written in the early 1960s when there was keen interest among psychologists in the process of visual-motor perception and in its relationship to learning problems. That was also the time when many school districts established special public-school classes for youngsters with learning disabilities. The book on the Bender Test and the Developmental Scoring System were readily accepted by a large number of clinical and school psychologists as a convenient and useful tool for assessing visual-motor function in children.

The Bender Test book also stimulated a considerable amount of new research that further increased our knowledge about the Bender Test. The findings from these investigations and my own experience as a school psychologist with a special-education program for children with learning disabilities led me in recent years to reexamine my earlier hypotheses and assumptions about the Bender Test. I discovered that most of my initial findings and formulations withstood critical reevaluations, but in some instances it was necessary to modify my earlier positions.

This volume presents the results of a systematic examination of the accumulated Bender Test research data from studies involving children, covering the period from 1963 through 1973. This is not a revision of my first book, but is rather a continuation of it; it should be used as a supplement to the earlier book. This is the second volume of *The Bender Gestalt Test for Young Children.* It was written especially for clinical and school psychologists and for other professionals working with children.

Hopefully, this volume, like its predecessor, will not only offer practical assistance to professional psychologists and diagnosticians but will also stimulate additional research so as to further increase our understanding of the Bender Test and to enhance our ability to help children to realize their full potential.

This book was made possible only because of the cooperation and support I received from many psychologists, teachers, school administrators, and others too numerous to mention here by name. I am deeply grateful to them all. However, I would be remiss if I did not express particular thanks to the following individuals who gave unselfishly of their time and effort: Above all, my husband, Werner J. Koppitz, who not only helped with the collection of the data and with the preparation of the manuscript but who also gave me unfailing support and encouragement throughout the many months I worked on the book. My friends and colleagues Barbara Keogh, Leonore Bravo, Ruth Tiedeman, Areta Stadler, Bertha Stavrianos, Jerry Adams, Alice Larking, and Serena Deutsch provided me with invaluable research information and Bender Test data. The late Margaret Jessen helped write the chapter "The Bender Test as a Group Test." William E. Caskey, Grant C. Dinmore, Ann Goff, Max Heinrich, Blanche Isaac, Dolly Moseley, Richard Walker, and Daniel B. Wile all generously shared with me the results of their doctoral dissertations.

Ole Varming from Denmark, Oddvar Vormeland from Norway, Tomio Sonoda, and Todayoshi Kai from Japan, and A. A. Weiss from Israel brought to my attention Bender Test studies from different parts of the world. Barbara Ayers and Helen Moloney located and obtained for me numerous articles and publications. The *Journal of Clinical Psychology* and the *Journal of Personality Assessment* gave me permission to reproduce two of their tables in this volume. Karen Dooley assisted in the preparation of the manuscript. And, of course, I am greatly indebted to the many boys and girls who produced Bender Test records and who taught me so much.

Mt. Kisco, New York   Elizabeth M. Koppitz
December 1974

The Bender Gestalt Test for Young Children
Volume II, Research and Application, 1963 – 1973

CHAPTER 1.
Introduction

"The Bender Gestalt Test . . . needs little introduction." So reads the opening sentence of *The Bender Gestalt Test for Young Children* (Koppitz, 1963). If this statement was true more than 10 years ago when I wrote it, it is even more true today. Recently Lubin et al. (1971) asked clinical psychologists to name the tests they employed in their practices or work. The survey revealed that the Bender Test, together with the TAT, ranked third from the top. Only the WAIS and the Rorschach were named more frequently. The investigators also inquired how frequently the various tests were used by the clinicians. The answers to this question showed that the Bender Test was the most frequently used test; it was mentioned most often as the test psychologists use with the majority of their clients.

The Bender Gestalt Test (Bender, 1938) has for many years been well established and accepted by clinicians working with adult patients. The greatest change during the past decade has been in the use of the Bender Test among psychologists and other professionals (speech and language therapists, pediatricians, educational diagnosticians, etc.) working with children. When I originally reviewed the research literature from 1938 to 1962, I could find only 29 studies dealing primarily with the use of the Bender Test with elementary-school-age children. During the years from 1963 to 1973 I collected over 200 published and unpublished studies and research papers that were concerned with children's performances on the Bender Test or that used the Bender Test as the main instrument of investigation. These studies came from all over the United States as well as from other countries, including Canada, Chile, Denmark, Germany, Great Britain, India, Israel, Japan, Mexico, and Norway.

In addition to research studies, a number of general surveys of the Bender Test literature have been published in recent years, both here and abroad (Billingslea, 1963; Koppitz, 1965; Landmark and Grinde, 1964; Sonoda, 1968; Tolor, 1968; Tolor and Schulberg, 1963).

Most noteworthy is the growing popularity of the Bender Test in schools. Formerly the test was used primarily by clinicians with children for diagnostic purposes. Now it is used more and more often as a developmental test of visual-motor perception for school beginners and as a screening test to identify children with learning problems. The growing awareness of and concern with learning disabilities and with poor school achievement have created a need for quick, easy-to-administer, reliable, inexpensive, and "safe" screening instruments and diagnostic tools. The Bender Test can qualify on all of those counts. The fact that it can be used both as an individual test and as a group test (see Chapter 12, p. 109) and the availability of simple objective scoring systems further enhance its

1

appeal for school psychologists and for others working in the schools. It is also important that children seem to enjoy the test and that it can be administered repeatedly without any apparent loss in validity.

The very fact that the Bender Test is so appealing and is so easy to administer presents a certain danger. Because it is so deceptively simple it is probably one of the most overrated, most misunderstood, and most maligned tests currently in use. Actually the Bender Test is not quite as simple or as easy to use as might appear to the casual observer. Psychological tests are, after all, nothing but tools; and a tool is, of course, only effective if the person handling it is skilled in its use. Bender (1965) pointed out that the use of the Visual Motor Gestalt Test requires that the person using it be "informed, interested, and experienced, as does any other scientific method." The values as well as the limitations of the Bender Test as a screening test for school children have been emphasized repeatedly (Keogh, 1968a; Koppitz, 1963, 1970b; 1975).

How useful, in fact, is the Bender Test? How can it be most effectively used with children? What can one accomplish with the test? And what cannot be accomplished with it? I tried to provide some of the answers to these questions in *The Bender Gestalt Test for Young Children* (Koppitz, 1963), but it seems that every answer or hypothesis advanced therein only raised new questions. It was most gratifying to discover that the book served to stimulate numerous new investigations. Many studies were specifically designed to test some of the hypotheses I had put forth. It therefore seems appropriate at this time to reexamine *The Bender Gestalt Test for Young Children* in light of the new studies and findings. What have we learned about the Bender Test during the past 10 years?

The present volume is not a revision of the earlier text. It is rather an addition to it. This new book begins where the other left off. This is the second volume of *The Bender Gestalt Test for Young Children*. It includes a detailed review of the Bender Test literature from 1963 through 1973 pertaining to children, as well as some of my own recent unpublished research with the Bender Test. It is hoped that this volume, like its predecessor, will contribute to a better understanding and more effective use of the Bender Test with children and that it, too, will serve as a catalyst to stimulate more research in the years to come.

CHAPTER 2.
The Bender Gestalt Test

DESCRIPTION OF THE BENDER GESTALT TEST

The Bender Gestalt Test or Visual Motor Gestalt Test, as developed by Lauretta Bender, consists of nine test cards (size 4 × 6 in.) with abstract designs on them. The nine designs are adapted from figures Wertheimer (1923) used in perceptual experiments. Children taking the test are asked to copy the designs, one at a time, with a number-2 pencil, on a single blank sheet of paper. If they so desire they can use more than one sheet of paper. There is no time limit on this test. A detailed discussion of the test administration has been given elsewhere (Bender, 1938, 1946; Koppitz, 1963) and will not be repeated here. Plate 1 shows the nine Bender Test figures as drawn by Alison, a well-functioning 9½-year-old girl of high-average mental ability.

The standard Bender Test cards have been published by the American Orthopsychiatric Association (Bender, 1946). All studies discussed in this book were conducted with the standard Bender Test cards and the standard Bender Test method of administration unless otherwise indicated.

Some people refer to the Bender Test as a test of visual perception (Zach and Kaufman, 1972); others think of it as a test of motor coordination. The Bender Test is neither. As I see it the Bender Test is a test of visual-motor integration. I like to hyphenate the term visual-motor in order to emphasize that we are dealing here with a higher level, integrative process. Bender (1970) speaks of the global nature of the Gestalt function and of the inseparableness of the perceptual and motor capacities. She takes exception to any effort to analyze this global function into its component parts, for obviously the integrative process is much more complex than either visual perception or motor coordination. Yet it stands to reason that a child with immature or defective visual perception will also have difficulty with visual-motor perception and will do poorly on the Bender Test (Plate 9). Good visual-motor perception and above-average Bender Test performance presupposes that the youngster also has relatively mature or adequate visual perception. The reverse, however, is not necessarily true. As was demonstrated by Fisher (1967) and by Newcomer and Hammill (1973), not all children with immature or defective Bender Test performances (Plate 8) necessarily have problems in visual perception.

A similar situation exists with regard to motor coordination. Only a child with good fine-motor coordination can execute a perfect Bender Test protocol. Youngsters with poor fine-muscle coordination will have difficulty drawing Bender Test designs without imperfections (Plate 14).

But not all children with immature or defective Bender Test performances are poorly coordinated (Plate 19). Support for these observations comes from several studies (Allen et al., 1971; Heinrich, 1968; Wedell and Horne, 1969; Zach and Kaufman, 1972). For a more detailed discussion of these studies see page 119.

Figure 1 shows a schematic representation of the visual-motor perception process involved in copying the Bender Test designs. At the top of the page is a stimulus card with Design A. This design or stimulus impinges on the child's retina and is transmitted to the brain; assuming that the child has normal vision, the design is seen by the youngster. But just

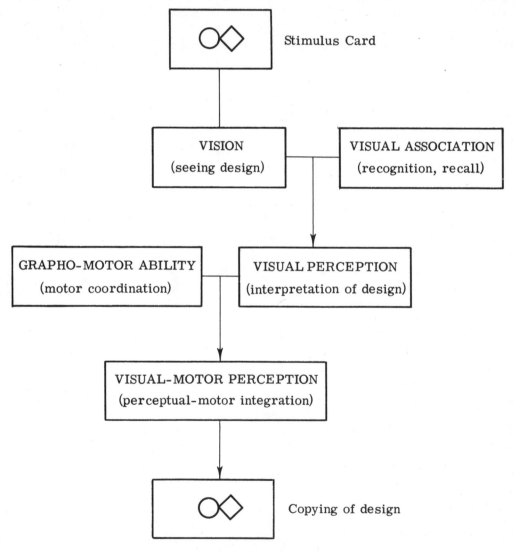

Figure 1. Visual-motor perception.

because the child can see the design does not mean that he can perceive or understand it. Perception, or the interpretation of what is seen, depends on maturation as well as on the child's experiences. We cannot say that our youngster is able to perceive Design A correctly until he can determine, consciously or unconsciously, that the design consists of a circle and a tilted square, not a diamond, and that they are of about equal size, arranged in the horizontal position, touching each other. When the child can do all that, we can speak of visual perception. But just because the child can perceive and can even describe or match correctly what he perceives does not necessarily mean that he can copy it. In order to copy it the child has to translate what he perceives into a motor activity—that is, he has to put it down on paper. The child is able to accomplish this task accurately only if the integration of his perception and motor coordination has matured to the level usually obtained by 8- or 9-year-old children. Prior to that age even normal youngsters tend to have difficulty copying the Bender Test designs without some imperfections.

Difficulties in copying the Bender Test figures, therefore, may result from immaturity or from malfunctioning in visual perception, in motor coordination, or in the integration of the two. A child who produces a poor Bender Test protocol may have difficulty in any one or two of these areas or in all three of them. However, the majority of school-age youngsters with immature Bender Test records do *not* have poor visual perception nor do they show difficulties with motor coordination, instead they have problems with perceptual–motor integration; that is, they still have difficulty with the higher level integrative function (Heinrich, 1968; Wedell and Horne, 1969).

INTERPRETATION OF THE BENDER TEST

The Bender Test, like most psychological tests, can be interpreted in several different ways. A trained and experienced examiner has the opportunity to observe and evaluate the subject's behavior while he is taking the test. In addition, the administration of the test results in a test protocol that can be analyzed both objectively and intuitively. In *The Bender Gestalt Test for Young Children* I dealt mostly with the interpretation of Bender Test records by means of the Developmental Scoring System and the Emotional Indicators. The child's behavior while taking the Bender Test was only briefly touched upon (Koppitz, 1963, p. 87). Controlled research studies with the Bender Test are by necessity limited to objective test data derived from the test protocols. But practicing psychologists are fortunately not limited by such restrictions. It is indeed sad when a clinical or school psychologist administers the Bender Test to a child and derives nothing from the test but a test score. Examiners often deprive themselves of valuable information regarding children's attitudes, self-concepts, inner control, ability to compensate for underlying perceptual–motor problems, and other factors that cannot be gleaned from the test scores or from the finished test protocols. There is much information that can be obtained only by observing the youngsters while they copy the designs.

BEHAVIOR OBSERVATIONS

Since the Bender Test bears little resemblance to schoolwork, it tends to be nonthreatening for most children. Most youngsters like to draw, and they enjoy copying the Bender Test designs. The test produces much less anxiety than would school-related tasks; because of this it offers the examiner a chance to watch the child's natural behavior when faced with a new task. I have found that a child's behavior while taking the Bender Test often provides valuable insights into *how* a child can best learn. The differences in attitude displayed by well-functioning pupils and by youngsters with behavior and learning problems are often striking.

I would like to suggest that clinical and school psychologists make it a point, every now and then, to administer the Bender Test to *good* pupils also, so that they can maintain a feeling for what is "normal." Examiners need to know how average children behave and function when they are faced with a perceptual–motor task. It is remarkable to see the ease and self-confidence with which bright, well-adjusted 6- and 7-year-olds sit down, pay attention, analyze the problem before them, and then proceed to copy the designs. Most of the youngsters show good control of the pencil and work carefully and deliberately without undue haste. Even very young children often show an awareness of imperfections on their Bender Test drawings and try to correct them spontaneously. These youngsters rarely ask for reassurance and are quite pleased with themselves and with their accomplishments.

By contrast, the youngsters referred to the psychologist because of behavior and/or learning difficulties tend to show a great variety of problems during the testing session. Some children will hesitate when first presented with the Bender Test. They will try to avoid possible failure by delaying the task. A child may first go to sharpen his pencil, then proceed to tell the examiner some lengthy story or experience he had, or he may offer to draw "a car" instead of the designs. Some children insist that the test is really "baby work" and "too easy." When they finally get around to taking the test they often dash off the drawings without ever stopping to look at and analyze the designs before they start copying them. Other children work very slowly, constantly checking and rechecking the number of dots and circles, while expressing much dissatisfaction with their work. Many insecure and anxious youngsters need repeated reassurances and encouragement before they can complete the test. Often after copying each Bender Test design they inquire: "Am I doing good?" Similar behavior patterns as those displayed during the testing situation also occur in the classroom and greatly influence the pupils' school functioning and achievement. It is therefore important that the examiner be aware of them.

Even a brief test like the Bender Test can be most frustrating for youngsters with poor inner control and immature visual-motor integration. Many a child will begin the Bender Test with great enthusiasm and will put forth much effort and good concentration only to tire or to get frustrated by the time he reaches Fig. 3 or Fig. 5. While Figs. A, 1, and 2 may be carefully drawn, Fig. 3 may start out with one small dot followed by a row of small circles succeeded by ever larger circles. As the test continues the drawings get more and more careless and larger (see Plate 16).

Only direct observation of the children at work enables one to differentiate with certainty between perfectionistic youngsters and those children who literally cannot concentrate for more than a few minutes at a time because of an extremely short attention span. Perfectionistic children sometimes give up trying when copying the Bender Test designs because they cannot meet their own unrealistically high standards, when in fact they do quite well. Children with short attention spans can realistically attend to their schoolwork only for brief periods to time. They dash through the Bender Test just as they rush through their schoolwork, displaying careless errors, substituting and omitting details, making shortcuts. Too often it is assumed that such children do poorly on the Bender Test because they have "perceptual problems" and need special training in this area, when they really need help in slowing down, in developing better inner controls, and in improving their work habits.

The finished Bender Test protocols of two youngsters may look very much alike; yet it makes a considerable difference whether a child completes the Bender Test in 4 min or in 10 or even 15 min. Some children with poor school achievement produce very good Bender Test records, provided they are given enough time. When rushed or pressured for time they get disorganized and anxious, and their test performance deteriorates. The same occurs in the classroom: These pupils can only complete their assignments when they are given extra time.

The amount of time a youngster requires to complete the Bender Test is highly significant. The findings in recent investigations by Ackerman et al. (1971) and Dykman et al. (1973) are in agreement with my earlier studies (Koppitz, 1963, p. 36). According to these studies most elementary-school-age children need approximately 6 min 20 sec to complete the Bender Test, whereas youngsters with learning and behavior problems tend to work much faster. Ackerman et al. reported that their subjects with learning disabilities finished the Bender Test on the average in 5 min 19 sec, while most of their hyperactive youngsters needed only 4 min 41 sec to copy the nine Bender Test designs.

I have repeatedly been impressed by the ability of some children to compensate for very real problems in visual-motor perception. These efforts are usually signs of good intelligence, but this can be appreciated only if one observes the youngsters at work. For instance, some children are distracted by visual stimuli; they prefer to work from recall. They will glance quickly at the stimulus card and put it aside, then they proceed to draw the design from memory. Other youngsters can draw only if they have some verbal cues to follow. They are often able to provide their own verbal instructions by translating what they see into words. They can be observed muttering to themselves or moving their lips, since they have to hear themselves, vocally or subvocally, before they can copy the Bender Test figures. Others first trace a design or draw it in the air with a finger before they can copy it with a pencil on paper. These children use kinesthetic sensations to help them integrate their visual perceptions and graphic motor expression.

"Anchoring" is another type of behavior that is characteristic of children who are compensating for weaknesses in the visual-motor area and in recall. This process involves placing a finger of one hand on the part of the design that is being copied while drawing the same with the other hand. By this method the child can keep track of where he or she is working and what portion of the design has already been completed. A less intelligent or younger child will count and recount the dots or circles after drawing each separate dot or circle; he keeps forgetting the number he counted and repeats the process over and over again only to end up, more likely than not, with an incorrect number of dots or circles on Figs. 1, 2, and 3. These same children are also apt to lose their place on a printed page when they are reading or forget a step when computing an arithmetic problem.

Sometimes very impulsive but intelligent children learn to control their impulsivity by means of compulsivity, which differs from the perfectionism mentioned above. Such impulsive youngsters may line up the Bender Test designs, neatly numbered at times, along the edge of the paper. They may work extremely slowly and carefully, putting forth a great deal of effort. Turning the paper and the stimulus card is another way in which a child may try to help himself when copying Bender Test figures, since it is easier to draw some designs in the vertical rather than the horizontal position. Bright children with poor visual-motor perception often develop spontaneous techniques that enable them to copy the Bender Test designs despite their awkwardness in performing such tasks. By observing these youngsters' work habits, the examiner can learn ways of helping not only the children under observation but also others who are unable to compensate on their own for difficulties in perceptual–motor integration.

Only observation of the child at work can determine the direction in which the youngster draws the Bender Test designs (Plate 7). Weiss (1969, 1971b) reported that kindergarten and first-grade pupils have no clearly preferred direction in which to draw Bender Test designs. Many children drew either from right to left or from left to right, or even in both directions. A definite shift toward the left–right direction was observed by age 7. Forty-eight percent of Israeli kindergarten pupils drew Figs. 1, 2, 3, and 6 on the Bender Test from left to right; by the ninth grade as many as 92% of the youngsters worked from left to right. These findings are especially interesting since Israeli children learn to read and write from right to left. It appears that directionality in drawing the Bender Test designs is independent of reading and writing habits.

ANALYSIS OF BENDER TEST PROTOCOLS

After a child has finished copying the nine Bender Test designs the examiner has a graphic record of the youngster's test performance. The Bender Test protocol can be analyzed and interpreted in different ways. The Bender Test record reflects the child's level of maturity in visual-motor perception and can reveal possible malfunction or impairment in visual-motor integration. In addition, the protocol can also be used as a personality test.

Both intuitive and clinical approaches, as well as objective scoring systems, have been developed to evaluate Bender Test records. The test protocols can also be used as projective materials or in any other way that provides the investigator with the insights he is seeking. Fisher (1973), for instance, does not analyze Bender Test records at all; instead she "goofs around" with the Bender Test, using it as an experience she shares with the child and as a starting point into further explorations of "contextual life events."

Bender (1965) prefers to evaluate the Visual Motor Gestalt Test protocols by means of "clinical inspection." She has some misgivings about formalized scoring systems. It is, of course, a fact that well-trained and highly skilled clinicians can derive much meaningful insight from Bender Test records by relying mainly on their intuition and experiences. But unfortunately a great many psychologists are not that skilled or experienced. Intuition can prove to be quite unreliable and even dangerous in the hands of less experienced or less proficient examiners. The fact that quite a number of scoring systems for the Bender Test have been developed over the years shows that psychologists have a real need for objective methods for interpreting Bender Test protocols.

Objective scoring systems that are standardized and validated have obvious advantages: They serve as a check and safeguard against the investigator's biases; they enable us to compare with confidence Bender Test data from different studies or groups of youngsters; they also let us assess a given child's rate of maturation in visual-motor perception by administering the Bender Test repeatedly over a period of time, comparing successive test scores; objective scoring systems make it possible for young and less experienced psychologists to use the Bender Test effectively even before they have accumulated years of practice and wisdom; finally, some sort of objective evaluation system is essential for well-designed and carefully controlled research studies whose results can be subjected to sound statistical analysis.

Most scoring systems for the Bender Test have been developed for specific populations or to evaluate specific functions. Evaluation of Bender Test records with different scoring systems leads to remarkably similar results when the scoring systems are appropriate for the same groups of children (i.e., normal school pupils, emotionally disturbed children, youngsters with learning disabilities, etc.) and for subjects of the same age level. Perhaps the best way to assess the usefulness of a Bender Test scoring system is to evaluate not only its reliability and validity but also to take into consideration the amount of time and effort it requires to analyze a single Bender Test record and the range of subjects and purposes it can be used with. A given scoring system may be excellent for one particular group or purpose, and yet its application may be so limited that it has little value for the practicing clinical or school psychologist.

Since the Bender Test is above all a developmental test for children, it is important to realize that scoring systems that are suitable for children may no longer be appropriate for normal adolescents or adults whose visual-motor perception has fully matured. The opposite also applies: scoring systems for Bender Test records of adults are not necessarily valid for children and should be used with caution.

During the past 10 years the majority of studies with children have employed the Developmental Scoring System for analyzing Bender Test records (Koppitz, 1963, p. 15). This method is quick and very easy to use; it has been standardized for children age 5 years 0 months to 10 years 11 months. However, the Koppitz scoring system is by no means the only Bender Test scoring system that has been mentioned in the recent research literature. The Developmental Scoring System will be discussed in some detail in Chapters 3, 4, and 5. The following is a brief account of other objective scoring methods for analyzing children's Bender Test records.

Next to the Koppitz system, the Bender Test scoring method most frequently referred to is that of Keogh and Smith (1961). This system was specifically developed to evaluate the Bender Test records of kindergarten and first-grade children. It correlates significantly with the Koppitz Developmental Scoring System, and both scoring methods are equally effective for use with school beginners.

The rather complex scoring system of Pascal and Suttell (1951) is most widely used with the Bender Test records of adult psychiatric patients. It was standardized for subjects age 15 to 50. Kawaguchi (1970) compared the Koppitz method and the Pascal and Suttell method on the Bender Test records of 477 children age 5 to 17. She found that with both systems the test scores markedly decreased between the ages of 5 and 6; Koppitz scores reached a plateau at age 9, while the Pascal and Suttell scores continued to decrease gradually until age 17. As would be expected, the Koppitz Developmental Scoring System is most appropriate for the age span for which it was designed; the system of Pascal and Suttell is better for older children. Cellura and Butterfield (1966) compared Pascal and Suttell scores with the Koppitz Developmental Scoring System scores of mentally retarded patients. The test scores of the two scoring systems correlated significantly.

Fromm (1966) used Pascal and Suttell's method with the Bender Test records of well-adjusted and poorly adjusted third-grade boys and found that it could differentiate between the two groups. Doubros and Mascarenhas (1969) obtained significant correlations between the Pascal-and-Suttell Bender Test scores and WISC IQ scores of young patients at a child-guidance clinic.

Elliott (1968) compared the Pascal and Suttell test scores and the Koppitz Emotional Indicators (see Chapter 10) on the Bender Test protocols of groups of youngsters age 11 and 14. He tried in effect to fill the age gap that exists between the two scoring methods. Elliott extended the use of the Pascal and Suttell scoring system downward to include younger children and extended the Koppitz system upward beyond age 10 to include teenagers. The results revealed that the Koppitz system of Emotional Indicators discriminated emotionally disturbed patients from a well-adjusted control group equally as well as the complicated and time-consuming Pascal and Suttell system.

In Lenstrup's study (1968) of the visual-motor function of 10 psychotic and 10 brain-damaged children, the Bender Test records were evaluated with the Pascal and Suttell scoring system only. No significant differences between the two groups of subjects were found.

Canter (1963) modified the Pascal and Suttell Bender Test scoring system for his study with the Background Interference Procedure (BIP) method on the Bender Test. Canter's scoring system was also used by Adams, Hayden, and others working with the BIP Bender (see p. 117). This particular Bender scoring system, just like the Pascal and Suttell system, is more appropriate for adults and older children than for younger children.

Mogin (1966) designed her own system for the objective scoring of Bender Test records when screening primary-grade children for emotional maladjustment, while Flint (1966) used the clinical signs of Hutt and Briskin (1960) on the Bender Test records of non-clinical groups of children age 10 to 11 and with young adults.

Quast (1961) designed a Bender Test scoring system for the specific purpose of identifying brain injury in patients. J. Holroyd (1966) made a cross-validation of the Quast and the Koppitz Bender Gestalt signs of cerebral dysfunctions. She found a high correlation between the two systems ($r = .93$), even though the latter system is quite simple and the former is very involved and time-consuming.

A number of investigators developed their own Bender Test scoring procedures for use in the particular studies they were conducting. Thus Wiener's (1966) scoring method was designed to correlate with signs of minimal brain dysfunction. Thweatt et al. (1972) devised a Bender Test scoring method that measured mainly the directional orientation to the task. Wile (1965) compared the Pascal and Suttell system, the Hain system (1964), and the Koppitz Developmental Scoring System with his own Bender Test scoring scales. His results show that his Primitivization and Motor Incoordination scales differentiate organic from nonorganic patients as well as do the other scoring systems.

Walker and Streff (1973) adapted the Koppitz Developmental Scoring

System to identify second-grade pupils in need of perceptual training. Lambert (1970, 1971) used an item-analysis procedure with second- and fifth-graders to determine the validity and reliability of a scoring system she developed for the Bender Test. The scoring system failed to predict pupil ability, general achievement, or social status, but it was related to arithmetic grades and behavior ratings of the pupils.

Most Bender Test scoring systems score for "errors": a low score is a good score, whereas a high Bender Test score indicates poor test performance. Maloney and Ward (1970), working with institutionalized mentally retarded subjects, modified the Koppitz scoring system and changed the test score from an "error" score to a "correct" score. They also gave credit for "discernible effort to reproduce figures." Satz et al. (1971) used a three-point rating system to analyze the Bender Test records of their subjects. They rated each test protocol, on the basis of clinical intuition, as good (three points), medium (two points), and poor (one point). Thus a high score is a good score in this rating system.

A radically different and most interesting scoring system for the Bender Test has been devised by Rimmer and Weiss (1972). They reinterpreted the Bender Test as a cognitive task and used Piaget's theory of arithmetic and geometric conceptual development as a theoretical basis for their scoring system. Each Bender Test design was analyzed for arithmetic concepts and geometric concepts. A total of 76 elements were scored, and they resulted in separate "profiles" for each Bender Test figure. With a sample of children ranging in age from 4 years 6 months to 13 years, significant correlations were found ($r = .50$ to $r = .65$) between the nine "profiles" for Figs. A to 8 and the youngsters' ages.

As with other Bender Test scoring systems, Rimmer and Weiss observed that there was a rapid improvement on the Bender Test performance between the ages of 4 and 6, while at age 10 to 12 the children reached a plateau in their Bender Test scores. Even though this scoring system proved highly reliable ($r = .90$), it seems to lack consistency. At each age level the children revealed a different "profile" for the nine Bender Test designs. Further research is needed to establish the validity of this scoring system.

CHAPTER 3.
The Developmental Bender Test
Scoring System

Part II of *The Bender Gestalt Test for Young Children* (Koppitz, 1963, p. 7) gives a detailed description of the construction of the Developmental Bender Test Scoring System. The scoring system was designed to assess the level of maturity in visual-motor perception of children age 5 to 10. By age 10 most normal youngsters can copy the Bender Test designs correctly without any difficulty. The Developmental Bender Test Scoring System is therefore only appropriate for elementary-school-age pupils. It has been standardized for ages 5 years 0 months to 10 years 11 months at 6-month intervals. As on all developmental tests, a child's Developmental Bender Test score can only be interpreted meaningfully when his chronological or mental age is taken into consideration. It is unfortunate that many investigators compare the Bender Test scores of groups of children from a wide range of age levels without carefully controlling or matching the youngsters' C.A. or M.A. A given Developmental Bender Test score has, for example, very different meanings for a 6-year-old and a 10-year-old.

Beyond the age of 10 the Bender Test can no longer be regarded as a developmental test for normal children. Once a youngster's visual-motor function has matured, his Bender Test record tends to be more or less perfect, and the test presents no problems for him. At that point the Developmental Bender Test Scoring System reaches its ceiling and can no longer discriminate between average and above-average Bender Test performances. Bright children reach this point by age 8 or 9. After age 10 only children with a marked immaturity or malfunction in visual-motor perception will show any meaningful scores on the Bender Test. The Developmental Bender Test Scoring System should not be used for groups of normal teenagers or for groups of youngsters ranging in age all the way from 8 to 13, or even from 6 to 20, as was the case in some recent Bender Test investigations. Failure to achieve significant findings in some research studies may not always be due to the Bender Test or to the scoring system involved; not infrequently such failure results from the incorrect use of the Bender Test and from inappropriate methods of interpreting the test results.

The current emphasis on pre-school education has led to an attempt to use the Bender Test with youngsters below the age of 5. These efforts have for the most part been unsuccessful. As Plenk and Jones (1967, 1968) showed, most 3- and 4-year-olds scribble and produce Bender Test protocols that defy scoring. Even those children who are able to make recognizable Bender Test figures tend to make primitive drawings lacking in scorable details. As a result they may obtain a lower (that is, a better)

Developmental Bender Test score than older children who draw more adequate Bender Test designs. An item can only be scored as being imperfect if all parts are present and distorted, not if they are omitted from the protocol. Furthermore, immaturity in visual-motor perception at the age of 3 or 4 is normal and is not necessarily related to later school functioning. Among very young children the exceptionally good Bender Test record has more predictive and diagnostic significance than an immature Bender Test record.

I recently tested 44 white middle-class kindergarten pupils with the Bender Test at the beginning and end of a school year. Of the 13 pupils with good Bender Test scores (10 points or less) in September, 12 also had good Bender Test scores (7 points or less) in June at the end of the school year. Of the 27 youngsters with average Bender Test scores (11 to 14 points) at the time of school entry, only 14 still had average Bender Test scores (8 to 11 points) 8 months later; 9 others obtained good Bender Test scores and 4 had poor test scores when they were retested. At the beginning of kindergarten 4 youngsters had below-average or poor Bender Test scores (15 points or more); by June 2 of them exhibited average performance on the Bender Test.

My own experience has been that the Developmental Bender Test Scoring System is useful and valid for 5-year-old youngsters of average or better than average ability; however, it is not very good for very immature children or for those with minimal brain dysfunction whose mental age is below the 5-year level. Plate 2 presents the good Bender Test record of Chris, a bright, well-integrated 5-year-old boy; by contrast, Plate 3 shows the Bender Test record drawn by Angelo, a very immature youngster of the same age.

It is sometimes incorrectly assumed that the Developmental Bender Test Scoring System was specifically designed to predict reading achievement or to diagnose brain dysfunction. This is not the case. The Developmental Scoring System was validated against general overall achievement in the primary grades (Koppitz, 1963, p. 12). Great pains were taken to exclude from the Developmental Scoring System all signs or scoring items that were not related to maturation in visual-motor perception and to achievement in the first and second grade.

Total Developmental Bender Test Score

According to the Developmental Bender Test Scoring System, each Bender Test design is scored, where appropriate, for distortion of shape, for rotation of the whole design or part of it, for failure to integrate the parts of the design, and for perseveration. There are 30 scoring items in all. Theoretically a child could obtain a Developmental score of 30, but actually a youngster rarely gets a score higher than 18 to 20. If a Bender Test score goes beyond 20, the protocol is most likely difficult to score, and all that can be said in such a case is that the child's visual-motor perception is as yet below the 4-year level. Plate 4 shows such an immature Bender Test record with a test score of 21. Ricki, a retarded youngster (WISC IQ 59), was 7 years 11 months old when he produced the protocol. At the time he was functioning on the 3½- to 4-year level.

Since the Bender Test records are scored for imperfections, a high Bender Test score indicates a poor Bender Test performance, while a low score reflects a good test performance. Bender Test protocols should always be evaluated by means of the *total* Developmental Bender Test score and not on the basis of individual scoring points. A child may vary in minor details when drawing the same design on different occasions. One time he may concentrate on the whole Gestalt of the design and omit some details; the next time he may carefully count dots and angles while rotating the whole figure or failing to integrate the parts. In each instance only one or two scoring points may be involved, and these may change; but the total Developmental score will usually remain the same.

The Bender Test record shown on Plate 5 illustrates this point well. It was drawn by Brian, a 7-year-old boy of average mental ability with a very low frustration tolerance. He was a neurologically impaired youngster with poor perceptual–motor integration and a serious expressive disorder in both the languages and visual-motor area. Brian started to draw the Bender Test with much enthusiasm and put forth much effort. On Fig. 1 he substituted dashes for dots, thereby revealing impulsivity, but he carefully counted them and produced the correct number. He also started counting the dots on Fig. 3. Brian concentrated so hard on the number of the dots that he totally lost track of the direction and the configuration of the design. When Brian looked at the drawing he became aware of his error; he tried to erase and correct the design but had little success in doing so. He got frustrated and wanted to destroy his paper just as he always destroyed his schoolwork because it never turned out the way he knew it should be. I reassured Brian and urged him to draw the design over again. Brian did so and concentrated this time on the shape of the design. As can be seen on Plate 5 he was quite successful in his endeavor, for the shape of Fig. 3 is now correct (unfortunately this time the design is rotated and solid lines are substituted for the dots).

Again Brian voiced his dismay and showed me with a hand movement the direction in which the design ought to go (horizontally). Brian's visual perception was good. He knew exactly what the design should look like, but he just could not get his hands to reproduce what he perceived correctly. Once again I encouraged Brian to draw the design over again. He complied and made a third drawing of Fig. 3, as shown on Plate 5. This time Brian concentrated on the direction of the figure and finally got it right, only this time he again lost the shape and the dots of Fig. 3!

Brian's three drawings of Fig. 3 differ greatly; yet each of them was scored for two points. The first drawing would be scored for rotation and distortion of shape (scoring points 11, 12a), the second drawing for rotation and lines instead of dots (scoring points 11, 12b), and the third for distortion of shape and lines instead of dots (scoring points 12a, 12b). Thus the total Developmental score remained the same even though particular scoring points varied. The important factor about Brian's Bender Test record is not a specific scoring point but rather the total Developmental score and his behavior during the drawing of the design. Here was a youngster whose visual perception was good but whose perceptual–motor integration was still so immature that he could only concentrate and work with one dimension at a time. He could either reproduce the exact number of details or the correct direction or the total configuration of the design, but he could not, as yet, manage to integrate all three at the same time. He was aware of his difficulties and got overly frustrated, since his inner control was weak. He tried to destroy his work and lost his temper. This type of behavior was duplicated many times each day in his classroom. The total Bender Test score showed Brian's level of maturity in perceptual–motor integration, while his behavior during the test administration gave clues for ways to help him and to make suggestions to his teacher to improve his school functioning. Brian could at this point handle only very brief, simple assignments that involved only *one* task at a time and not two or three. Too often we expect children to listen and to remember and to think and to write all at the same time long before they can do so, even though they may be able to cope with each dimension separately.

Several recent studies by other investigators offer support for my observation that the total Developmental Bender Test score is consistently more meaningful than separate scoring items. Each scoring item is important and cannot or should not be omitted; yet none of them has any special significance by itself. Obrzut et al. (1972) examined the relationship of single items on the Developmental Bender Test Scoring System and reading achievement of children from the first, third, and sixth grades. Nine of the thirty scoring items correlated significantly ($p < .05$) with first-grade reading; four scoring items correlated with the reading achievement of the third-graders; five items were found to be related to sixth-grade reading. For all three grade levels the total Developmental Bender Test score showed a closer relationship to reading achievement ($p < .01$) than any of the individual Bender Test scoring items.

Connor (1969) compared good and poor second-grade readers, all of whom were of at least average intelligence. The two groups differed significantly on the total Developmental Bender Test score and on the distortion of designs, but there was no significant difference on the number of rotations, perseverations, and integration scores.

Ackerman et al. (1971) found that the total Developmental Bender Test score was better than individual scoring items in discriminating third-grade boys of normal intelligence with learning disabilities from those without learning disabilities. Similar results were obtained by Keogh (1965) with kindergarten and third-grade pupils. She, too, found that the total Developmental Bender Test score was a better predictor of reading achievement than individual scoring items.

BENDER TEST SCORE TRANSFORMATIONS

The total Developmental Bender Test score is a negative score, since it records imperfections instead of giving credit for accomplishment in the drawing of Bender Test designs. Most psychological tests have positive scores, so that a subject's good performance is rewarded with a high test score. In contrast, a perfect Developmental Bender Test score is zero. This represents some complications for statistical analysis and for comparisons of Bender Test data with the results from other tests. A correlation between Bender Test scores and scores from tests of mental ability or achievement, for instance, is usually negative. The combination of test scores or an analysis of variance with Developmental Bender Test scores and other test scores is difficult. Some investigators tried to resolve this problem by transforming the Bender Test raw scores into scale scores or standard scores.

Hartlage and Lucas (1971) prorated Koppitz's normative data by months to provide a continuous distribution of year and month expectancy levels for boys and girls separately. Expectancy scores were developed to be used as a numerator in the determination of a given child's scale score, while the youngster's number of errors served as the denominator. This ratio, when multiplied by 100, produced the *scale score*.

Furr (1970) published a table of *standard scores* for the Developmental Bender Test Scoring System based on Koppitz's normative data. He set the mean at 100 and one standard deviation at 15. R. J. Holroyd (1971) questions the use of standard scores with the Koppitz normative data, since there is some skewing in the distribution of the test scores.

Because of the nature of the Bender Test, standard scores seem to be appropriate only for young children, age 5 to 7 or 8 years, whose visual-motor perception is still immature. At this age range one usually finds an approximately normal distribution of test scores. Only a few children in the primary grades are able to produce perfect Bender Test records. However, by age 9 most youngsters of average mental ability tend to have adequate visual-motor integration, so that they can obtain a perfect or near-perfect Developmental Bender Test score. At this point the Bender Test scores can only discriminate between children with average and below-average visual-motor perception; they can no longer differentiate between average and above-average Bender Test performances. Since the Developmental Bender Test scores are limited by a ceiling, the test-score distribution for youngsters age 8 and older becomes progressively more skewed. It would seem, therefore, that standard scores cannot be recommended for children beyond the primary grade level.

In order to obtain a better indication of the relative standing of a child, I computed *percentile scores* based on my 1974 normative data (see p. 34). Table 15 in Appendix E shows the Bender Test percentile scores for children age 5 to 11. Here, too, we find that percentile scores are most appropriate for the younger children and for older pupils with below-average visual-motor integration. Percentile scores are of little value for youngsters age 8 and older, if they are of average or better than average mental ability. The ceiling of the Bender Test scoring system prevents discrimination between mature children in the upper portion of the distribution.

INTERSCORER RELIABILITY FOR DEVELOPMENTAL SCORES

When the Developmental Bender Test Scoring System was published in 1963 there was only one study available that reported on the interscorer reliability of the scoring system. Miller et al. (1963) showed that the interscorer correlations for five different scorers who evaluated 30 Bender Test protocols ranged from $r = .83$ to $r = .96$. During the past 10 years quite a number of studies have included reports on the reliability of the Developmental Scoring System.

Table 1 gives the findings of these studies. Listed are the interscorer

Table 1.
Interscorer Correlations for Developmental Bender Test Scores

Investigator(s)	Number of Scorers	Tests Scored	Subjects	Correlations
Caskey (1973)	2	193	K pupils	.99
Cellura & Butterfield (1966)	2	20	MR pupils	.91
Dibner & Korn (1969)	2	492	K–4th grade	.95
Dinmore (1972)	3	30	K–4th grade	.97, .95, .93
Egeland et al. (1967)	3	80	MR children	.90, .91, .91
Giebink & Birch (1970)	2	98	K pupils	.84
Giebink & Birch (1970)	2	111	1st grade	.93
Heinrich (1968)	2	20	2nd & 6th grade	.80
Kaspar & Lampel (1971)	2	28	ages 5 to 8	.90
Marsh (1972)	2	21	ages 6 to 13	.96
Mlodnosky (1972)	2	30	1st grade	.96
Moseley (1969)	1*	80	3rd grade	.91
Moseley (1969)	2	25	3rd grade	.89
Obrzut et al. (1972)	2	54	1st, 3rd, 6th grade	.98
Ryckman et al. (1972)	2	20	2nd grade	.85
Ryckman et al. (1972)	2	24	4th grade	.79
Ryckman et al. (1972)	2	27	6th grade	.80
Snyder & Kalil (1969)	3	418	1st grade	.91, .96, .93
Sonoda (1971)	3	37	K pupils	.89, .90, .86
Taylor & Thweatt (1972)	2	50	ages 6 to 12	.96
Vormeland (1968)	1†	281	1st grade	.92
Vormeland (1968)	2	281	1st grade	.89
Wile (1965)	2	50	children & adults	.91

*Investigator rescored Bender Test records 1 year later.
†Investigator rescored Bender Test records 6 months later.

correlations for the Bender Test scores together with the names of the investigators, the number of scorers, the number of Bender Test records evaluated, and the group of subjects involved in each of the studies. The 31 interscorer correlations presented range from .79 to .99. Twenty-five of them, or 81% of the correlations, are at .89 or better. Thus there appears to be a high likelihood that two scorers evaluating a child's Bender Test record with the Developmental Scoring System will obtain approximately the same test score.

ANALYSIS OF SCORING PROBLEMS ON THE DEVELOPMENTAL SCORING SYSTEM

Despite the high interscorer reliability of the total Developmental Bender Test scores, some psychologists have expressed uncertainty or confusion about specific scoring items—especially troublesome has been the scoring of rotations on the Bender Test records.

In the study of Egeland et al. (1967) three scorers rated Bender Test protocols of mentally retarded subjects. The results showed a high inter-scorer correlation for the total Developmental Bender Test score ($r = .90$), but when the four scoring categories were examined separately, a significant difference between the three judges was found in the mean scores for the categories Rotation and Perseveration. The scorers did not differ significantly in their mean scores for the categories Distortion and Integration.

Snyder and Kalil (1968) analyzed each scoring point on the Developmental Scoring System and examined problems in scoring Bender Test records of 6-year-old children. Three examiners evaluated 654 Bender Test protocols of first-grade pupils in nine different schools. They found that the frequency of occurrence of imperfections on the Bender Test records varied greatly. Some scoring items were scored on 92% of the Bender Test protocols; others were present only on 1% of the records. Most difficult to score were, in descending order, scoring items 22, 1a, 18a, 3, 14, 12a, 21a, 21b, 13, 16, 23, and 20 (Appendix A). The greatest disagreement among the three examiners occurred on number 22—that is, on rotation of Fig. 7. It seems that some clarification of the instructions for the scoring of angles on Fig. 6 and for the scoring of "circles instead of dots" on Figs. 1, 3, and 5 (scoring points 4, 10, 15) would also be helpful.

Six sources of error in scoring Bender Test records were identified by Snyder and Kalil. They were (1) overscoring; (2) instructions not detailed enough; (3) lack of care by the scorer in counting dots and circles; (4) poor motor skills of children, making it difficult to differentiate circles and dots; (5) oversight of a design by the scorer; (6) fine lines, overlapping designs, and erasures that interfere with the clarity of a protocol.

All these points are well taken and suggest that the two main sources of scoring error are the scorer and the scoring manual. Psychologists who overscore Bender Test records tend to fall into two groups. One group is made up of perfectionists. These scorers are very exact and set extremely high standards. They tend to penalize children for minor irregularities on Bender Test drawings that are common among immature youngsters and that are of no diagnostic significance. When it comes to scoring Bender Test records of children, one should not be rigid. As I emphasized earlier, *only clear-cut errors or imperfections should be scored. In case of doubt, do not score* (Koppitz, 1963, p. 15). The other group of examiners who at times overscore children's Bender Test protocols are those who expect too much from the Bender Test. They assume that they will be able to diagnose brain injury with the Bender Test, predict reading achievement, and identify emotional problems. When these results are not forthcoming they tend to blame the scoring system, and many seriously believe that a more exact scoring system will bring about better results. They treat a Bender Test record as they would a precision instrument and base their diagnosis on whether a line is 1/16 in. longer or shorter, or whether a design is rotated by 3 deg more or less. They regard the Bender Test protocol as a final statement, when in fact it is only a child's response at a given moment. A youngster rarely if ever produces two identical Bender Test protocols. A Developmental Bender Test score is never absolute; it is merely a guideline that offers tentative information on which the examiner can build hypotheses. Minor details on a child's Bender Test record will vary; their importance should not be exaggerated. Even though a child's Bender Test performance reflects primarily his level of maturation in visual-motor perception, it is also somewhat influenced by the youngster's mood and attitude, by his ability to concentrate at the time of testing, and by extraneous factors in the testing situation, such as the time of day, the temperature, distracting noises, etc.

The opposite of the perfectionist is the casual examiner who fails to observe the child at work and who does not bother to make notations when a youngster turns the paper or overlaps designs. Unless notes are kept it is sometimes impossible to tell later whether a design was rotated or whether the paper was turned or just where one drawing of a figure ends and another one begins. Plates 28 and 29 are two cases in point. It would indeed be difficult to score Fig. 2 and Fig. 3 on Plate 28 if one had not observed Edgar at work. What looks like an arbitrary confusion of large circles represents in fact a very deliberate effort by Edgar, age 6 years, to draw the correct number of dots (circles) of Fig. 3 between the correct number of circles of Fig. 2. He succeeded remarkably well considering that he was at that time very immature and impulsive.

Lori, age 6 years 2 months, also failed to distinguish between dots and circles on Figs. 2 and 3, as shown on Plate 29. She drew circles on both designs and placed them in such a way that it would be difficult to tell where one leaves off and the other begins, unless one had watched Lori copy the figures.

Some psychologists are careless about counting dots and circles and angles. They score by intuition. There is nothing wrong with using an intuitive approach in the evaluation of Bender Test protocols (see p. 9), but in such cases no objective scoring system should be used. If the Developmental Scoring System or any other scoring system for the Bender Test is used, then it should be used correctly, or else the results will lack validity and will remain doubtful.

But even conscientious, noncompulsive psychologists or examiners sometimes have difficulties with the scoring of specific Bender Test scoring items. Indeed, some of the instructions for scoring Bender Test records are not as explicit as they might be. Therefore I made a revision of the scoring manual for the Developmental Bender Test Scoring System. No changes were made on the thirty scoring items themselves. The revision of the scoring manual is an attempt to refine and to sharpen the instructions so that the scoring of Bender Test protocols will be easier and scoring errors can be minimized. The Revised Scoring Manual for the Developmental Bender Test Scoring System is presented in Appendix A.

Rotation of Bender Test Designs

Since the scoring of rotations of Bender Test figures seems to present some difficulties, it may be in order to discuss rotations on the Bender Test in some detail. I have become aware that the examiner sometimes unwittingly contributes to the production of rotations on the protocol by a failure to provide structure for a child during the test administration. I have found that a consistent method of presentation of both the Bender Test cards and the drawing paper helps to diminish the number of rotations a child will produce. I personally prefer always to use the vertical orientation of the drawing paper, since such an orientation resembles most closely a notebook leaf and the printed page with which the youngster is familiar and with which he has learned to work.

Many children like to pick up Bender Test cards and rotate either the stimulus cards or the drawing paper or both. Bender (Tolor and Schulberg, 1963, p. XV) concedes that a different orientation between the background shape of the test cards and the drawing paper may well facilitate the drawing of designs in a rotated position. Bravo (1972) observed that many of her gifted subjects preferred to use the horizontal position of the drawing paper, which more nearly equals the shape of the stimulus cards. These gifted youngsters rarely if ever drew rotations on their Bender Test protocols, but neither do bright children who are required to keep the drawing paper in a vertical position.

I have developed the following standard method for administering the Bender Test that seems to reduce the number of rotations that occur on children's test protocols:

1. Place drawing paper in vertical position in front of child. Let the youngster adjust the angle of the paper to suit his own convenience, provided the long axis of the paper is still more nearly vertical than hori-

zontal. The paper doesn't have to be placed at a right angle with the table top. Left-handed children often draw better when the paper is placed at a slight angle.

2. After the drawing paper has been put into place, align the stimulus card horizontally with the top of the drawing paper.

3. Let the children pick up and manipulate the stimulus cards if they so desire, but insist that the card be replaced in the original position. Do not let children copy a design from a rotated card. If need be, reemphasize that you want the youngsters to copy the design exactly the way you presented it in the first place.

4. If the children insist on rotating or turning the paper while copying a design, let them do it. But after the design has been drawn return paper to its original position. In this manner, the children begin the copying of each design with the paper and the stimulus card in the same position.

If given complete freedom to turn the cards and the paper, a youngster may change the position of the paper for practically each drawing of a design. Plate 7, drawn by David, age 8, is an example of the kind of confusion that might ensue under such circumstances. At first glance it appears that several designs on Plate 7 are rotated. Actually, with the exception of Fig. A, the drawings are not rotated, but the designs are oriented in five different directions. It is important to make notations when a child rotates the paper, so that the examiner can tell later whether a rotated design on a Bender Test record was actually drawn upside down or rotated, or whether the paper was turned and the design was drawn correctly.

Some youngsters rotate only Fig. 3. In such cases I have learned to ask the child what the design looks like. Almost invariably the reply will be: "It's a Christmas tree, it should be like this," the design pointing upward. In fact, some children announce spontaneously upon seeing Fig. 3 that it is a Christmas tree and turn the card automatically to its "correct" position. Thus the youngsters seem to respond to the perceived content of the design and try to copy it as they think it ought to be. After all, everybody knows that a Christmas tree is supposed to stand upright.

The same process sometimes occurs with Fig. 5. Children who rotate only Fig. 5 often say that it is "a Y upside down." They are not the ones who rotate the design; on the contrary, the youngsters are certain that it was the stupid examiner who did not know any better than to place the Y upside down. When copying Fig. 5 the child is therefore only trying to correct the examiner's mistake. Obviously there is nothing amiss with the child's visual perception.

When children who did not rotate Fig. 5 on their Bender Test record were asked what the design looked like, they replied that it was "a tunnel with a chimney," "a tank," "a chair," "an igloo," or the like. All these answers referred to objects that were "right-side up" as far as Fig. 5 was concerned.

Moeller (1972) did an interesting study with 4- and 5-year-old children. The subjects were required to copy eleven abstract designs that had been consistently rated as "upside down" or "right-side up." Rotations on the children's drawings occurred most often when the figures were presented "upside down," not when they were shown "right-side up." When the figures were considered to have a low preference of right-side up or down, then they were seldom drawn in rotated positions.

The same principle seems to operate on the Bender Test. I have observed that some very young or very concretistic boys and girls have difficulty copying the abstract Bender designs until they attach a verbal label to the figures. Then suddenly the designs no longer present any serious problems for them. The label a youngster selects will of course influence the drawing. Thus a boy said that Fig. 4 was an "upside-down table" and "girl's hair." He did not perceive the design as one total Gestalt, but rather as two different and distinct objects; he then proceeded to draw them as such. First he drew the table "right-side up," correcting, thereby, the examiner's "error" of placing the table upside down. Then he copied the girl's hair some distance from the table. Most children who did not have a need to label the designs or who saw nothing in the figures but a "design" had no difficulty copying them without rotations or fragmentations.

Plate 8 shows an example of a Bender Test record with rotation. It was made by John, age 10 years 9 months, a very concretistic, immature youngster of normal mental ability with minimal brain dysfunction. He rotated Fig. 3 and Fig. 4 on the Bender Test. When asked what Fig. 3 looked like, John said emphatically, "A tree," and added a trunk to the drawing to make the apparent even more obvious. When asked about Fig. 4, John declared, "You turned the box upside down." After John was told that Fig. 4 was just "a design" and that he should copy it *exactly* as it was shown on the card, he did so without effort.

When a child tells me that Fig. 3 is a "lying-down Christmas tree" or that Fig. 5 is an "upside-down Y," I make a point of saying, "Yes, it does look like that, but it is really just a design. I would like you to make the design exactly as it appears on the card." When the youngster then redraws the design, he usually does so without any rotations. It would appear, therefore, that for these particular youngsters the rotations on Figs. 3, 4, and 5 are due more to problems in conceptualization of visual impressions than to difficulties in visual perception as such. The children can perceive the Gestalten correctly, but they need to interpret them in a concrete way that fits into their own realm of experience. They are not comfortable with abstract designs. Rock (1974) demonstrated that perception of form involves the automatic assignment of a top, a bottom, and sides to the form. The results of Rock's study concur with my own observations: *Form perception in general seems to be based to a much greater extent on cognitive processes than most current theories maintain.*

There are, of course, also some youngsters who in fact have poor visual perception. These children perceive the Bender Test designs in a distorted or rotated fashion and tend to show one or more rotations on their test protocols. When questioned about their drawings they are usually quite unaware of the rotations and distortions. When they are asked to draw the designs over again they tend to repeat the same distortions and rotations.

Plates 9 and 10 are examples of Bender Test records with five and six rotations, respectively. Both of these test protocols were drawn by Glenn, an impulsive, hypersensitive, angry youngster of low-average mental ability with minimal brain dysfunction. Glenn suffered from serious disturbances in time and space perception and from malfunction in visual-motor integration and directionality. As a result he was utterly confused and frustrated when attending a big school with hundreds of pupils and a large regular classroom buzzing with activities. Glenn had a long history of behavior and learning difficulties when, at age 9½, he was referred to the special classes for children with learning disabilities.

The Bender Test record shown on Plate 9 was produced by Glenn when he first came to the LD program. He announced at once: "I don't draw very well." His main concern was his difficulty in drawing angles and curves, while he seemed unaware of the fact that he rotated Figs. A, 1, 2, 3, 4, and 5. Eight months later, when Glenn was 10 years 2 months old, I administered the Bender Test a second time. By this time Glenn had made a good adjustment to the special classes for children with learning disabilities and was much less explosive and impulsive; he had also made satisfactory academic progress. His reading and comprehension had greatly improved; however, he continued to be weak in arithmetic. Arithmetic is, of course, related to part–whole relationships and to space perception, and these were among Glenn's main areas of weakness. Plate 10 shows Glenn's second Bender Test record, which revealed quite clearly his underlying problems with space perception and directionality.

A Bender Test record reflects a child's overall functioning in school rather than specific achievement (see p. 64). Thus it was found that Glenn was unable to return to regular school classes even in subsequent years when his achievement was almost up to grade level. He was so vulnerable that he could only function in a small, self-contained, highly structured special class. He needed the calm and supportive setting this class could offer in order to be able to concentrate and to compensate for his perceptual difficulties. In the small class he continued to do well, while in a large, loosely structured class Glenn got confused and quickly regressed to his former disturbing behavior and poor achievement. At his own request Glenn remained in the special class until he graduated from high school.

Weiss (1971c) observed that the incidence of rotation is a developmental phenomenon. It decreases as children get older. But the rate of decrease in rotations is unequal for different Bender Test figures. Figures A, 3, and 4 retain "rotational pull" longest. Black (1973) also found that a reduction in the frequency of rotations on the Bender Test was associated with an increase in age and achievement for children 6 to 9 years old.

CHAPTER 4.
Reliability of Bender Test Performance

Before we can assess the reliability of the Bender Test performance, it is essential to demonstrate that the Bender Test really is a developmental test of visual-motor perception and not just a test of learned skills that reflects primarily a youngster's experience and motivation for paper-and-pencil tasks. The execution of the Bender Test presupposes that a child is able to manipulate a pencil and that he is able to perceive and copy visual designs. Does this mean that the test puts a young child from a deprived, low socioeconomic background at a disadvantage compared with middle-class children who usually have ample experience with paper and crayons prior to coming to school? Does familiarity with and practice on visual-motor tasks, and specifically with the Bender Test, improve a youngster's test performance? Several investigators have explored these questions by trying to improve children's Bender Test performances by means of increasing their motivation and by specific training techniques.

Effect of Motivation on Bender Test Performance

Isaac (1973) administered the Bender Test first in standard fashion to a group of first-graders. Just prior to having them redraw the designs she promised her subjects candy as an added incentive to get the youngsters to try harder on the second administration of the Bender Test. Despite the added inducement of candy, no significant improvement was found between the first and second Bender Test records. Most children enjoy the Bender Test and do as well as they can even without candy or special rewards. Lack of motivation rarely accounts for immaturity or imperfections in young children's Bender Test drawings.

Effect of Familiarization on Bender Test Performance

Isaac (1973) not only tried to increase her subjects' motivation, she also tried to improve their Bender Test performance by familiarizing them with the Bender Test figures prior to having them copy the designs. The youngsters were asked to match Bender Test designs in a multiple-choice task. This required close inspection and manipulation of the figures and was supposed to aid their perception and analysis of the Bender Test designs. Results showed that children who had the opportunity to familiarize themselves with the test designs did not have significantly better Bender Test performance than a matched group of youngsters who did not have this chance.

The findings are in agreement with those of Zach and Kaufman (1972). They reported that discrimination tasks on a multiple-choice Bender Test are not necessarily related to the copying tasks on the standard Bender Test.

Effect of Verbal Labeling on Bender Test Performance

Some children spontaneously verbalize instructions to themselves when copying Bender Test designs. This process seems to facilitate their ability to draw. Zach and Kaufman (1969) used this same procedure in a formal study. They instructed 48 kindergarten pupils (24 black deprived Ss, 24 white middle-class Ss) to use verbal labels to describe the Bender Test task. A control group of 48 matched subjects received no such instructions. Three weeks later the Bender Test was again administered to all 96 subjects. Both experimental and control groups (both black and white Ss) showed improvement on their second Bender Test record. However, the use of verbal labels with the Bender Test did not result in significantly greater improvement. Thus verbal mediation may help a few youngsters who do it more or less spontaneously, but it does not seem to have any significant effect on the Bender Test performance of most kindergarten pupils in general.

Effects of Tracing and Copying on Bender Test Performance

Vega and Powell (1970) conducted a study with 19 black youngsters in a compensatory pre-primary education program. The children received 33 ½-hr training sessions in tracing and copying designs. A control group received no such training. Both groups were tested with the Bender Test twice, once before and once after the training period. At the end of the training period the experimental group showed slightly more improvement on the Bender Test than the control group, but this difference was not statistically significant.

Effect of Perceptual–Motor Training on Bender Test Performance

Rice (1972) gave the Bender Test to 22 5-year-old Headstart children. Eleven of them received perceptual–motor training for 6 weeks; the other youngsters served as controls. When the Bender Test was readministered, 4 of the experimental subjects showed significantly greater improvement on the Bender Test than did their controls. The other 7 experimental subjects did not reveal significantly greater improvement than their controls. The results are, at best, inconclusive.

Keim (1970) worked with 74 kindergarten pupils who were divided into two groups on the basis of their initial Bender Test performances. The experimental group received perceptual–motor training (Winter Haven program, McQuarrie, 1967); the control group did not. When the Bender Test was readministered no statistically significant differences were found between the test performances of the experimental and control groups. Most children with difficulties in visual-motor perception still had problems in this area. However, teachers reported that the perceptual–motor training program improved the youngsters' behavior.

Walker and Streff (1973) found that second-graders who were given perceptual–motor training did improve on their Bender Test performance more than did the control subjects. This improvement did not occur in any specific aspect of visual-motor function, for different children improved in different areas. According to Ames (1969), children with immature Bender Test performances also lag behind developmentally. Perceptual training in the classroom may facilitate the youngsters' perceptual–motor development and behavioral growth. However, despite such training, they will continue to be more immature than their peers; yet without the special help they appear to fall even farther behind.

Effects of Motivation and Training on Bender Test Performance: Summary

In summing up the findings reported above, one might conclude that most young children who have never seen the Bender Test improve their Bender Test performance somewhat if they are allowed to take the test over again. This is true both for advantaged and disadvantaged youngsters of pre-school age. Children who do well on the first Bender Test do even better on the second test administration. Children who do poorly on the initial Bender Test may do somewhat less poorly when the Bender Test is repeated; but even then their test performance will still be below average. Increase in motivation, instructions in matching, tracing, copying, and labeling the Bender Test designs, and perceptual–motor training appear to have little effect on the test performance of groups of children, in general, although individual children might profit somewhat from one training procedure or the other. Without special help, some youngsters may fall even farther behind in visual-motor perception. The Bender Test performance of young children reflects primarily their level of maturation in perceptual–motor integration and to a much lesser extent their experience with learned visual-motor tasks. Minor changes from one test administration to the next within a short time interval are to be expected and rarely affect the conclusions one can draw from the test performance.

TEST–RETEST WITH THE BENDER TEST

As Bender (1967) pointed out, no matter how often a child performs the Visual Motor Gestalt Test the results are never the same. The situation differs, the child differs, and the test results inevitably differ, too. Since children's Bender Test performances vary from one test administration to the next, the question of test score reliability is important; for if the

Bender Test and the Developmental Bender Test scores are not reliable, they cannot be valid diagnostic and clinical instruments.

The reliability of Bender Test scores can be determined by repeated administration of the Bender Test within a relatively short period of time. Nine studies have been reported that offer data on test–retest with the Bender Test for normal elementary-school children. Table 2 gives the summary of the findings.

In Isaac's study (1973) each of her 180 first-graders was tested twice with the Bender Test on the same day. She found no significant differences between the first and second test scores. Ryckman et al. (1972) tested lower middle-class children in the second, fourth, and sixth grades and retested them a week later. The test–retest correlations for the Bender Test scores ranged from .53 to .76 (p <.05 to p <.01).

A time interval of 10 days to 2 weeks between test and retest was used by Caskey (1973) and McCarthy (1972). McCarthy's test–retest correlation for his first-graders was much higher than that for his second-graders. Caskey administered the Bender Test to 193 kindergarten pupils both as an individual and as a group test. Correlation between individually administered Bender Tests was .63, while the group administration yielded a correlation of .83 between the first and second test scores.

Table 2.
Test–Retest with the Bender Test

Investigator(s)	N	Subjects	Time Interval	Correlations
Isaac (1973)	180	1st gr.	same day	no sig. diff.
Ryckman et al. (1972)	20	2nd gr.	1 week	.53*
	24	4th gr.	1 week	.56
	27	6th gr.	1 week	.76
McCarthy (1972)	19	1st gr.	1–2 weeks	.88
	31	2nd gr.	1–2 weeks	.56
Caskey (1973)	193	K pupils	10–14 days	.63 (indiv. test)
	193	K pupils	10–14 days	.83 (group test)
Goff & Parker (1969)	25	K pupils	2 weeks	.90
	29	1st gr.	2 weeks	.81
	29	2nd gr.	2 weeks	.85
	28	3rd gr.	2 weeks	.83
	29	4th gr.	2 weeks	.85
Ruckhaber (1964)	24	K pupils	6 weeks	.84, .80, .87
	24	K pupils	12 weeks	.81, .75
	24	K pupils	18 weeks	.77
Sonoda (1971)	37	K pupils	3 months	.63, .53, .60
Keogh & Smith (1968)†	140	K pupils	2 months (Sep/Nov)	.57
	140	K pupils	5 months (Sep/Feb)	.65
	140	K pupils	8 months (Sep/May)	.56
Koppitz, 1974	44	K pupils	8 months (Oct/Jan)	.50

*Significant at .05 level, all other r's significant at .01 level or better.

†The Keogh scoring system was used in this study; in all other studies the Developmental Bender Test Scoring System was used.

Goff and Parker (1969) tested pupils ranging from kindergarten to the fourth grade, with a 2-week interval between Bender Test administrations. They obtained correlations between Bender Test scores from .83 to .90; all of them were significant at the .001 level. Corresponding results were found by Ruckhaber (1964), who tested 24 kindergarten pupils four times at 6-week intervals using alternately individual and group administration of the Bender Test. There was little difference between the test scores obtained with the group and the individual testing methods. However, the magnitude of the correlations between the Bender Test scores decreased somewhat as the interval between test administrations increased.

Keogh and Smith (1968), using the Keogh Bender Test scoring system, tested a single group of kindergarten pupils four times over an 8-month period. Their correlations between Bender Test scores are slightly lower than Ruckhaber's correlations, but they are still significant at the .01 level. In Japan, Sonoda (1971) tested and retested 37 kindergarten pupils with a 3-month interval between tests. Three qualified psychologists scored the two sets of Bender Test records independently. The correlations they obtained between the Bender Test scores were .53, .60, and .63; all were significant at the .001 level.

As indicated earlier (p. 14), I administered the Bender Test to 44 white, middle-class kindergarten pupils at the beginning (October) and end (June) of the school year. The correlation between the two sets of test scores for the entire group was .50 (p <.01). Children who obtained very good Bender Test scores in the fall also had very good scores 10 months later. The test scores of the youngsters who showed average or below-average Bender Test performance at the beginning of the school year were less reliable. Of this group of 31 children, 35% produced above-average Bender Test scores by the end of the school year; 45% had average Bender Test scores by June; 20% were scoring poorly on the Bender Test 10 months later.

Results from these nine studies indicate that the total Developmental Bender Test scores of normal elementary-school children were reasonably stable and that the Bender Test scores are quite reliable. One would expect, of course, more instability on the Bender Test scores of children with minimal brain dysfunction and/or emotional problems. Minor changes on the Bender Test records of average children have relatively little effect on the test–retest scores when the interval between the test administrations does not exceed 3 months. Details on a Bender Test protocol may vary from one test administration to the next, as was shown above (p. 15). It is imperative, therefore, not to attach too much significance to minor imperfections or to a single Bender Test scoring point. Certainly no diagnosis or major decision should ever be made on the basis of a single scoring point, nor for that matter on the basis of a youngster's total Developmental Bender Test score.

A given Bender Test performance reflects a child's current state of maturity in visual-motor perception as well as his current attitudes and emotional state. As these change and as the youngster matures, his Bender Test performance will also change and mature. A Bender Test can provide valid and reliable information concerning the child's status at the particular time of the test administration. For most normal children, grades 1 to 6, the Bender Test scores improve at the expected rate and the correlations between earlier and later Bender Test scores remain significant.

Children with developmental lags or with minimal brain dysfunction tend to mature at a slower and often uneven rate; they are also apt to show instability and unevenness on repeated Bender Test performances. Therefore a child's rate of improvement on the Bender Test scores is highly significant from a diagnostic point of view. Erratic, inconsistent progress on the Bender Test reflects a child's unstable functioning and is not due to unreliability on the part of the Bender Test scoring system. Research findings showed conclusively that Bender Test scores of normal elementary-school pupils (end of kindergarten to sixth grade) are reliable.

CHAPTER 5.
Normative Data for the Developmental Bender Test Scoring System

SEX DIFFERENCES ON THE BENDER TEST

The original normative data for the Developmental Bender Test Scoring System (Koppitz, 1963, p. 33) showed no statistically significant differences between test scores for boys and girls. In consequence, only one set of normative data was presented for both boys and girls. A number of recent Bender Test studies offer support for the earlier findings. One set of norms for boys and girls seems quite sufficient, since there seem to be no sex differences on the Developmental Bender Test scores of elementary-school children from the end of kindergarten through the fifth grade. For beginning kindergarten pupils, the findings are less clear-cut.

The following is a list of the investigators who reported no statistically significant differences between the Developmental Bender Test scores of the boys and girls they examined:

Investigators	Subjects
Baer and Gale (1967)	First grade
Condell (1963)	Mentally retarded
Dibner and Korn (1969)	K to fourth grade
Dinmore (1972)	First to fourth grade
Fiedler and Schmidt (1969)	Age 7–0
Goff (1968)	K to fourth grade
Hammer (1967)	First grade
Isaac (1971)	First grade
Keogh and Vormeland (1970)	K to fourth grade
Koppitz (1973)	Beginning K
Murphy (1964)	First grade
Savering (1968)	First grade
Singh (1965)	Ages 6 to 11
Smith and Keogh (1963)	K, second, third grade
Stadler (1966)	First grade
Taylor and Thweatt (1972)	Ages 6, 7, 11, and 12
Vormeland (1968)	First grade
Wedell and Horne (1969)	Age 5–3 to 5–9

There seems to be some evidence that girls mature a little earlier than boys in visual-motor perception (Koppitz, 1963, p. 35). This difference is usually little more than a trend with very young children. Vormeland (1968) found that among Norwegian first-graders girls did better than boys on the Bender Test, but this difference was not statistically significant.

31

Fiedler and Schmidt (1969) discovered that the Bender Test scores of their 7-year-old boys were more variable than those of the girls, but once again the difference between the sexes was not statistically significant. On the other hand, Caskey's (1973) kindergarten girls did significantly better ($p <.05$) than his boys. The girls also had a slightly higher mean IQ, but this difference was not significant.

As youngsters mature, any difference that might have existed initially disappears. Keogh and Smith (1968) tested kindergarten youngsters twice, once in November and again in February. There was a significant difference between the Bender Test scores of the boys and girls in November, but none in February.

Dinmore (1972) encountered significant differences between the Bender Test performances of his male and female kindergarten pupils in both educationally deprived and in educationally adequate school settings. However, sex differences on the Bender Test scores were no longer in evidence in the first grade. Between the beginning of kindergarten and the end of the first grade marked maturation takes place in the visual-motor perception of both boys and girls. During this period the boys seem to catch up with the girls, so that there is no longer any significant difference on their Developmental Bender Test scores.

The discussion of sex differences on the Bender Test scores has dealt so far only with the Bender Test performance of normal public-school pupils. It appears that average boys and girls in the first to fifth grades do not differ on their Developmental Bender Test scores. The findings, however, do not necessarily apply also to children with emotional and learning problems. Sabatino and Ysseldyke (1972) reported considerable differences in the Bender Test performance of boys and girls who were referred to the psychologist because of severe learning disabilities. In this study the boys did significantly better on the Bender Test than the girls. The same was discovered by Dierks and Cushna (1969) with clinic patients. The Bender Test scores of the boys were far superior to those of the girls.

These results seem to reflect the double standard that has existed up to the present in our middle-class culture. There are indications that this situation is now changing, but these changes are still too new to be revealed in the research literature. Until recently boys were more readily referred for psychological evaluation and treatment than girls. Girls tended to be more protected than boys and were exposed to less pressure for achievement. Because of this, only girls with very serious problems were referred for special help. A girl with moderate learning and behavior problems was most often accepted at home and in school, therefore she experienced less frustration than would a boy with the same difficulties. In consequence, a comparison of boys and girls among clinic patients and psychiatric referrals reveals that boys outnumber girls by a considerable margin, while girls tend to show more serious impairment and pathology than do boys. Their Bender Test performances are also inferior to those of the boys. However, I found that this difference between the Bender Test scores disappears when the boys and girls are carefully matched for age and mental ability. Neither Dierks and Cushna nor Sabatino and Ysseldyke matched their subjects for chronological age and IQ scores.

I conducted a study to determine whether, in fact, any significant difference exists between the Bender Test performances of boys and girls with emotional and learning difficulties. The subjects for this study were all the female special-class pupils with behavior and learning problems I had worked with during the past 10 years who met the following criteria: They had to be between 8 and 10 years 11 months old, and their WISC Full Scale IQ score had to be at least 80 or better. Thirty-two girls met these criteria. Thereafter, I matched the girls for exact C.A. and WISC FS IQ scores with 32 male special-class pupils. Each group of subjects had an age mean of 9 years 8 months and an IQ mean score of 89.4 (range 80 to 110).

After the boys and girls had been selected from my files on the basis of their C.A. and IQ scores, I pulled out their Bender Test records and compared their Bender Test scores. All Bender Test records had been scored previously at the time of initial evaluation of the youngsters. The Bender Test mean score for all 32 boys was 5.6 (range 1 to 13), and that for all 32 girls was 5.2 (range 0 to 11). The difference between the Bender Test mean scores of the two groups was not statistically significant. Separate test scores for the subjects 8, 9, and 10 years old again yielded no statistically significant differences between the boys and girls. There was also no difference between the number of boys and girls whose test scores fell above or below the Bender Test mean score for their age level. Thus it appears that there is no significant difference between the Bender Test scores of boys and girls regardless of whether they are average public-school pupils or children with emotional and learning problems, provided the groups are matched for age and mental ability.

BENDER TEST NORMATIVE DATA BY AGE LEVEL

The normative data for the Developmental Bender Test Scoring System as presented in *The Bender Gestalt Test for Young Children* (Koppitz, 1963, Table 6 and Figure 1) show a somewhat uneven distribution of test scores. Choynowski (1970) applied a curve-fitting method to the normative data that smoothes out the distribution of test scores and makes them more readily available for the application to individual Bender Test records. Table 3 shows both the original and the adjusted set of mean Developmental Bender Test scores for children age 5 years to 10 years 11 months.

The normative data shown in Table 3 were derived from 1104 public-school pupils, kindergarten to fifth grade. An attempt was made to include in the normative sample a socioeconomic cross-section of elementary-school children from urban, suburban, small-town, and rural

Table 3.
Empirical and Adjusted Bender Test Means and Standard
Deviations*

	Empirical		Adjusted	
Age	Mean	SD	Mean	SD
5–0/5–5	13.6	3.6	13.2	3.8
5–6/5–11	9.8	3.7	10.2	3.8
6–0/6–5	8.4	4.1	8.0	3.8
6–6/6–11	6.4	3.8	6.4	3.8
7–0/7–5	4.8	3.6	5.1	3.6
7–6/7–11	4.7	3.3	4.2	3.4
8–0/8–5	3.7	3.6	3.4	3.1
8–6/8–11	2.5	3.0	2.7	2.8
9–0/9–5	1.7	1.8	2.2	2.5
9–6/9–11	1.6	1.7	1.8	2.2
10–0/10–5	1.6	1.7	1.5	1.8
10–6/10–11	1.5	2.1	1.2	1.5

*Reproduced by permission from Choynowski M: Curve-fitting as a method of statistical correction of developmental norms, shown on the example of the Bender-Koppitz Test. J Clin Psychol 26:140, 1970.

areas. Although a few black youngsters were included in the sample, there was a marked underrepresentation of minority students in the normative sample. The normative data are, in fact, typical only of white school children. In order to include a more representative cross-section of American school children, I conducted a new normative study for the Developmental Bender Test Scoring System.

The 1974 normative sample includes 975 elementary-school pupils, age 5 to 11, from the West (15%), from the South (2%), and from the Northeast (83%). Of these youngsters, 86% were white, 8.5% black, 4.5% Mexican-American and Puerto Rican, 1% oriental. The youngsters lived in rural areas (7%), in small towns (31%), in suburbs (36%), and in large metropolitan centers (26%). The mean Bender Test scores for different age levels of this new normative sample are shown in Tables 4 and 5 and in Appendix B and Appendix C. The percentile scores for the Bender Test in Table 15, Appendix E, are also based on the data from the new normative study.

Gifted children would be expected to perform considerably above the level of the normative data, while many youngsters from deprived areas and those with limited ability or specific learning problems would be expected to function below the average level. For psychologists working in a given socioeconomic or ethnic area it is always helpful to establish appropriate norms for that given setting or to have available "typical" Bender Test scores for that particular population. A child whose Bender Test score is average for his social group and his age level cannot be considered to have serious problems in the visual-motor area, even if his performance on the Bender Test is more immature than the norm for his age level.

Recent Bender Test literature offers a wealth of data for school children from advantaged and from disadvantaged communities, and for youngsters from different regional, national, and ethnic backgrounds. The findings from various studies are shown in Tables 4 and 5. Table 4 shows the Bender Test mean scores for children age 5 to 11 at 6-month intervals—that is, in the same fashion as the Bender Test normative data in Table 3 and Table 13. Table 5 gives the Bender Test mean scores for children age 6 to 11 at 12-month intervals since several investigators reported their findings for groups of pupils whose age range extended over a 12-month period (C.A. 5–0 to 5–11, 6–0 to 6–11, etc.) or whose age span was limited to the middle 6 months of the year (5–3 to 5–9, 6–3 to 6–9, etc.). Table 4 and Table 5 are presented separately in order to avoid confusion when comparing the Bender Test scores of groups of children whose age spans differ.

For research purposes pupils age 6 years 0 months to 6 years 5 months (with an age mean of 6 years 3 months and a Bender Test mean

Table 4.

Bender Test Mean Scores for Ages 5 to 10 in 6-Month Intervals

Age	Investigator(s)	N	Subjects	Bender Test Mean Score
5–0/5–5	Koppitz (1963)	81	cross-section, white	13.2
	Koppitz , 1974	47	cross-section, wh. & bl.	13.7
5–6/5–11	Dibner & Korn (1969)	55	white, high IQ	9.0
	Koppitz, 1974	130	cross-section, wh. & bl.	9.7
	Koppitz (1963)	128	cross-section, white	10.2
6–0/6–5	Greene & Clark (1973)	22	Anglo, New Mexico	5.3
	Greene & Clark (1973)	40	Chicano, New Mexico	7.4
	Koppitz (1963)	155	cross-section, white	8.0
	Koppitz, 1974	175	cross-section, wh. & bl.	8.6
	Dibner & Korn (1969)	49	white, high IQ	8.7
6–6/6–11	Greene & Clark (1973)	35	Anglo, New Mexico	4.2
	Dibner & Korn (1969)	48	white, high IQ	5.4
	Henderson et al. (1969)	120	low socioecon., white	6.0
	Greene & Clark (1973)	78	Chicano, New Mexico	6.0
	Koppitz (1963)	180	cross-section, white	6.4
	Koppitz, 1974	60	cross-section, wh. & bl.	7.2
	Henderson et al. (1969)	83	low socioecon., black	8.1
7–0/7–5	Greene & Clark (1973)	22	Anglo, New Mexico	4.4
	Dibner & Korn (1969)	48	white, high IQ	4.6
	Solomon (1969)	15	low middle-class	4.8
	Greene & Clark (1973)	78	Chicano, New Mexico	5.1
	Koppitz (1963)	156	cross-section, white	5.1
	Koppitz, 1974	61	cross-section, wh. & bl.	5.8

Table 4. (continued)
Bender Test Mean Scores for Ages 5 to 10 in 6-Month Intervals

Age	Investigator(s)	N	Subjects	Bender Test Mean Score
7–6/7–11	Dibner & Korn (1969)	60	white, high IQ	3.4
	Greene & Clark (1973)	25	Anglo, New Mexico	3.4
	Koppitz (1963)	110	cross-section, white	4.2
	Solomon (1969)	50	low middle-class	4.5
	Koppitz, 1974	47	cross-section, wh. & bl.	4.6
	Greene & Clark (1973)	86	Chicano, New Mexico	4.7
8–0/8–5	Greene & Clark (1973)	34	Anglo, New Mexico	2.9
	Moseley (1969)	22	non-deprived, white	2.9
	Dibner & Korn (1969)	51	white, high IQ	3.0
	Moseley (1969)	12	deprived, white	3.3
	Koppitz (1963)	62	cross-section, white	3.4
	Solomon (1969)	43	low middle-class	3.5
	Greene & Clark (1973)	63	Chicano, New Mexico	3.6
	Koppitz, 1974	53	cross-section, wh. & bl.	4.2
	Moseley (1969)	12	deprived, black	6.0
8–6/8–11	Greene & Clark (1973)	34	Anglo, New Mexico	2.4
	Moseley (1969)	39	non-deprived, white	2.6
	Koppitz (1963)	60	cross-section, white	2.7
	Koppitz, 1974	60	cross-section, wh. & bl.	3.0
	Dibner & Korn (1969)	51	white, high IQ	3.0
	Moseley (1969)	69	deprived, white	3.6
	Greene & Clark (1973)	78	Chicano, New Mexico	3.8
	Moseley (1969)	29	deprived, black	4.6
9–0/9–5	Dibner & Korn (1969)	42	white, high IQ	2.0
	Moseley (1969)	64	non-deprived, white	2.0
	Koppitz (1963)	65	cross-section, white	2.2
	Koppitz, 1974	78	cross-section, wh. & bl.	2.8
	Moseley (1969)	78	deprived, white	2.9
	Moseley (1969)	62	deprived, black	4.7
9–6/9–11	Koppitz (1963)	49	cross-section, white	1.8
	Dibner & Korn (1969)	33	white, high IQ	2.0
	Moseley (1969)	33	non-deprived, white	2.2
	Koppitz, 1974	47	cross-section, wh. & bl.	2.3
	Moseley (1969)	88	deprived, white	3.0
	Moseley (1969)	99	deprived, black	4.6
10–0/10–5	Bravo (1972)	22	gifted children	1.2
	Koppitz (1963)	27	cross-section, white	1.5
	Dibner & Korn (1969)	37	white, high IQ	1.6
	Koppitz, 1974	76	cross-section, wh. & bl.	1.9
	Moseley (1969)	37	non-deprived, white	2.3
	Moseley (1969)	18	deprived, white	2.6
	Moseley (1969)	45	deprived, black	4.7
10–6/10–11	Koppitz (1963)	31	cross-section, white	1.2
	Dibner & Korn (1969)	15	white, high IQ	1.4
	Bravo (1972)	22	gifted children	1.5
	Koppitz, 1974	64	cross-section, wh. & bl.	1.8
	Moseley (1969)	25	deprived, white	1.8

Table 5.
Bender Test Mean Scores for Ages 5 to 10 in 12-Month Intervals

Age	Investigator(s)	N	Subjects	Bender Test Mean Score
5–0/5–11	Koppitz, 1974	177	cross-section, wh. & bl.	10.6
	Koppitz (1963)	209	cross-section, white	11.3
	Keogh (1968b)	69	urban cross-sec., England	11.3
	Sabatino & Becker (1969)	38	lower-class, white	15.2
	Goff (1969)	20	cross-section, wh. & bl.	15.6
6–0/6–11	Sabatino & Becker (1969)	39	lower-class, white	7.1
	Koppitz (1963)	335	cross-section, white	7.3
	Obrzut et al. (1972)	48	cross-section	7.4
	Koppitz, 1974	235	cross-section, wh. & bl.	8.2
	Keogh (1968b)	64	urban cross-sec., England	8.6
	Keogh & Vormeland (1970)	46	cross-section, Norway	9.0
	Goff (1969)	30	cross-section, wh. & bl.	9.7
7–0/7–11	Koppitz (1963)	266	cross-section, white	4.8
	Sabatino & Becker (1969)	48	lower-class, white	5.0
	Koppitz, 1974	108	cross-section, wh. & bl.	5.3
	Keogh & Vormeland (1970)	71	cross-section, Norway	5.9
	Goff (1969)	30	cross-section, wh. & bl.	6.0
	Keogh (1968b)	78	urban cross-sec., England	6.2
	Obrzut et al. (1972)	40	cross-section	6.2
8–0/8–11	Sabatino & Becker (1969)	36	lower-class, white	2.7
	Koppitz (1963)	122	cross-section, white	3.1
	Koppitz, 1974	133	cross-section, wh. & bl.	3.6
	Bravo (1971)	76	cross-section, Mexico	3.7
	Goff (1969)	25	cross-section, wh. & bl.	3.8
	Obrzut et al. (1972)	50	cross-section	4.0
	Keogh (1968b)	67	urban cross-sec., England	4.2
	Keogh & Vormeland (1970)	100	urban cross-sec., Norway	5.0
9–0/9–11	Koppitz (1963)	114	cross-section, white	2.1
	Koppitz, 1974	125	cross-section, wh. & bl.	2.5
	Bravo (1971)	139	cross-section, Mexico	2.6
	Goff (1969)	25	cross-section, wh. & bl.	3.8
	Obrzut et al. (1972)	50	cross-section	3.8
	Keogh & Vormeland (1970)	48	urban cross-sec., Norway	4.0
	Keogh (1968b)	64	urban cross-sec., England	4.2
10–0/10–11	Bravo (1972)	44	gifted children	1.4
	Koppitz (1963)	58	cross-section, white	1.5
	Koppitz, 1974	144	cross-section, wh. & bl.	1.9
	Bravo (1971)	123	cross-section, Mexico	2.9
11–0/11–11	Koppitz, 1974	73	cross-section, wh. & bl.	1.4

score of 8) are not comparable to a group of youngsters age 6 years 0 months to 6 years 11 months (with an age mean of 6 years 6 months and a Bender Test mean score of 7.3). Any significant difference on the Bender Test performance of two such disparate groups of subjects may be nothing more than a reflection of their age differences.

The differences of Bender Test mean scores for different age levels diminish as the youngsters grow older. By age 9 most children are able to execute the Bender Test without major imperfections, so that precise age groupings of older pupils become less crucial in research studies. By age 9 the Developmental Bender Test scores reach a plateau and no longer discriminate between average and above-average Bender Test performance. By age 10 the Bender Test ceases to be significant as a test of perceptual–motor development for normal children. The function of the test changes. The Developmental Bender Test scores are meaningful only for older pupils if the youngsters' perceptual–motor integration functions below the 9-year level.

The range of Bender Test mean scores at each age level gradually diminishes as the age of the children increases. Table 5 reveals a range of mean scores for 5-year-old children that extends over five points, from 10.6 for average youngsters to 15.6 for deprived children. At age 8 and 9 the differences in Bender Test mean scores for various groups of pupils extend only over 2.5 points, while by age 10 there appears to be no difference to speak of between the Bender Test mean scores of average and gifted pupils and only a 1.5-point difference between the highest and the lowest mean scores.

BENDER TEST NORMATIVE DATA
BY GRADE LEVEL

Bender Test scores of individuals or of groups of children can be compared with scores of other children of the same age level or with the test scores of pupils attending the same grade level. Normative data for kindergarten through fourth grade were provided earlier (Koppitz, 1963, p. 188). However, these data were obtained at the beginning of the school year and therefore do not show improvement on the Bender Test in the course of a given grade level.

During the past 10 years I have collected findings from various studies that taken together give a rather comprehensive picture of the Bender Test mean scores of different groups of children at the beginning, the middle, and the end of each grade from kindergarten through sixth grade. Table 6 presents the Bender Test mean scores for the different grade levels. Just as with the age-level norms, each grade level reveals a considerable range of mean Bender Test scores, reflecting the children's ages and socioeconomic and cultural backgrounds. Thus we find that the Bender Test mean scores for beginning first-graders from high socio-

Table 6.
Bender Test Mean Scores by Grade Level

Investigator(s)	N	Subjects	Bender Test Mean	S.D.
		Beginning Kindergarten (August–November)		
Koppitz, 1974	45	middle-class, white	12.1	
Koppitz (1963)	38	cross-section, white	13.5	3.6
		Middle Kindergarten (December–March)		
Becker & Sabatino (1973)	154	upper middle-class, white	8.9	3.4
Hammer (1967)	43	middle-class, white	11.2	3.4
Kerr (1972)	64	cross-section	12.2	
Dinmore (1972)	20	disadvantaged, black	12.8	3.9
Dinmore (1972)	20	advantaged, black	12.9	4.2
Vega & Powell (1972)	33	COPE, deprived, black	13.5	
Goff (1969)	25	urban & rural, wh. & bl.	14.6	
		End of Kindergarten (April–June)		
Sonoda (1973)	122	cross-section, Japan	6.8	2.8
Dibner & Korn (1969)	114	suburban, white, high IQ	8.8	
Koppitz, 1974	146	middle-class, white	9.1	3.4
Smith & Keogh (1963)	117	middle-class, white	9.4	3.7
Wise (1968)	79	middle-class, white	9.6	
Caskey (1973)	201	lower middle-class	9.8	2.4
Zach & Kaufman (1969)	48	middle-class, white	10.2	
Giebink & Birch (1970)	98	semi-rural, white	11.5	
Zach & Kaufman (1969)	48	lower-class, black	15.9	
		Beginning First Grade (August–November)		
Pope & Snyder (1970)	30	middle-class, white	5.4	
Oberstein (1968)	50	suburban, white	5.9	
Vormeland (1968)	547	cross-section, Norway	6.7	3.3
Koppitz (1963)	153	cross-section, white	8.1	4.4
Thweatt (1963)	64	middle-class, white	8.8	
Cabrini (1968)	90	parochial school, white	8.8	3.8
Norfleet (1973)	311	middle-class, white	9.4	4.1
Stadler (1966)	70	middle-class, white	10.3	3.2
Hammer (1967)	126	middle-class, white	10.5	3.1
Mlodnosky (1972)	93	deprived, black	11.9	3.6
Hammer (1967)	216	deprived, white	13.1	3.9
		Middle First Grade (December–March)		
Wile (1965)	45	middle-class, white, high IQ	4.5	2.3
Isaac (1971)	20	advantaged, white	4.6	2.6
Isaac (1971)	20	disadvantaged, white	6.0	3.1
Dinmore (1972)	20	advantaged, black	6.4	2.6
Kerr (1972)	100	cross-section	7.2	
Isaac (1971)	20	disadvantaged, black	8.4	3.4
Goff (1969)	29	cross-section, wh. & bl.	8.5	
Dinmore (1972)	20	deprived, black	9.2	3.1

Table 6. (continued)
Bender Test Mean Scores by Grade Level

Investigator(s)	N	Subjects	Bender Test	
			Mean	S.D.
End of First Grade (April–June)				
Dibner & Korn (1969)	103	suburban, white, high IQ	4.4	2.2
Sonoda (1973)	133	cross-section, Japan	4.7	3.1
Giebink & Birch (1970)	111	semi-rural, white	5.3	
Hammer (1972)	126	middle-class, white	6.4	2.7
Snyder & Freud (1967)	667	middle-class, white	7.6	3.9
Hammer (1972)	216	deprived, white	8.4	3.4
Beginning Second Grade (August–November)				
Koppitz (1963)	141	cross-section, white	4.7	3.2
Middle Second Grade (December–March)				
Wile (1965)	45	middle-class, white, high IQ	3.8	1.8
Koppitz, 1974	24	cross-section, wh. & bl.	4.0	
Heinrich (1968)	57	middle-class, white	4.2	2.6
Kerr (1972)	92	cross-section	4.2	
Isaac (1971)	20	advantaged, white	4.5	2.6
Goff (1969)	29	cross-section, wh. & bl.	5.2	
Isaac (1971)	20	disadvantaged, white	5.5	2.7
Dinmore (1972)	20	advantaged, black	5.9	3.1
Dinmore (1972)	20	disadvantaged, black	7.0	3.0
Isaac (1971)	20	disadvantaged, black	8.0	3.0
End of Second Grade (April–June)				
Sonoda (1973)	60	urban, Japan	2.3	2.3
Sonoda (1973)	54	rural, Japan	2.8	2.5
Dibner & Korn (1969)	109	suburban, white, high IQ	3.2	2.2
Smith & Keogh (1963)	117	middle-class, white	5.8	2.8
Beginning Third Grade (August–November)				
Oberstein (1968)	50	suburban, white, high IQ	3.0	
Middle Third Grade (December–March)				
Wile (1965)	45	middle-class, white, high IQ	2.0	1.9
Koppitz (1963)	40	middle-class, white	2.2	2.0
Bravo (1971)	469	cross-section, Mexico	3.3	
Goff (1969)	28	cross-section, wh. & bl.	3.5	
Dinmore (1972)	20	advantaged, black	3.8	2.1
Howard (1970)	42	suburban, white	4.6	
Dinmore (1972)	20	disadvantaged, black	6.8	2.8
End of Third Grade (April–June)				
Sonoda (1973)	49	urban, Japan	.9	.9
Sonoda (1973)	55	rural, Japan	2.0	2.0
Dibner & Korn (1969)	106	suburban, white, high IQ	2.3	1.8
Koppitz, 1974	26	cross-section, wh. & bl.	2.6	

Table 6. (continued)
Bender Test Mean Scores by Grade Level

Investigator(s)	N	Subjects	Bender Test	
			Mean	S.D.
Smith & Keogh (1963)	117	middle-class, white	4.9	2.5
Moseley (1969)	76	deprived, rural, black	6.5	3.0
Middle Fourth Grade (December–March)				
Wile (1965)	45	middle-class, white, high IQ	1.0	1.1
Koppitz (1963)	39	cross-section, white	1.5	1.9
Dinmore (1972)	20	advantaged, black	3.0	2.5
Goff (1969)	29	cross-section, wh. & bl.	3.5	
Dinmore (1972)	20	disadvantaged, black	5.4	3.0
End of Fourth Grade (April–June)				
Sonoda (1973)	65	urban, Japan	.9	1.4
Sonoda (1973)	56	rural, Japan	1.5	2.0
Dibner & Korn (1969)	60	suburban, white, high IQ	1.7	1.5
Middle Fifth Grade (December–March)				
Wile (1965)	45	middle-class, white, high IQ	2.0	1.6
Sixth Grade (January–June)				
Heinrich (1968)	41	middle-class, white	1.2	.1
Keogh (1968)	127	middle-class, white	2.3	2.0

economic areas range from 5 to 9; middle-class children typically have
Bender Test scores between 8 and 10; youngsters from deprived areas are
likely to have Bender Test mean scores between 10 and 13. By the end of
the first grade advantaged youngsters obtained a Bender Test mean score
of 4.4; middle-class pupils had mean scores from 5 to 7; deprived children
showed a Bender Test mean score of 8.4. Both the magnitude and range of
the Bender Test scores decrease markedly between kindergarten and the
second grade. Thereafter, the range of the Bender Test mean scores diminishes gradually until it stabilizes by fourth grade to a span of only one
or two scoring points for most groups of youngsters.

Interpretation of Individual Bender Test Scores of Primary-Grade Pupils

When interpreting the Bender Test scores of a given child in school,
it is important to know not only the pupil's age and socioeconomic and
cultural background but also when the test was administered. As was
pointed out earlier, it makes a difference whether the Bender Test was
administered at the beginning or the end of the school year. For example,

Johnny, a deprived youngster, obtained a Bender Test score of 8. If he
had made that score at the beginning of the first grade, he would have
been typical of middle-class youngsters and would have been above average for his particular group. But as it happened Johnny was 7 years 3
months old and was tested during May, at the end of the school year. This
changes the picture. We can now conclude from Johnny's Bender Test
score of 8 that his visual-motor perception is somewhat immature for his
age level, since it resembles that of 6-year-old pupils (Tables 4 and 5).
The Bender Test score of 8 is on the level of advantaged pupils entering
the first grade, of middle-class children at the middle of the first grade,
and of disadvantaged youngsters at the end of the first grade (Table 6). It
follows, therefore, that Johnny's Bender Test performance is immature
when compared to that of most 7-year-olds, but not when compared to the
particular group he comes from.

CHAPTER 6.
The Bender Test
and Social and Cultural Factors

Several recent studies have concerned themselves with the relationship of performance on the Bender Test and social and cultural background factors among school children.

DEPRIVED VERSUS NONDEPRIVED CHILDREN

There is a consensus that the Bender Test performances of groups of white middle-class pupils, kindergarten to third grade, are significantly better than those of deprived Indian children (Hoffman, 1966) and of disadvantaged black youngsters (Hammer, 1967; Hoffman, 1966; Isaac, 1973; Mlodnosky, 1972; Zach and Kaufman, 1969).

Dinmore (1972) reported that Bender Test scores did not discriminate between black kindergarten pupils from educationally adequate and educationally deprived school settings. However, in grades one to four Dinmore's black youngsters from the adequate school settings did significantly better on the Bender Test than did the black children from deprived school settings.

Both Hoffman (1966) and Isaac (1973) failed to find any statistically significant differences between the Bender Test performances of white advantaged and white disadvantaged pupils.

Deprivation, Ethnic Group, and Sex

Henderson et al. (1969), Isaac (1973), and Moseley (1969) all used children from low socioeconomic areas as subjects in their Bender Test studies. A comparison of deprived black and deprived white youngsters revealed that the Bender Test performance of the white group was markedly better than that of the black youngsters. The study of Adams and Lieb (1973) showed that white Headstart boys did better on the Bender Test than black Headstart boys, but there was no significant difference between the Bender Test scores of the black and white Headstart girls.

ETHNIC GROUP AND RATE OF MATURATION

Research findings suggest that the rate of development in visual-motor perception differs among children of various ethnic groups. The Bender Test performances of young Puerto Rican, Indian, and black children, both advantaged and disadvantaged, seem to mature at a somewhat slower rate than those of white youngsters. Marmorale and Brown (1974) showed significant differences between the Bender Test scores of groups of white, black, and Puerto Rican first-grade pupils. By the end of the third grade the youngsters in all three groups showed marked improvement in their Bender Test performances. The Puerto Rican youngsters seemed to benefit most from the school experience and made the biggest gains on the Bender Test; the black children made the least gains in Bender Test scores. The gap between the Bender Test scores of all three groups of pupils diminished drastically during the 3-year period of the study.

Taylor and Thweatt (1972) discovered that 6- and 7-year-old Navajo children lagged behind a Caucasian control group in visual-motor perception as measured on the Bender Test. But by age 11 to 12 the differences between the Bender Test performances of the Navajo and the white children had disappeared. Both groups had matured in the visual-motor area and were able to copy the Bender Test designs with few, if any, errors.

Greene and Clark (1973) found that Spanish-American and Anglo youngsters in New Mexico differed significantly in their Bender Test scores at age 6. Thereafter the discrepancies between the Bender Test scores of the two groups of children diminished and were no longer significant (Table 4).

The rate of maturation in visual-motor perception seems to be accelerated among oriental children, especially among pupils in Japan. Tiedeman (1971) collected Bender Test protocols from 7-year-old children in the United States and in thirteen different countries in Africa, Asia, and Europe. The Bender Test performances of the children in Japan were far superior to those of 7-year-olds in all the other countries, including the United States. The Bender Test scores of the Chinese children were second best. Results from Sonoda's study (1973) concur with Tiedeman's findings. Sonoda examined young urban and rural children in Kumamoto City and surroundings on Kyushu Island, Japan. As shown in Table 6, Sonoda's kindergarten pupils obtained Bender Test scores that were on the level of American first-graders; the Japanese first-graders functioned on the Bender Test more like second-graders in the United States; the second-graders in Japan resembled third-graders in this country; and the Bender Test records of the Japanese third-graders were similar to those of most American fourth-graders. But by fourth grade or at age 9 the difference between the Bender Test scores of the Japanese and the American children were no longer statistically significant.

Tiedeman's study raises an interesting question: To what extent do early childhood training and the values of a given culture affect the rate of development in visual-motor perception? We know that specific training in visual-motor perception of school-age children has only a limited impact.

In both China and Japan the visual arts have been developed to the highest level and have flourished since prehistoric times. One might surmise either that the people of Japan and China are inherently gifted in the visual-motor area or that they have developed over the centuries ways of rearing their children so as to facilitate the maturation of perceptual-motor integration. If, indeed, early and outstanding performance in visual-motor perception, as measured on the Bender Test, is a genetic trait in Japanese and Chinese youngsters, then it should manifest itself in children of Japanese and Chinese ancestry, no matter where they might reside. But this is not the case.

Tiedeman showed a significant difference in the Bender Test scores of Japanese children in Japan and of American youngsters of Japanese ancestry in San Jose, California. On the other hand, she found no statistically significant difference between the Bender Test performances of American children of Japanese and of European background. She also noted that the Japanese-American children were well adapted to American life and resembled other American youngsters more than they did the children of Japan.

A different picture presented itself when Tiedeman administered the Bender Test to 7-year-old Chinese children in Taipei, in Fiji, and in a Chinese area of San Francisco. Although the children in these three groups lived far apart, all of them had been reared in close-knit Chinese families and were educated and brought up in traditional Chinese ways. Tiedeman found that the three groups of youngsters did equally well on the Bender Test; there were no significant differences between their Bender Test scores.

How can we account for the differences in the Bender Test performances of the children of Japanese ancestry in Japan and in this country, and for the similarity between the Bender Test scores of the Chinese children living in different parts of the world? Tiedeman suggests that the rate of development in visual-motor perception may be at least in part determined by the child-rearing practices of a people and by the values they place on certain abilities and skills. Tiedeman hypothesizes that the training the children in Japan receive from infancy in the areas of visual awareness, appreciation of beauty, and motor control all contribute to the development of perceptual–motor integration at an earlier age. In this country more emphasis is placed on verbal skills than on visual-motor skills. Japanese-American children who are reared more nearly like other American youngsters also develop similar strengths and weaknesses as their Caucasian counterparts. Until recently many Chinese families continued to adhere closely to their traditional ways, regardless of where they lived. Their child-rearing practices seem to favor the development of visual-motor integration, be it in Taipei, in Fiji, or in San Francisco.

Tiedeman's study is most thought-provoking. Would it be possible, for instance, to improve the rate of development in visual-motor perception in socially and economically deprived youngsters by modifying their early childhood training? The recent study of Kagan and Klein (1973) with Guatemalan children seems to support such a hypothesis. They found that various cognitive functions emerged somewhat later in certain groups of

children than in others. But by age 11 to 12 the slowly maturing youngsters were able to perform the basic cognitive tasks as well as the early
maturing youngsters. Kagan and Klein concluded that experiential factors
seemed to influence the time at which these cognitive functions emerged.

SUMMARY

Results from recent Bender Test studies with deprived youngsters
show that disadvantaged black children do significantly less well on the
Bender Test than do advantaged black youngsters and both deprived and
nondeprived white children. No significant differences were found on the
Bender Test scores of disadvantaged and advantaged white pupils.

Indian and Chicano youngsters seem to mature in visual-motor perception at a somewhat slower rate than Anglo children; differences that
were found on Bender Test scores at age 6 or 7 disappear as the children
grow older.

Research findings suggest that child-rearing practices in Chinese
families and in families in Japan favor an early development in perceptual–motor integration. Young children in Japan show an accelerated
rate of maturation on the Bender Test; by age 9, however, the discrepancies between the Bender Test scores of Japanese and American youngsters disappear. The Bender Test performances of 7-year-old children of
Japanese ancestry reared in the United States are no different from those
of other 7-year-old American pupils. In contrast, Chinese-American
youngsters reared in traditional Chinese families in San Francisco differed from other American children; they revealed the same accelerated
rate of development on the Bender Test as did Chinese children in
Taipei. This raises the intriguing question: Will a change in child-rearing
practices in this country also improve the rate of development in
perceptual–motor integration of children, especially of socially deprived
youngsters?

CHAPTER 7.
The Bender Test and IQ Scores

The statement "the Bender Gestalt Test can be used with some degree of confidence as a short nonverbal intelligence test for young children, particularly for screening purposes" (Koppitz, 1963, p. 50) has been supported by a number of recent studies. But as I previously suggested, the Bender Test should if possible be combined with a brief verbal test.

CORRELATIONS BETWEEN BENDER
AND IQ TEST SCORES

Table 7 shows the correlations between the Bender Test scores and IQ scores of primary-grade pupils as reported in recent investigations. The highest correlations in Table 7 are those between the test scores of very young children and those of less advantaged youngsters (Baer and Gale, 1967; Caskey, 1973; Henderson et al., 1969; McNamara et al., 1969). All but two of the thirteen correlations in Table 7 are statistically significant at the .01 level or better, indicating that the Bender Test scores are indeed closely related to average or below-average IQ test scores.

The two nonsignificant correlations in Table 7 were derived from the Bender Test scores of white middle-class pupils with above-average mental ability. One of these correlations came from the study of Baer and Gale (1967); the other is part of my own investigation. These studies show quite similar results: Correlations between Bender Test and IQ scores of pupils with average mental ability were statistically significant, while the Bender Test and IQ scores of youngsters with superior intelligence were not significantly related.

The subjects of Baer and Gale were 32 first-graders of average mental ability (CTMM mean IQ 96), who lived in a Catholic Charities Care Home, and a group of 69 bright first-graders (CTMM mean IQ 120) from a parochial school. The correlation between the Bender Test and the IQ scores for the average pupils was $-.54$ ($p < .01$), whereas the correlation for the test scores of the bright pupils was only $-.23$ and was not significant.

In my own study I administered the Bender Test to two first-grade classes ($N = 44$) in a suburban school at the beginning of the school year. At the end of the following year I tested two kindergarten classes ($N = 52$) in the same school. Both groups of children were given the California Test of Mental Maturity (CTMM) when they were in the second grade. Either because of the redistricting of school populations that had occurred between the testing of the first-graders and the kindergarten group or because of chance fluctuations the two samples of pupils from the same

Table 7.
Relationship beteeen Bender Test and IQ Scores

Investigator(s)	N	Age	Subjects and IQ Tests	Bender & IQ test	
				r	p
Mc Namara et al. (1969)	42	M 5–8	Headstart, black, WPPSI IQ M 84	−.62*	0.001
Caskey (1973)	193	K (group)	small-town, Otis-Len. IQ M 105	−.66	0.001
	193	K (indiv.)	small-town, Otis-Len. IQ M 105	−.51	0.001
Becker & Sabatino (1973)	154	K	Suburb, white, Am. Sch. Int. T. M IQ 104	−.35	0.001
Koppitz	52	K	suburb , white, CTMM M IQ 109	−.36	0.01
	44	1 st gr.	suburb, white, CTMM M IQ 119	−.19	NS
Baer & Gale (1967)	69	1st gr.	parochial sch., CTMM M IQ 120	−.23	NS
	32	1 st gr.	Cath. Ch. Care Home, CTMM M IQ 96	−.54	0.01
Vormeland (1968)	281	1 st gr.	Oslo, Norway, Kuhlman-Anderson IQ	−.48	0.01
	691	1 st gr.	Oslo, Norway, Kuhlman-Anderson IQ	−.49	0.01
Henderson et al. (1969)	120	6–9/7–0	lower-class, white, WISC M IQ 99	−.51	0.01
	83	6–9/7–0	lower-class, non-white, WISC M IQ 92	−.48	0.01
Keogh (1965)	127	3rd gr.	middle-class, white, CTMM M IQ 106	−.24	0.01

*Correlations are negative since the Bender Test is scored for imperfections; hence a high score is a poor score.

school differed markedly in their IQ scores. The first-graders obtained a CTMM mean IQ of 118.6 and were obviously of above-average mental ability; the correlation between their Bender Test and IQ scores was −.19 and was not statistically significant. By contrast, the pupils I tested in kindergarten had only a CTMM mean IQ score of 108.6; the correlation between their Bender Test and IQ scores was −.36. While the magnitude of the correlation is not very high, it is statistically significant at the .01 level.

Hutton's findings (1966) also clearly demonstrate a close relationship between Bender Test scores and IQ test scores for groups of young clinic patients. His 6- and 7-year-old children with IQ scores of 40 to 69 had a Bender Test mean score of 12.4; those with IQ scores between 70 and 89 had a Bender Test mean score of 10.9; those with average mental ability (IQ 90 and up) had a Bender Test mean score of 5.3. For 8- and 9-year-old patients and for the 10- to 12-year-olds similar improvements on the Bender Test mean scores were found as the youngsters' IQ scores increased.

Table 10 and Figure 2 show similar results for children with learning disabilities; for a more complete discussion thereof see page 65. Ackerman et al. (1971) found that among third-grade boys with learning disabilities the youngsters with good Bender Test scores also had significantly higher WISC IQ scores than the boys with poor Bender Test scores.

BENDER TEST AND SUPERIOR MENTAL ABILITY

Bravo (1972) tested over 200 fifth-graders (including black, white, Chicano, and oriental boys and girls) who had been referred by their classroom teachers for possible inclusion into a program for gifted children. All youngsters were good students and read at least one to three years above grade level; all were thought to be of superior intelligence. I had the opportunity to examine the Bender Test records of 75 of these excellent pupils. Their Stanford-Binet IQ scores ranged from 121 to 180. It was interesting to discover that 70 of the 75 Bender Test protocols were as outstanding as one might have expected. These 70 bright children scored either 0, 1, or at most 2 on the Bender Test; only a few scores of 3 were found. Thus 93% of the outstanding pupils also produced exceptionally good Bender Test records. But how do we explain the failure of the remaining five bright youngsters to do well on the Bender Test? These five pupils with superior mental ability produced Bender Test records that were far from perfect. Their Bender Test scores were 4, 5 and 9. Four of the test protocols strongly resembled the Bender Test records of children with minimal brain dysfunction. The fifth Bender Test record showed signs of extreme anxiety and emotional disturbance. A closer look at the youngsters' test files showed that two boys had very good visual perception but poor visual-motor coordination and control. The two boys were exceedingly bright (both had IQ scores of 140) and excelled in abstract reasoning, in language ability, and in recall. The boys were so outstanding in most areas that the teachers evidently made allowances for their impulsivity, restlessness, and poor motor coordination. It is also quite probable that these 10-year-old pupils had learned in time to control their behavior even though the underlying impulsivity was still reflected on the Bender Test records.

The two bright girls with poor Bender Test records appeared to be good in just about everything but visual-motor perception. Their IQ scores were 131 and 135; they showed good motivation and control. Their language abilities were superior, and they had learned to compensate for most of their immaturity in the visual-motor area. The Bender Test protocols showed this quite clearly. The youngsters used guidelines on their drawings and corrected them spontaneously. Even so, some distortions and rotations were evident on the Bender Test records. However, this did not seem to interfere with their overall functioning. A child who has a weakness only in visual-motor perception is usually able to get along quite well, provided all else is good or outstanding (p. 60).

The fifth child with superior mental ability (IQ 133) and a poor Bender Test score was a 10-year-old boy. He had good achievement, but otherwise he was withdrawn and emotionally quite maladjusted. There was no evidence of any serious problem in perceptual–motor integration; instead he showed signs of extreme anxiety. This could, of course, have been a temporary condition, since he knew he was being tested for admission to a special program. Without having seen the youngster at work it is difficult to determine from the single Bender Test record whether the child's state of anxiety had been of long duration or was a response to the immediate situation. The Bender Test record in question showed at least six instances where the boy had attempted to copy a design only to abandon the drawing and start all over again. He made second and third tries to copy a given design, and he reworked other drawings. Every single figure was either corrected or redrawn. Even so, some of the worked-over designs were immature and showed regressive features such as the substitution of circles for dots.

It was the excessive amount of erasing and redrawing that made his Bender Test record so unusual. A moderate amount of erasing and redrawing of Bender Test figures was characteristic of many of Bravo's 75 bright youngsters. In my experience, excessive erasing and redrawing of Bender Test figures occurs only among severely upset and extremely anxious youngsters.

It was obvious that the true mental ability of the five bright children with poor Bender Test scores could not be assessed from their Bender Test record alone. For a valid evaluation of their ability it was also essential to get information about their verbal ability, their ability to conceptualize and recall, their emotional adjustment, and their inner control.

Chang and Chang (1967) used second- and third-graders of superior intelligence as subjects for their study. They divided the pupils into four groups according to their grade level and Bender Test scores. Two groups included bright second- and third-graders with *good* Bender Test scores, while the other two groups included second- and third-graders with *immature* Bender Test scores. Chang and Chang found, as would be expected, that the correlations between the test scores of these four groups of children, with fairly homogeneous IQ and Bender Test scores, were markedly higher (.46, .50, .31, and .35) than if the subjects had not been grouped according to their Bender Test scores. The correlations for the second-graders were higher than those for the third-graders.

Research findings and experience reveal at least three major reasons why the relationship between the Bender Test scores and IQ scores of bright schoolchildren is not as close as that for children with only average or below-average mental ability: (1) Some bright school beginners, especially boys, are young for their class or have a minor developmental lag in visual-motor perception. As a result, their Bender Test scores are still quite immature at the time of school entry. However, as the youngsters get older and mature, their Bender Test performances improve rapidly and are usually quite in keeping with their IQ levels by the time they are 8 or 9 years old. (2) Some bright youngsters excel in just about everything except visual-motor perception. Because of their high intelligence they can in time overcome and/or compensate for this specific weakness. Therefore they will do well in school even though their Bender Test records may still be immature. (3) As was discussed earlier (p. 13), the ceiling on the Bender Test is so low that it may be difficult or even impossible to discriminate between the Bender Test records of average, superior, and very superior pupils age 8 or older. Once children are able to copy the Bender Test designs without imperfections and obtain test scores of 0 or 1, they can no longer improve their scores even though they will continue to grow in age and in mental ability for many years to come.

BENDER TEST, AGE, AND IQ SCORES

In order to determine whether the relationship of Bender Test scores and WISC IQ scores remains stable for children of different age levels, I conducted a study involving pupils with learning disabilities. The subjects for this study were three groups of 75 children each, matched for WISC Full Scale IQ scores. The groups represented three different age levels. In one group the learning-disabled youngsters were 7 years 6 months to 7 years 11 months old; the second group was age 8 years 6 months to 8 years 11 months; the third group ranged in age from 10 years 6 months to 10 years 11 months. Between the ages of 7 and 10, children's visual-motor perceptions tend to mature greatly, so that the three groups of subjects differed markedly in their Bender Test performances. The 75 subjects at each age level were further divided on the basis of their IQ scores into a group with average and high average mental ability (IQ 90 to 118) and a group with below-average mental ability (IQ 59 to 89). Table 8 shows the Bender Test and IQ scores for the six subgroups and the correlations between their Bender Test and IQ scores. It is shown that the Bender Test scores of the subjects with below-average mental ability correlate significantly with their IQ scores at all three of the age levels ($r = -.42, -.43, -.53; p < .005$). The same was not the case for the young-

Table 8.
Relationship of Bender Test and IQ Scores at Different Age Levels

Age	N	WISC IQ M	Bender M	r	p	N	WISC IQ M	Bender M	r	p
7–6/7–11	36	99.0	7.9	−.19	NS	42	76.7	12.3	−.42	.005
8–6/8–11	36	98.7	5.6	−.30	.05	42	76.2	8.5	−.43	.005
10–6/10–11	36	98.9	3.0	−.21	NS	42	76.4	6.9	−.53	.005

sters of average and above-average mental ability. Two of the three correlations for the learning-disabled pupils with IQ scores of 90 or better were not significant. The third one, for the 8½-year-olds, was significant ($r = -.30$; $p < .05$), but to a much lesser degree than the correlations for the subjects with below-average ability. The findings concur with those discussed above and indicate a relatively stable relationship between Bender Test scores and IQ scores of elementary-school pupils at different age levels.

Although Bender Test and IQ scores of most children are closely related at each age level from 5 to 10 years, this does not mean that one can correlate the test scores of groups of youngsters with a wide age range. As shown in Table 8, the Bender Test scores differ greatly at different age levels even when the IQ scores are held constant. Hartman (1972), too, showed that age is closely related to children's Bender Test scores ($r = -.56$; $p < .01$) and can, therefore, not be ignored when selecting subjects for an investigation. A number of interesting studies have been published reporting, among other things, positive relationships between Bender Test and IQ scores for groups of clinic patients and for children with and without learning problems (Cerbus and Oziel, 1971; Culbertson and Gunn, 1966; Doubros and Mascarenhas, 1969; Marsh, 1972; Routh and Roberts, 1972; Skore, 1971). Unfortunately the results of these studies are inconclusive, despite their statistical significance, since the subjects involved range in age from 6 years to 11 or even to 13 years.

Only subjects with a limited age range, or from a single grade level, should be used when correlating Bender Test scores with IQ scores. Research with Bender Test scores is usually carried out with Bender Test raw scores, which cannot be used in the same manner as the deviation scores or scale scores of IQ tests (see p. 17). For instance, a WISC or a Binet IQ score of 100 means the same for a youngster age 5 or age 10; a score of 100 always signifies that the child's test performance is average. With the Bender Test, on the other hand, a score of 5 would be a very good score for a 6-year-old child, while the same score of 5 would be quite poor for a 9-year-old. The score of 5 would correlate, therefore, most likely with a high IQ score for school beginners and with a low IQ score for fourth-graders. It follows that if a study includes both 6- and 9-year-old children among its subjects, then a given Bender Test score would reflect different levels of maturity in visual-motor integration and the results obtained from the study would be quite confusing.

Skore (1971) reported that good Bender Test scores of 71 culturally disadvantaged children were not so much related to the levels of their IQ scores as to their rates of improvement on CTMM IQ scores during a 2½-year period.

Bender Test and Verbal versus Performance IQ Scores

The Bender Test is a paper-and-pencil test that involves no language skills; most IQ tests include both visual-motor and language items. How does the Bender Test relate to the language and the non-language parts of full-scale IQ tests? The relationship of the WISC Verbal and Performance IQ scores and Bender Test scores was discussed in some detail previously (Koppitz, 1963, p. 48). At that time it was found that both IQ scores were positively related to Bender Test scores but that the correlation between the Bender Test scores and the Performance IQ scores was significantly higher than the correlation with the Verbal IQ scores. Similar findings were reported in four recent studies. McNamara et al. (1969) tested 42 black Headstart children with the WPPSI. The youngsters' Verbal mean IQ was 83.9 and their Performance mean IQ was 87.0. The correlations between the Bender Test and IQ scores were −.47 for the Verbal IQ and −.62 for the Performance IQ scores. The correlations were significant at the .01 and .001 levels, respectively.

Cerbus and Oziel (1971) tested black pupils from the first to fourth grades with the Bender Test and the WISC. They obtained the following correlations:

Grade Level	N	Bender and Verbal IQ	Bender and Performance IQ
1st and 2nd	20	$r = -.32$, not significant	$r = -.66$, $p < .01$
3rd and 4th	20	$r = -.32$, not significant	$r = -.78$, $p < .01$

Ackerman et al. (1971) reported that learning-disabled pupils with *good* Bender Test scores had *low* Verbal IQ scores, whereas the well-functioning control group had good Bender Test scores as well as good Verbal IQ scores. Using 74 moderately retarded youngsters age 6 to 10 years as subjects, Kelly and Amble (1970) found that the Bender Test scores correlated significantly with the WISC Performance IQ but not with the WISC Verbal IQ.

QUALITY OF BENDER RECORDS AND IQ SCORES

This chapter has focused so far only on the relationship of the Developmental Bender Test scores and IQ scores. It should be pointed out, however, that the way in which the Bender Test designs are copied also has a significant relationship to children's mental ability. As mentioned above, Bravo (1972) tested over 200 fifth-graders of superior intelligence who came from different cultural and social backgrounds. Despite these differences the youngsters revealed certain common characteristics on their Bender Test records. Bravo found that most Bender Test protocols showed an absence of distortions and an "orderly, logical, and intelligent approach to copying the Bender Test designs." When I studied the Bender Test protocols of 75 of Bravo's outstanding pupils, I observed the same qualities. Almost all of the youngsters showed the following: (1) The Bender Test designs were well organized and carefully spaced on the page. (2) Most youngsters used less than the whole page for their drawings. The nine designs covered most often only the upper or left-hand half to two-thirds of the piece of paper. (3) The children were aware of the imperfections in their drawings and tried to correct them spontaneously. No less than 84% of the bright youngsters erased part or all of one or more Bender Test designs before completing them. In addition, 25% of the pupils tried to correct their figures by carefully drawing over part of the designs. (4) The Bender Test records showed neither excessively heavy pencil lines nor unduly fine ones.

It would appear, therefore, that good organization and good placement of Bender Test designs, spontaneous erasures and careful correction of imperfections on the drawings, and fairly small figures are all associated with high IQ scores. Plate 1 shows the Bender Test record of Alison, a bright, well-adjusted 9½-year-old girl. The protocol displays all of these characteristics with the exception of erasures.

BENDER TEST AND MENTAL RETARDATION

The relationship of the Bender Test and mental retardation in school children was discussed in some detail in Part V of *The Bender Gestalt Test for Young Children* (Koppitz, 1963, pp. 107–122). Since that chapter seems still to be quite up to date and valid, there is no need at this time for another complete chapter on the subject. During the past 10 years few new studies have appeared that deal specifically with retarded children and the Bender Test, and none of these has produced any results different from those of earlier studies. The same is true of my recent observations and work with moderately retarded youngsters; therefore only a short report of recent findings will be given.

The Bender Test can be used most effectively with retarded youngsters as a test of mental maturity (Condell, 1963). The Bender Test scores are more closely related to the mental ages of retarded children than to their chronological ages. The Bender Test scores of retarded youngsters improve gradually as the children get older (Kelly and Amble, 1970), but at a much slower rate than do the scores of children with normal mental ability. As shown in Figure 9 and Table 10 (p. 66), most retarded youngsters, and even those of borderline intelligence, are at age 14 not yet able to copy the nine Bender Test designs without imperfections.

Only minimal improvement on test–retest with the Bender Test is characteristic of mentally retarded children. Plates 11, 12, and 13 show the Bender Test records Rocco produced over a 5-year period. Rocco was a small, attractive, friendly youngster with moderate mental retardation. His WISC IQ scores were Verbal 66, Performance 79, Full Scale IQ 68. He had serious difficulties with sequencing and recall, with auditory perception, with both oral and written expression, and with abstract reasoning. Rocco was very impulsive and restless, and socially and emotionally immature. He tended to be moody, and he vacillated between outgoingness and sullen withdrawal.

When he was 7 years old Rocco drew the Bender Test record shown on Plate 11. Its outstanding features are the combination of the very large drawing of Fig. 2 with impulsive dashes instead of circles and the tiny, constricted drawings of Figs. 4, 5, 6, and 7. Rocco also showed perseveration on Figs. 1, 2, and 3; his angles and curves are primitive. His Developmental Bender Test score of 13 was on the level of a 5-year-old child. At age 9 years 10 months Rocco produced the Bender Test protocol shown on Plate 12. By then Rocco had become less impulsive and restless, but he was still quite immature and moody, and he had failed to make any academic progress at all during the nearly 3-year interval between the drawing of his first and second Bender Test records. His Bender Test score was 13, or identical with the earlier Bender Test score. Only the quality of the Bender Test drawings had improved somewhat, showing less impulsivity. Yet the same striking characteristics were present on Rocco's second Bender Test record: very large drawings (Figs. A, 3, and 5) interspersed with small drawings (Figs. 1, 4, and 6), reflecting his unevenness in functioning, his moodiness, and a tendency toward perseveration (Figs. 1 and 6).

Not until age 12 did Rocco begin to show some maturation in visual-motor perception, as can be seen on Plate 13. This Bender Test protocol reveals much better organization, and the Bender Test score was 9, or on the level of a 5½- to 6-year-old child, which corresponded to Rocco's achievement level. Interestingly enough, even on this protocol the unevenness in the size of the Bender Test figures persists: Figs. 5 and 9 are unusually large while Figs. A and 4 are unusually small. Thus we find that the Bender Test scores reflect Rocco's slow mental development, while the quality of the drawings reflects his unstable, labile personality.

There are no significant sex differences between the Bender Test scores of retarded boys and girls (Condell, 1963). The Developmental Bender Test scores did not differentiate successfully between groups of "familial" and "organic" retarded children and adolescents (Adams, 1970; Sternlicht et al., 1968). By modifying the Bender Test scoring system (p. 12) Maloney and Ward (1970) obtained significant differences between the Bender Test scores of functional and organic retarded male adolescents, but there was much overlap between test scores of the two groups.

No special signs or deviations have been found on the Bender Test that distinguish retarded youngsters with emotional problems from children with emotional problems who are not retarded. One possible exception may be the Emotional Indicator "Expansion"—that is, the use of two or more sheets of paper to complete all nine Bender Test designs (see p. 86). Plate 4 shows an example of such an expansive Bender Test record. It was made by Ricki, a 7½-year-old retarded boy (WISC IQ 59) who copied Figs. A, 1, 2, 3, 4, and 5 on one side of the paper and Figs. 6, 7, and 8 on the other side of the paper. In recent years I have obtained nine Bender Test records that used from two to six pieces of paper; 8 of the 9 youngsters who produced them were retarded; all of them were also very impulsive, acting-out children with minimal brain dysfunction.

The relationship of Bender Test performance and school achievement of retarded youngsters is no different from that of pupils who are not retarded. Bender Test scores are more closely related to achievement in arithmetic than to reading achievement, and even this relationship decreases when variations in age and IQ levels of the retarded children are controlled (Kelly and Amble, 1970; Morgenstern and McIvor, 1973).

In general, it appears that the Bender Test records of retarded youngsters can and should be evaluated in the same manner as Bender Test records of children who are not retarded.

SUMMARY

Recent research findings show that:

1.   Children with good Bender Test performances also tend to have average or above-average IQ scores; however, the Bender Test scores cannot discriminate between high-average and superior mental ability.

2.   Children with immature Bender Test scores may have high or low IQ scores depending on what other factors are present.

3.   Children with average or better IQ scores may have good or immature Bender Test scores, but most often they show good Bender Test performance.

4.   Children with below-average IQ scores also tend to have immature or poor Bender Test scores.

5.   The Bender Test is a good screening instrument of mental ability for very young and for disadvantaged children and for youngsters of average or below-average intelligence. It is less useful for screening groups of children of above-average mental ability.

6.   The Bender Test's effectiveness as a measure of mental ability is greatly enhanced when it is combined with a test of verbal ability, of visual–oral integration, and of recall.

7.   Not only the Developmental Bender Test score but also the quality of Bender Test records is related to children's mental ability. Of particular significance are the organization and placement of the Bender Test designs on the paper, spontaneous erasures and corrections, and the size of the figures.

8.   Bender Test scores of retarded pupils are usually more closely related to their M.A. than to their C.A. In every other way their protocols should be evaluated just like the Bender Test records of pupils who are not retarded. Expansiveness on the Bender Test seems to occur most often on the records of impulsive, poorly controlled retarded children.

CHAPTER 8.
The Bender Test
and School Achievement

Since the Developmental Bender Test Scoring System was validated against overall school achievement in the first and second grades (Koppitz, 1963, p. 12), Part III of *The Bender Gestalt Test for Young Children* (Koppitz, 1963, pp. 52ff) recommended the Bender Test as a useful tool for screening school beginners. It was further shown that the Bender Test was related to success and failure in reading and arithmetic. During the past 10 years a number of studies have investigated the relationship of the Bender Test and school achievement more fully. This chapter will discuss the findings of recent studies.

There is a consensus that the total Developmental Bender Test score is more closely related to school achievement than any single Bender Test sign or score (Ackerman et al., 1971; Connor, 1969; Keogh, 1965b; Obrzut et al., 1972). Emotional Indicators on the Bender Test (p. 84) do not seem to be good indicators of achievement (Ackerman et al., 1971; Dibner and Korn, 1969). I concur with the observations of Keogh (1968a) and Bravo (1972) that erasures and careful overwork are found most often on the Bender Test records of good students.

DEVELOPMENTAL SCORE AND ACHIEVEMENT

Results from recent studies support the claim that the total Developmental Bender Test scores can discriminate between groups of well-functioning pupils and groups of children with reading disabilities (Ackerman et al., 1971; Connor, 1969; Fisher, 1967; Hunter and Johnson, 1971; Kerr, 1972; Nielsen and Ringe, 1969; Stavrianos, 1971; Van de Voort and Senf, 1973). In comparisons of good pupils and poor pupils, good students were found to exhibit good Bender Test performances, while most children with poor reading achievement also had poor Bender Test scores. These findings do not mean, however, that there is a one-to-one relationship between Bender Test scores and reading achievement; and of course most youngsters are neither particularly outstanding nor very poor students, the majority functioning in the average range. How successful is the Bender Test in predicting the achievement of a whole class of unselected elementary-school pupils? Any meaningful screening of schoolchildren has to deal with whole groups or classes, and not just with the top and the bottom 10% of a class; it is usually quite obvious who the most outstanding and who the worst students in a class are even without special screening or testing.

Dibner and Korn (1969) suggest that the end of kindergarten is the best time for using the Bender Test as a screening instrument to predict school achievement. I tend to agree with Hammer (1967) that it really makes no difference whether the testing is done at the end of kindergarten or at the beginning of the first grade. But the beginning of the first grade is better than the end of the first grade, since the Bender Test seems to be especially effective as a predictive instrument for children between the ages of 5½ and 6½. Screening at the end of kindergarten has the advantage that the findings or test results can be used to help with the planning for the youngsters' placement and curriculum in the year ahead.

Table 9 summarizes the findings of recent studies on the relationship between Bender Test scores and achievement for entire elementary-school classes from kindergarten through sixth grade. An analysis of the data in Table 9 suggests that several factors influence the magnitude and level of significance of the correlations. Some measures of achievement (reading versus arithmetic, achievement test versus teacher ratings, etc.) correlate better with the Bender Test scores than others; the youngsters' socioeconomic backgrounds, their levels of mental ability, their ages and grade levels at the time of testing, and the number of subjects included in a study all have an effect on the correlations and their significance.

Several investigators have reported achievement scores for both reading and arithmetic for the same group of pupils (Dibner and Korn, 1969; Greene and Clark, 1973; Henderson et al., 1969; Keogh and Smith, 1967; Vormeland, 1968). It was shown that Bender Test scores are more closely related to first-to-third-grade arithmetic than to reading achievement.

Of the 54 correlations in Table 9, 33 are statistically significant at the .01 level, 13 at the .05 level, and 8 are not significant. A recent study also shows a significant correlation between kindergarten Bender Test scores and seventh- and eighth-grade achievement (Koppitz, 1973b). It is scarcely possible to deny a positive relationship between Bender Test

Table 9.
Relationship between Bender Test and School Achievement

Investigator(s)	N	Time & Measure of Achievement	r	p
		Kindergarten Bender Test and Achievement		
Jessen & Prendergast (1965)	140	Kindergarten, Lee-Clark Read. T.	−.34*	.01
Cabrini (1968)	90	1st gr., Met. Readiness Test	−.39	.01
Cabrini (1968)	90	1st gr., Gates Primary Test	−.29	.01
Giebink & Birch (1970)	98	2nd gr., Calif. Achiev. Test	−.19	NS
Keogh (1965)	127	3rd gr., Calif. Reading Test	−.29	.01
Keogh (1967)	73	3rd gr., Calif. Ach. T., read.	−.24	.05
Keogh (1969)	21	4th gr., arithmetic	−.51	.02
Keogh (1969)	21	5th gr., arithmetic	−.46	.05
Keogh (1967)	73	6th gr., Iowa Bas. Skills, read.	−.57	.01
Keogh (1967)	73	6th gr., Iowa Bas. Sk., arith.	−.37	.01
Dibner & Korn (1969)	492	K to 4th, teacher rating, read.	−.28	.01
Dibner & Korn (1969)	492	K to 4th, teacher rating, arith.	−.25	.01

Table 9. (continued)
Relationship between Bender Test and School Achievement

Investigator(s)	N	Time & Measure of Achievement	r	p
First-Grade Bender Test and Achievement				
Snyder & Freud (1967)	667	1st gr., Lee-Clark Readiness	−.47	.01
Greene & Clark (1973)	263	1st gr., Stan. Ach. T., reading	−.17	NS
Greene & Clark (1973)	263	1st gr., Stan. Ach. T., arith.	−.27	.01
Hammer (1967)	213	1st gr., Sur. Prim, read. dev.	−.21	.05
Henderson et al. (1969)	120	1st gr., reading	−.26	.01
Henderson et al. (1969)	83	1st gr., reading	−.32	.01
Henderson et al. (1969)	120	1st gr., arithmetic	−.41	.01
Henderson et al. (1969)	83	1st gr., arithmetic	−.36	.01
Jessen & Prendergast (1965)	105	1st gr., Gates Reading Test	−.49	.01
Mlodnosky (1972)	93	1st gr., classroom reading	−.38	.01
Oberstein (1968)	50	1st gr., N.Y.S. Reading Ach.	−.58	.01
Obrzut et al. (1972)	99	1st gr., Stan. Ach. Test, read.	−.32	.01
Stadler (1966)	74	1st gr., Modif. Ginn Read. Test	−.46	.01
Vormeland (1968)	574	1st gr., reading	−.29	.01
Vormeland (1968)	574	1st gr., arithmetic	−.49	.01
Vormeland (1968)	574	2nd gr., reading	−.20	.05
Vormeland (1968)	574	2nd gr., arithmetic	−.40	.01
Giebink & Birch (1970)	111	2nd gr., reading	−.17	NS
Second-Grade Bender Test and Achievement				
Chang & Chang (1967)	27	2nd gr., good Bender & reading	−.39	.05
Chang & Chang (1967)	23	2nd gr., poor Bender & reading	−.46	.05
Greene & Clark (1973)	234	2nd gr., Stan. Ach. T. reading	−.21	.05
Greene & Clark (1973)	234	2nd gr., Stan. Ach. T., arith.	−.37	.01
Heinrich (1968)	57	2nd gr., Stan. Ach. T. reading	−.37	.01
Vormeland (1968)	547	2nd gr., reading	−.22	.05
Vormeland (1968)	547	2nd gr., arithmetic	−.37	.01
Third-Grade Bender Test and Achievement				
Chang & Chang (1967)	26	3rd gr., good Bender & reading	−.29	NS
Chang & Chang (1967)	24	3rd gr., poor Bender & reading	−.32	NS
Greene & Clark (1970)	118	3rd gr., Stan. Ach. T., reading	−.23	.02
Greene & Clark (1970)	118	3rd gr., Stan. Ach. T., arithmetic	−.13	NS
Oberstein (1968)	50	3rd gr., N.Y.S. Read. Achiev.	−.46	.01
Obrzut et al. (1972)	98	3rd gr., Stan. Ach. T., reading	−.22	.05
Keogh (1967)	127	3rd gr., Cal. Reading Test	−.23	.02
Keogh (1967)	73	3rd gr., Cal. Ach. T., reading	−.21	NS
Keogh (1969)	21	3rd gr., Cal. Ach. T., reading	−.51	.02
Keogh (1969)	21	4th gr., Cal. Ach. T., reading	−.58	.01
Keogh (1969)	21	5th gr., Cal. Ach. T., reading	−.57	.01
Keogh (1967)	73	6th gr., Cal. Ach. T., reading	−.31	.01
Keogh (1967)	73	6th gr., Cal. Ach. T., arith.	−.49	.01
Sixth-Grade Bender Test and Achievement				
Heinrich (1968)	41	6th gr., Stan. Ach. T., reading	−.14	NS
Keogh (1967)	73	6th gr., Cal. Ach. T., reading	−.46	.01
Keogh (1967)	73	6th gr., Cal. Ach. T., arithmetic	−.34	.01
Obrzut et al. (1972)	92	6th gr., Stan. Ach. T., reading	−.37	.01

*All correlations are negative since the Bender Test is scored for imperfections; hence a high score is a poor score.

scores and school achievement against such an amount of evidence. Yet most of the reported correlations are too low to be of much practical value for the school psychologist trying to make predictions about an individual child's school achievement. What specific conclusions can be drawn from the research findings that can be of assistance to the practitioner in the field?

The 9-year study (Koppitz, 1973b) of Bender Test performance and school achievement mentioned above may offer some answers to this question. The findings are quite similar to those of other investigators (Keogh, 1965a; Norfleet, 1973; Thweatt, 1963). A good Bender Test record at the time of school entry tends to be a good predictor of later school success. A good Bender Test score is of course also associated with good intersensory integration and good mental ability; it is obvious that brighter children also tend more often to be good students.

An immature or poor Bender Test score, on the other hand, may be associated with either good, average, or poor school achievement. Children who fail in school tend to have poor Bender Test scores. This includes youngsters with limited mental ability as well as those with normal intelligence but with specific learning problems. However, an immature or even poor Bender Test record at the end of kindergarten or at the beginning of the first grade does not by itself necessarily imply that a child will fail. Some school beginners with poor Bender Test scores are merely young or immature for their class; they may be normal youngsters with developmental lags. There is nothing "wrong" with these children; they just need a little more time than most children to mature. They are not yet ready to cope with schoolwork at the time the law requires that they begin formal schooling (Snyder and Freud, 1967). Given the extra time they need to mature, many of these children get to be average or even outstanding students.

Some children with poor Bender Test scores are not just immature; they suffer from real malfunction in visual-motor perception or in intersensory integration. Yet if they are bright, if they have good language ability and recall, if they are well motivated, if they have no major behavior problems, and if they have supportive parents and teachers, they can overcome or compensate for perceptual–motor problems and may in time turn into good pupils. On the other hand, children with poor visual-motor perception who also have problems in several other areas may not be able to overcome their perceptual–motor difficulties and may develop serious learning disabilities.

Children's successes or failures in school depend only partially on their visual-motor integration; many factors influence the youngsters' school functioning. In retrospect, I seem to have overestimated in the earlier studies the significance of visual-motor perception for school achievement. As intervening research and experience with the Bender Test have demonstrated, one cannot neglect other equally important factors, especially language development, oral–visual integration, sequencing, recall of symbols and information, and concept formation. Children's ages, attitudes, gender, and family and social backgrounds also influence their achievement in varying degrees. A youngster's progress in school depends on a combination and interaction of all of these factors.

Sex Differences and Achievement

One important factor to consider when predicting long-range school achievement with the Bender Test is the child's gender. Even though the research data show conclusively (p. 31) that there is no statistically significant difference between the Bender Test scores of school-age boys and girls, boys and girls do differ in their behavior and school achievement. For instance, in a recent study (Koppitz, 1973b) 13 of the 15 pupils with poor kindergarten Bender Test records who developed into good eighth-grade students were girls. This was not chance. There is a significant difference in the relationships of Bender Test scores of boys and girls and school achievement. This difference is not due to any difference in visual-motor function, but to some of the other factors that affect school progress.

Keogh and Smith (1969) found that the Bender Test is more successful in predicting school achievement for boys than for girls. Norfleet (1973) observed that the Bender Test is best at predicting good reading for girls, and poor reading for boys. This concurs with my own observation that boys with immature Bender Test scores are usually poor readers, while girls with immature Bender Test scores may have either high or low achievement in reading. Since girls tend to be better controlled, less hyperactive, more advanced in language development, and more striving than boys, they are also better able to overcome or to compensate for problems in the visual-motor area. Therefore, many girls are successful in their schoolwork despite immature Bender Test records at the time of school entry. Little boys, however, are often impulsive and restless. Even without specific difficulties in perceptual–motor integration they are often at a disadvantage in school. To date, many school activities and requirements in the primary grades still favor girls over boys. The boys' nonconforming behavior not only interferes with their classroom learning but also influences the teacher's attitude toward them. When such immature, restless boys also suffer from poor perceptual–motor integration, then their school progress will inevitably be slow and painful, and compensation for poor visual-motor perception will be difficult. Therefore, a boy with immature Bender Test performance is more likely to have poor achievement than a girl with a poor Bender Test score, even when their Bender Test scores and their IQ scores are the same.

Oberstein's (1968) study illustrates this point well. She reported a correlation of −.55 between Bender Test scores and reading test scores for first-grade boys, compared to a correlation of only −.39 for the girls. For her third-grade pupils the correlation between test scores was −.48 for the boys and −.24 for the girls.

Reading, Arithmetic, and General Achievement

There is obviously no one-to-one relationship between Bender Test scores and reading. Among youngsters with immature Bender Test records can be found both good and poor readers, and not all children with good Bender Test records are necessarily good readers. Heinrich (1968) investigated second- and sixth-grade boys with poor Bender Test scores. He found that the poor readers with poor Bender Test records suffered from difficulties in visual-motor integration, whereas the good readers with poor Bender Test scores had more problems in motor coordination.

Similar results were obtained by Brenner et al. (1967). They studied English schoolchildren, of whom 6.7% exhibited both poor Bender Test scores and high verbal scores. These youngsters were described as being good readers; however, they also exhibited poor motor coordination, they were clumsy and sloppy, and they had difficulty with writing and arithmetic. Their school performances were unsatisfactory. They were poor at games, lacked self-confidence, and were not popular with their peers. The Bender Test scores were more closely related to their overall school functioning than to achievement, especially reading achievement.

As was mentioned earlier (Table 9), the Bender Test correlates better with arithmetic than with reading; this concurs with my own earlier findings (Koppitz, 1963, p. 62) and with the results of the studies of Kelly and Amble (1970) and Morgenstern and McIvor (1973) on achievement and Bender Test performance of retarded children. Arithmetic achievement resembles the Bender Test in that it, too, is mainly related to visual-motor perception and to part–whole and space relationships; unlike reading, arithmetic is not dependent on sound discrimination, visual–oral integration and recall.

A similar relationship between Bender Test scores and general school functioning can also be observed among many learning-disabled youngsters. Plate 14, for example, shows the grossly inadequate Bender Test record of Sharon, a 10-year-old, neurologically impaired, moderately retarded girl (WISC Verbal IQ 72, Performance IQ 57, Full Scale IQ 62). Sharon was a poorly coordinated, clumsy, impulsive child whose handwriting was practically unintelligible and who had severe problems in arithmetic and in social relationships. Despite these difficulties Sharon's ability to read printed material was on grade level; however, her reading comprehension was low and in keeping with her mental ability. Sharon's Bender Test record reflected her immaturity and impulsivity, her limited intelligence, her extremely poor motor coordination, and her generally poor level of functioning. It did not reflect her reading skill, which depended on her good visual and auditory perception and on her excellent visual–oral integration and oral recall.

In contrast to Sharon, Susano, a 10-year-old boy, was well coordinated and of normal intelligence (WISC Verbal IQ 86, Performance IQ 99, Full Scale IQ 91). His very good Bender Test record is shown on Plate 15. Susano's reasoning ability and his visual-motor perception were average for his age level, but he suffered from serious problems in receptive and expressive language, in visual–oral integration, and in recall. He was for practical purposes a nonreader. Susano's reading skill was limited to a few sight words only; he also had a very poor vocabulary. His Bender Test score reflected his good overall adjustment, general school functioning, and average intelligence, while his reading disability resulted from a combination of difficulties in sound discrimination, association of sounds and symbols, and severe problems in sequencing and memory. None of these are measured by the Bender Test or by any other test of visual-motor perception.

Results from the study of Satz et al. (1971) suggest that the Bender Test is better able to detect reading problems in younger children (age 7 to 8 years) than in older pupils (age 11 to 12 years).

Werner et al. (1967) found that reading problems were more closely related to socioeconomic background, to mental ability, and to language skills than to visual-motor perception. They studied all 750 of the 10- and 11-year-old children on the island of Kauai, Hawaii. Test results showed that Bender Test scores were able to discriminate significantly between youngsters with and without reading problems, when all of the children were included. But when the youngsters were divided into four groups according to their Primary Mental Ability IQ levels, then the Bender Test scores no longer discriminated between the high and low readers in three of the four groups. In fact, there is serious doubt whether the Bender Test is at all related to reading, although both the Bender Test and reading require that children have a minimum level of maturity in visual-motor perception. A child whose level of visual-motor integration is still below that of a 5½-year-old will have difficulty with both the Bender Test and with reading, regardless of whether he is immature because he is young, or because he shows a developmental lag, or because he suffers from minimal brain dysfunction.

Both reading and Bender Test performance are greatly influenced by a child's age and mental ability. Once the subjects in an investigation are matched for age and IQ scores, then the relationship between reading and the Bender Test scores disappears, especially if the youngsters under investigation are atypical (Cellura and Butterfield, 1966; Clarke and Leslie, 1971; Connor, 1969; Kelly and Amble, 1970; Morgenstern and McIvor, 1973; Routh and Roberts, 1972; Sabatino and Ysseldyke, 1972; Silberberg and Feldt, 1968). Clinic patients, retarded youngsters, and children with learning disabilities are all atypical. Groups of such youngsters invariably tend to show immature performances on the Bender Test as well as poor overall school functioning, but not all of them are necessarily poor readers. The Bender Test is clearly more closely related to children's general school performances then to reading in particular.

According to Black (1973), rotations on the Bender Test correlated significantly ($r = .39$; $p < .05$) with the Wide Range Achievement Test (Jastak et al., 1965) reading recognition scores of 200 6- to 9-year-old children of normal ability. However, rotations were not able to discriminate between the 100 youngsters who were average readers and the 100 moderately retarded readers. The two groups of 100 youngsters were matched for C.A., grade level, and for WISC Full Scale IQ scores.

The Bender Test is not a good test for the assessment of a child's reading ability. Schoolcraft (1972) reported that the knowledge of letter names was a better predictor of reading achievement for rural first-graders than was their Bender Test performance. Hammer (1967) discovered that the Bender Test scores of kindergarten and first-grade pupils are more effective in predicting a child's gain in reading than his actual reading level.

A recent study (Koppitz, 1975) supports the finding that Bender Test scores are related to general school functioning rather than to reading as such. Two groups of special-class pupils with learning disabilities and a control group of average pupils served as subjects for the study. All subjects were white middle-class youngsters. The 23 pupils in each of the two learning-disability groups (Group A and Group B) were matched for age and IQ scores. Their age mean was 9 years 0 months (range 8–1 to 9–11) and their WISC Full Scale IQ mean score was 100.1 (range 91 to 118). The 30 control subjects had an age mean of 9 years 2 months (range 8–2 to 9–10), and their CTMM IQ mean was 104.4 (range 88 to 122). The Bender Test and the Visual Aural Digit Span Test (Koppitz, 1972) were administered to each child individually in school.

A comparison of the Bender Test scores of Groups A and B with the scores of the control group by means of Chi-square tests yielded highly significant results for both groups (Group A, $p = <.001$; Group B, $p = <.05$). The Bender Test performances of the learning-disabled youngsters were greatly inferior to those of average pupils, even though they were all matched for age and IQ scores and came from similar socioeconomic backgrounds. This is one more bit of evidence supporting the finding that the Bender Test scores can discriminate between groups of well-functioning pupils and children with learning problems.

Later the Bender Test performances of Group A and Group B were compared. Group A included only children who had some knowledge of reading. Their mean reading recognition score on the Wide Range Achievement Test was 3.9 (range 2.7 to 7.0). Group B included only non-readers; their mean reading score was only 1.6 (range 0.8 to 2.1). None of the youngsters in Group B had more than a few sight words, and none was able to sound out words. A Chi-square was computed comparing the youngsters in Group A and Group B with Bender Test scores of 3 or less and those with scores of 4 or more. No significant difference was found between the Bender Test performances of the two groups of learning-disabled pupils. The Bender Test scores were unable to discriminate between the youngsters with and without serious reading problems. The children in Group A and Group B were all special-class pupils, and most of them had poor overall school functioning regardless of whether they could read or not. Therefore it comes as no surprise that no less than 75%

of the youngsters in both groups had below-average or poor Bender Test scores.

In contrast to the results of the Bender Test, the children in Group A and Group B differed significantly (p <.001) in visual–oral integration and recall as measured on the Visual Aural Digit Span Test (VADS). Thus the VADS Test seems to be more closely related to reading achievement, while the Bender Test is more closely related to children's overall functioning—the two tests seem to complement each other. In fact, I have used the Bender Test and the VADS Test together with the Human Figure Drawings (Koppitz, 1968) as an effective screening battery for school beginners (see Chapter 11).

Seifert (1968) has suggested using the Reading Eye Camera together with the Bender Test to identify children with reading disabilities. She investigated visual-motor perception and speed of eye movements of a group of poor readers and of a control group. She found that poor readers have slower reaction times to print than good readers; the former did less well on the Bender Test. The Bender Test alone was able to identify more of the poor readers than the Reading Eye Camera; both tests together were 100% successful in classifying all the children with reading disabilities.

BENDER TEST AND LEARNING DISABILITIES

The relationship of Bender Test scores to age and IQ scores for children in general was discussed in some detail in Chapter 7. The Bender Test scores of children with learning disabilities (LD) are also related to age and mental ability. Table 10 shows the Bender Test score means for four groups of learning-disabled youngsters age 6 to 14 years, with different levels of IQ scores. The data in Table 10 are based on over 1200 Bender Test records collected during the past 10 years from over 500 special-class pupils. Many of the youngsters contributed two or three Bender Test protocols to this study, but never more than one at any age level. Seventy-five percent of the special-class pupils were white, 22% were black, and 3% were Puerto Rican. Five percent of the children came from upper-middle-class families, 45% came from middle-class homes, and 50% came from low socioeconomic backgrounds.

The data presented in Table 10 are shown in graph form in Figure 2. These data are highly significant and have serious implications for the education of children with learning disabilities. The data show convincingly that visual-motor integration of LD pupils matures at a rate slower than normal. The rate of development depends on the youngster's age and mental ability. This is a fact, and it must be taken into account when planning a curriculum for educationally handicapped children. Too often special-education programs are designed with the idea that there is something one can do to help children with learning problems "catch up" with

Table 10.
Bender Test Mean Scores of Children with Learning Disabilities by Age and IQ Levels

		Bender Test Means and SD											
		Ss with WISC IQ 100 up			Ss with WISC IQ 85–99			Ss with WISC IQ 70–84			Ss with WISC IQ 69 down		
Age	Normative Data	N	M	SD	N	M	SD	N	M	SD	N	M	SD
5-0/5-5	13.6												
5-6/5-11	10.2												
6-0/6-5	8.0	6	10.0	3.5	8	12.8	3.7	9	14.1	1.5	3	20.0	
6-6/6-11	6.4	7	8.2	2.3	13	12.2	2.7	12	12.1	3.1	4	15.8	1.9
7-0/7-5	5.1	16	7.4	3.8	23	10.4	3.0	20	11.5	4.1	7	16.6	1.0
7-6/7-11	4.2	17	6.8	3.5	33	8.8	2.6	26	12.0	4.5	10	13.9	3.4
8-0/8-5	3.4	13	5.0	3.6	44	6.9	2.5	43	10.1	3.3	15	12.3	3.8
8-6/8-11	2.7	21	4.7	2.2	49	6.1	2.9	42	8.4	3.4	15	12.0	4.3
9-0/9-5	2.2	19	3.6	2.5	48	4.6	2.5	44	7.2	2.7	14	11.4	3.5
9-6/9-11	1.8	17	2.9	2.4	43	4.8	2.7	39	6.5	3.1	12	9.9	3.2
10-0/10-5	1.5	17	2.9	2.1	34	4.1	3.0	43	6.4	3.0	11	9.5	3.6
10-6/10-11	1.2	15	2.4	1.3	36	3.6	2.5	36	6.6	2.8	11	10.3	4.0
11-0/11-11		22	1.8	1.6	41	3.8	2.4	63	5.3	3.0	20	9.6	2.9
12-0/12-11		16	1.1	1.3	31	2.9	2.0	38	4.7	2.6	15	8.9	4.6
13-0/14-11		3	1.0	.8	30	1.9	1.5	29	4.1	2.4	9	6.7	3.7

66

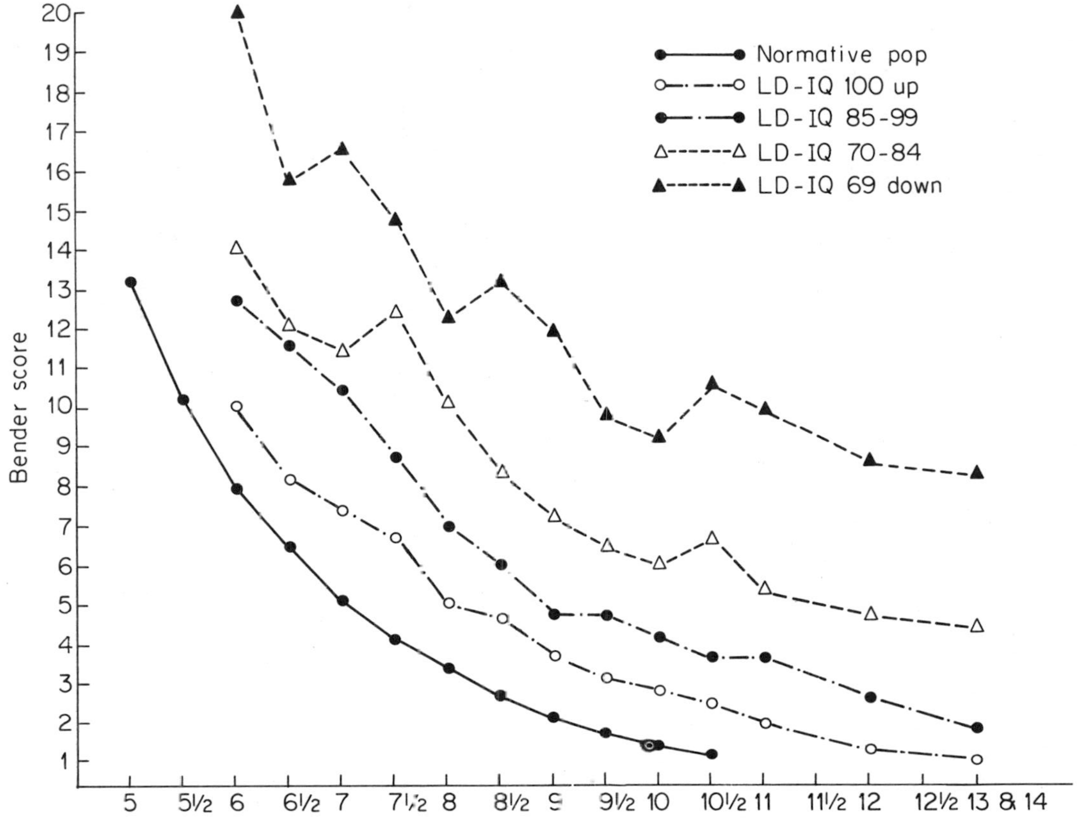

Normative pop
LD-IQ 100 up
LD-IQ 85-99
LD-IQ 70-84
LD-IQ 69 down
Bender score
20
19
18
17
16
15
14
13
12
11
10
9
8
7
6
5
4
3
2
1
5
5½
6
6½
7
7½
8
8½
9
9½
10
10½
11
11½
12
12½
13 & 14

Figure 2. Bender Test mean scores for LD pupils.

well-functioning pupils, help them speed up their slower development. Even LD pupils with average or above-average mental ability require extra time before they can develop sufficient maturity in perceptual–motor integration to cope with formal school learning, but given this extra time most can succeed quite well. To date, efforts to speed up the rate of development of a slowly maturing child have produced, at best, only some immediate short-lived improvements; they have failed to result in any permanent increase in the rate of maturation.

As shown in Table 10, most average youngsters obtained at age 5½ (C.A. 5–6 to 5–11) a Bender Test score of 10; this is also the level at which they are ready to start schoolwork. LD pupils with IQ scores of 100 or better did not reach this level of maturation in visual-motor integration until age 6 (C.A. 6–0 to 6–5). Those with IQ scores of 85 to 99 did not obtain a mean Bender Test score of 10 until they were 7 years old (C.A. 7–0 to 7–5). LD youngsters of borderline mental ability (IQ 70–84) were 8 years old (C.A. 8–0 to 8–5) before their Bender Test mean score was 10. Finally, we see in Table 10 that moderately retarded children (IQ 50–69) did not achieve a Bender Test score of 10 until age 9½ or 10 (C.A. 9–6 to 10–11).

Normal pupils tend to show a marked spurt in learning and achievement in the third grade when they are 8 years old and when their Bender Test score is 3 or 4. LD pupils of average or above-average mental ability do not usually show real progress in learning until they are about 9 years old; this is also the time when they tend to show a marked improvement in their Bender Test performance. Educationally, handicapped children with low-average IQ scores do not usually reveal any significant improvement on their Bender Test scores and in their achievement until they are 10½ or even 11 years old, while borderline youngsters need until age 12 or even 13 or 14 before they approach this level of maturity in visual-motor integration and achievement. Most retarded pupils do not reach a Bender Test score of 3 or 4 even at age 14. Rocco's Bender Test records shown on Plates 11, 12, and 13, have already been mentioned as examples of the slow rate of improvement of retarded youngsters. The Bender Test performance of slow children does improve, but at a much slower rate than that of more capable children. The data in Table 10 are Bender Test mean scores and apply to groups of children; there is of course some variation in Bender Test scores among individual children at the various age levels and intelligence levels.

A slower rate of maturation on the Bender Test for educationally handicapped children was also described by Dykman et al. (1973). They found a significant difference between the Bender Test scores of pupils age 9 to 11 with learning disabilities and those of a normal control group. But when the youngsters were retested at age 14 the Bender Test scores no longer discriminated between the two groups.

The Bender Test records shown on Plates 16, 17, and 18 illustrate the rate of progress in visual-motor perception of a learning-disabled youngster of average mental ability (WISC IQ 99). The Bender Test protocols were produced by Kevin, a youngster with minimal brain dysfunction. When Kevin was first referred to a special class for LD youngsters he was extremely immature and restless and had emotional and behavioral problems, infantile speech, and poor auditory and visual-motor perception and integration. Even though he had repeated the first grade, his academic achievement was minimal. Plate 16 shows the Bender Test protocol Kevin drew at age 7 years 11 months. He had a Bender Test score of 15—that is, his level of functioning in visual-motor perception was still on the 4½-year-old level and lagged 3 years behind his chronological age. Kevin's functioning at the time was on the kindergarten level. His Bender Test record shows poor integration of parts, perseveration, and immaturity in the drawing of dots, angles, and curves.

Not until Kevin was 9½ years old did his Bender Test performance reach the 5½- to 6-year level (Plate 17), which is the minimal level for coping with schoolwork. At that time Kevin first began to make substantial progress in his achievement and was able to do first-grade work with comprehension. Kevin continued to progress in school achievement from then on, but at a slow rate. By age 12, Kevin's Bender Test record (Plate 18) resembled that of an average 9-year-old pupil, while his reading and arithmetic were on the fourth-grade level. As Kevin matured in the visual-motor area, his impulse control and motor coordination also improved. With sufficient time for maturation, with the help of special education in a highly structured but noncompetitive class, and with constant encouragement and support from his parents Kevin was gradually able to overcome or compensate for many of his difficulties in perceptual–motor integration and school achievement. The three Bender Test records he produced at ages 7, 9, and 12 reflect this progress.

The Bender Test performance of a child with learning disabilities gives a good indication of his level of maturation in perceptual–motor integration and of the level at which the curriculum for the child should be aimed. A great deal is being said and written these days about individualized instruction in the classroom; yet too often teachers and administrators expect all children to achieve at the same rate. Repeated administration of the Bender Test will provide a record of a given child's rate of maturation and can be of help in setting up realistic expectations for achievement for that youngster. It is absurd to expect a child to achieve on the fourth-grade level when his level of perceptual–motor integration is still at the first-grade level.

A single Bender Test can only indicate a child's current level of functioning; it cannot predict his level of achievement five years hence. This was shown in my follow-up study of children with learning disabilities (Koppitz, 1971). However, repeated administration of the Bender Test enables the examiner to evaluate a given LD child's rate of maturation in visual-motor perception and allows him to make long-term predictions about the youngster's achievement.

SUMMARY

The total Developmental Bender Test score can discriminate significantly between groups of good and poor students. There is also a positive correlation between the Bender Test performance and school achievement of groups of normal public-school pupils, kindergarten to eighth grade. However, there is no one-to-one relationship between the Bender Test scores of individual children and their achievement.

For individual pupils a good Bender Test performance seems to forecast good achievement. Good students tend to erase more often than poor students while drawing Bender Test designs. Most poor students have poor Bender Test scores, but a single poor Bender Test score is not by itself a good predictor of a child's success or failure in school. A youngster's age, sex, mental ability, language skills, memory, behavior, and home background all have to be taken into account when predicting school achievement. In general, girls are better able to compensate for problems in visual-motor perception than boys; therefore a poor Bender Test score correlates better with the schoolwork of boys than of girls.

The Bender Test is more closely associated with arithmetic than with reading. When the C.A. and IQ scores of pupils are controlled, then the Bender Test performance can no longer differentiate between groups of good and poor readers. The Bender Test is not closely related to reading per se.

The Bender Test scores appear to be most successful in predicting overall school functioning and rate of progress in total achievement. A child with a marked discrepancy between IQ and Bender Test scores usually has specific learning difficulties. LD pupils and slow learners mature at a significantly slower rate in visual-motor integration, as measured on the Bender Test, than do well-functioning children. Scores from repeated administrations of the Bender Test are good indicators of the rate of progress a child is making, and they are helpful in planning an individualized educational program.

CHAPTER 9.
The Bender Test
and Minimal Brain Dysfunction

From the outset the Bender Test has been regarded as a valuable aid in diagnosing brain injury in adults (Bender, 1938). Part IV of *The Bender Gestalt Test for Young Children* (Koppitz, 1963, pp. 71–106) focused on the use of the Bender Test as an instrument for diagnosing brain injury in children. In the early 1960s there was a growing awareness and concern among clinicians and educators about the relationship of neurological impairment or brain injury to learning and behavior problems in children. But a survey of the literature in 1962 revealed only three studies that dealt with the Bender Test and brain injury in children (Hanvick, 1953; Shaw and Cruickshank, 1956; Wewetzer, 1959). To obtain more information at that time, I conducted a number of studies and explored more fully the diagnostic effectiveness of the Bender Test with neurologically impaired youngsters.

BRAIN INJURY VERSUS MINIMAL BRAIN DYSFUNCTION

During the past decade I have had the opportunity to work with hundreds of pupils with serious behavior and learning problems. Most of them exhibited so-called "soft" signs and "organic" indicators in their behavior and on test results. However, even though the children showed many characteristics of children with neurological impairment, the majority of them had no history of brain injury, nor did they reveal any positive signs on neurological examinations or have abnormal EEGs. Obviously the children were not "brain-injured" and could not be diagnosed as such by means of medical examinations. Yet these youngsters were obviously suffering from some kind of brain dysfunction that did not necessarily result from a demonstrable brain lesion or from brain trauma. Other investigators came to similar conclusions, and increasingly the concept of Minimal Brain Dysfunction (MBD), due to any number of different causes, became a meaningful diagnosis for learning-disabled and emotionally disturbed children.

Some clinicians try to limit the diagnosis of MBD to cases with specific "hard" neurological indicators. I prefer to use the term MBD in its broadest sense and include in this category children with both "soft" and "hard" neurological signs. For me the diagnosis of MBD implies that a child's learning and behavior difficulties have, at least in part, an organic basis, even though frustration and social factors might have resulted in additional secondary emotional and learning problems. I always base a diagnosis of MBD on a combination of several factors: a youngster's developmental, medical, and social history, his school functioning, behavior observations, and of course psychological test results including his performance on the Bender Test. A diagnosis of brain injury implies the presence of a brain lesion; this is not the case with MBD. MBD can result from prenatal or birth trauma, from accidents or illnesses, from genetic factors, from severe early emotional or physical deprivation and neglect, or from other known or unknown causes.

Since brain injury is a medical diagnosis, it can be made only by a qualified physician. MBD, on the other hand, can be diagnosed by a qualified physician as well as by a qualified psychologist. Signs of MBD may manifest themselves on both neurological and psychological examinations or only on one or the other method of evaluation, as was shown in the study of Klatskin et al. (1972). The Bender Test can be of considerable help in diagnosing MBD, but it is not possible to determine the etiology of MBD from children's Bender Test records (Koppitz, 1970b).

Plates 19 and 20 show the Bender Test protocols of two learning-disabled boys with MBD. Jim (Plate 19) had a history of prenatal and birth trauma, while Tom (Plate 20) received a medical diagnosis of "MBD due to unknown cause." His developmental and medical history as well as a neurological examination proved negative. Both children were extremely vulnerable and immature; they had difficulty in perceptual–motor integration, in the language area and in sequencing and recall, and both were nonreaders. There can be no doubt that the learning problems of both youngsters had organic bases.

The title of this chapter reflects my current point of view. Instead of discussing the Bender as a test for diagnosing brain injury, as I did in my first book (Koppitz, 1963, p. 71), we shall explore at this time the relationship between the Bender Test and minimal brain dysfunction. With this in mind, I would like to review the findings of recent Bender Test studies dealing with children with MBD.

DEVELOPMENTAL BENDER TEST SCORES VERSUS INDICATORS OF BRAIN INJURY

One of my earlier studies showed that 91% of the brain-injured children had poor Bender Test scores, but so did 24% of the control group. I concluded, "It appears safe therefore, to state that a poor Bender record may be thought of as indicating the possibility of brain injury especially if the Bender score is more than minus one standard deviation from the mean normative Bender Score for a given age group. But a definite diagnosis of brain injury should never be made solely on the basis of a single Bender Test score or, for that matter, on the basis of *any single* psychological test score. Nor can the presence of neurological impairment be definitely ruled out because of a good Bender Test performance" (Koppitz, 1963, p. 75). This statement is still true today; I would only like to substitute the term MBD for the term brain injury. Today I would further hypothesize that some of the control subjects with poor Bender Test scores were suffering from MBD even though they could not be medically diagnosed as brain-damaged.

A search for signs on the Bender Test that were specifically related to brain dysfunction resulted in a list of Neurological Indicators (Koppitz, 1963, p. 189). Since these signs occurred more often on the Bender Test records of brain-injured youngsters, I made the statement, "The validity of a diagnosis of brain injury is greatly enhanced when a Bender record is examined for both the total Bender score and for individual scoring items which are associated with neurological impairment" (Koppitz, 1963, p. 81). At present I am no longer convinced that this statement is necessarily valid, especially when diagnosing MBD rather than brain injury in children. Based on my experiences during the past 10 years I have found that total Developmental Bender Test scores and the Neurological Indicators are able to differentiate equally well between the Bender Test records of groups of youngsters with and without MBD; little is added by using both the Neurological Indicators and the Developmental Bender Test scores. Ackerman et al. (1971), McConnell (1967), and Stavrianos (1971) all came to similar conclusions.

Oliver and Kronenberger (1971) compared the Bender Test records of three groups of adolescents who were brain-damaged, emotionally disturbed, and normal (age 11 to 15). They found that both the Developmental Bender Test scores and the Indicators of Brain Injury could differentiate significantly between the three groups of youngsters, but the Developmental Scoring System was the more effective of the two measures. The Developmental Bender Test scores were also able to discriminate significantly between "neurologically suspect" children and normal pupils in the study of Henderson et al. (1969) and between brain-damaged and control subjects in Bravo's investigation (1973).

Rotations and MBD

Rotations on the Bender Test have been discussed in detail in Chapter 3. Smith and Martin (1967) observed that a group of neurologically impaired youngsters made a significantly greater number of rotations on the Bender Test and required a greater number of learning cues to correct the rotations than did a control group of learning-disabled youngsters without neurological impairment. They concluded that the ability to correct rotations was an even more discriminating index of neurological impairment than the frequency of rotations on a given Bender Test protocol. Weiss (1971c) indicated that rotations on the Bender Test records of average school children are a developmental phenomenon and are not necessarily linked with brain damage in children.

OTHER BENDER TEST SCORING SYSTEMS AND MBD

Most investigators have used the Developmental Bender Test Scoring System to evaluate Bender Test records of neurologically impaired youngsters. But other methods of assessing Bender Test protocols are also effective in discriminating between children with and without MBD. Quast's scoring method (1961), for instance, includes ten specific signs that differentiate brain-damaged children from emotionally disturbed children. J. Holroyd (1966) found no significant difference in the number of youngsters with MBD who were correctly identified by means of the Developmental Scoring System and the Quast Scoring System, even though the two systems did not identify all of the same children.

Adams et al. (1973) reported that both the standard Bender Test copying method, scored by Canter's system, and Canter's Background Interference Procedure (p. 117) were able to discriminate children with cerebral dysfunction from groups of emotionally disturbed youngsters and from normal control subjects. No significant difference was found between the Bender Test performances of the latter two groups.

In Germany, the Göttinger Formreproduktions Test, using the standard Bender Test stimulus cards, was developed by Schlange et al. (1972); it is a modified Bender Test scoring system for the specific purpose of diagnosing brain injury in children. The investigators showed that their scoring system was able to differentiate between three groups of clinic patients: children without brain injury (IQ mean 113.6), children with medically diagnosed brain injury (IQ mean 92.6), and patients who were suspected of having brain dysfunction even though no clear-cut medical evidence was found (IQ mean 100.8).

Lauretta Bender and some other clinicians prefer to use clinical judgment rather than a formal scoring system with the Bender Test when diagnosing brain pathology in children or adolescents. Wagner and Murray (1969) explored the accuracy of the clinical judgment of five raters who had compared the Bender Test records of 32 medically diagnosed "organic" children (age 6 to 16) and the Bender Test protocols of 32 good pupils without neurological problems. Each pair of Bender Test records was judged as organic or nonorganic. From 27 to 30 pairs of Bender Test records were judged correctly by the different raters.

DIAGNOSING DEGREE OF ORGANIC IMPAIRMENT

There can be little doubt that the Bender Test performances of most children with medical diagnoses of neurological impairment (Plates 14 and 22) are grossly inferior to those of good students (Plates 1 and 31) and that their records can be readily recognized no matter how the Bender Test protocols are analyzed or interpreted. Differential diagnosis is more difficult when the Bender Test records of different groups of clinic pa-

Table 11.
Bender Test Performance of Three Groups of Clinic Patients*

Group	Age 6 to 8			Age 8½ to 11½		
	N	IQ M	Bender M	N	IQ M	Bender M
A. Neurological impairment	34	107	11.2	56	108	7.8
B. Perceptual–motor problem	37	111	9.5	53	112	6.3
C. Emotional Disturbance	33	112	7.5	45	113	4.5
D. Control	34	116	6.1	33	115	2.9

*Reproduced by permission from Stavrianos BK: Can projective test measures aid in the detection and differential diagnosis of reading deficits? Projective Techniq Person Asses 35:80–91, 1971.

tients are compared. McConnell's study (1967) showed that the Developmental Bender Test scores could discriminate significantly between groups of clinic patients with varying degrees of organic involvement. McConnell's subjects were three groups of children who were diagnosed "substantial brain damage," "minimal brain damage," and "nonorganic." The youngsters were matched for mental age, and none of them had any gross motor or sensory impairment.

Similar results were obtained in the well-controlled investigation of Stavrianos (1971). She studied four groups of children matched for age and IQ scores. The four groups included children with medical diagnoses of neurological impairment, children with perceptual–motor problems without brain injury, children with emotional disturbance without brain injury, and a well-functioning control group. As can be seen in Table 11, the three clinical groups differed significantly from the control group in their Bender Test performances. They also differed from each other. Thus the control group did better on the Bender Test than did the emotionally disturbed children, who in turn showed fewer imperfections on the Bender Test than the children with perceptual–motor problems, while the neurologically impaired group did poorest on the Bender Test.

AGE AND MBD

Children with MBD are usually more immature and tend to have a slower than average rate of maturation in visual-motor integration. The study of Stavrianos (1971) illustrates this point well. Table 11 shows the Bender Test mean scores for her four groups of subjects. As would be expected, the Bender Test scores of Stavrianos' older subjects (age 8½ to 11½) were significantly better, in all four diagnostic categories, than the test scores of the corresponding groups of young subjects (age 6 to 8). Maturation in visual-motor perception was evident between the two age levels; only the rate of maturation differed for the four diagnostic categories. For example, the 6- to 8-year-old control subjects had a mean Bender Test score of 6; the children with perceptual–motor problems did not obtain a Bender Test score of 6 until they were 8½ to 11½ years old.

As was shown earlier in Table 10 and Figure 2, retarded children fail to show significant improvement on their Bender Test records for long periods of time, while youngsters of normal mental ability with MBD show gradual but continued improvement in visual-motor perception until they reach maturation in this function and can copy the Bender Test designs without any marked distortions. Adults with brain dysfunction sustained later in life may regress in their visual-motor functioning until their Bender Test records once again resemble those of immature children. Wile (1965) observed that the Bender Test scores of his adult organic V.A. patients were similar to those of bright, well-functioning school children (first- to fifth-graders). But there was a significant difference between the Bender Test scores of the children and those of the adult schizophrenic patients and of the normal adults (college students). Both of these adult groups produced Bender Test records that were superior to those of well-functioning children.

It is unfortunate that so many investigators fail to control the age level of their subjects. As was pointed out earlier (p. 13), a large age range within a group of subjects inevitably affects the validity of the findings of a study. Routh and Roberts (1972), for instance, used 89 clinic patients age 6 years 5 months to 13 years 8 months as subjects in their study. They found that the Bender Test scores for this group of youngsters correlated significantly with neurological signs, with speech, with the digit span test, with arithmetic computations, and with reading recognition. The Bender Test scores also correlated significantly with the youngsters' ages ($r = -.49$) and with their IQ scores ($r = -.37$). In fact, it seems that the Bender Test was primarily related to age and mental ability in this group of children. Once the C.A. and the IQ of the subjects were partialled out, the Bender Test scores no longer correlated significantly with any of the other measures.

Ackerman et al. (1971) used learning-disabled boys age 8 years to 11 years 11 months as subjects; Friedman et al. (1967) used clinic patients age 5 years to 10 years; Hayden et al. (1970) studied 48 emotionally disturbed patients in a residential treatment center, age 7 years 10 months to 13 years 5 months: None of these investigators found any significant differences between the Bender Test scores of children with neurological impairment and those of the control groups. I suspect that this lack of significant results is at least partially due to the wide age range of the subjects used in the studies and to failure to control the age levels of the clinic patients and the control groups.

In order to test this hypothesis, I selected from the study of Hayden et al. 17 subjects with MBD and matched them for exact age with 17 other subjects from this study without MBD. A comparison of the Bender Test scores of these two matched groups of youngsters showed a significant difference between them:

Bender Score	Ss with MBD	Ss without MBD	χ^2	p
$\leqslant3$	9	15		
			3.54	$<.05$
$\geqslant4$	8	2		

Since all of the subjects in this study were emotionally disturbed and vulnerable, most of them functioned on the Bender Test below their age levels; but the group of children without neurological impairment did significantly better on the test than did the group of youngsters with MBD.

Henderson et al. (1969) found significant differences on the Bender Test scores of their "neurologically suspect" youngsters and their normal control group. In this study, 203 lower-class schoolchildren served as subjects; their age range extended only from 6 years 9 months to 7 years. Of this group, 28 children (14%) revealed abnormal signs on a neurological examination. The mean Bender Test score for the subjects with MBD was 9.6 as compared to 6.4 for the youngsters without neurological signs.

IQ AND MBD

As discussed earlier (p. 47), Bender Test scores are closely related to IQ scores of average public-school pupils. One of the characteristics of children with MBD is that "as a group [they] tend to do poorly on the Bender Test regardless of their IQ scores" (Koppitz, 1963, p. 83). A marked discrepancy between a child's mental age derived from his IQ score and his perceptual–motor age derived from the Bender Test score tends to be one of several indications that the youngster may have MBD. Supporting evidence for this claim comes from the studies of Stavrianos (1971) and Hartlage and Lucas (1971). In Stavrianos' investigation subjects of average mental ability with MBD did significantly less well on the Bender Test than did children of the same age and mental ability without MBD (see Table 11).

Hartlage and Lucas administered the Bender Test to 30 young clinic patients with a diagnosis of neurological impairment and to 30 patients who were free from neurological impairment. The two groups of subjects were matched for age and IQ level. The investigators converted the Bender Test scores into Scale Scores (p. 17) so that they could be compared with the subjects' WISC IQ scores. Results showed that a discrepancy of 29 points between the Bender Test Scale Scores and the WISC IQ scores correctly identified 25 of the 30 neurologically impaired subjects ($p < .001$) and ruled out neurological impairment in 28 of the 30 control subjects ($p < .001$).

MEDICAL PROBLEMS AND MBD

A number of recent studies deal with the Bender Test performance of youngsters with specific types of neurological problems or medical conditions that appear to be related to MBD:

Low birth weight. An important series of studies by Wiener et al. (1965, 1968) followed 500 children with low birth weight (LBW ≤ 2500 g) and 492 full-term controls from birth to age 10. The youngsters were given repeated neurological and psychological evaluations. When the children were 6 and 7 years old, data were obtained from 442 LBW youngsters and from 415 control subjects. None of the children had any gross sensory motor handicap nor a WISC IQ score of less than 60. The LBW youngsters showed marked impairment in the following areas: performance on the Bender Test, comprehension and abstract reasoning, perseveration, gross motor development, speech, and IQ scores. The youngsters with the lowest birth weight showed the greatest degree of impairment at ages 6 and 7. Low birth weight was also associated with a higher "index of perinatal trauma" and with neurological damage. Thus it appears that poor Bender Test performance and neurological damage were correlated and both were related to low birth weight.

By the time the children reached age 8 to 10 it was found that the WISC Full Scale IQ score was better able to discriminate between the LBW children and the control group than was the Bender Test. However, performance on the Bender Test was still the best single indicator of neurological impairment among the white LBW youngsters. For black LBW children the WISC Performance Scale was most closely associated with brain damage.

Cerebral palsy. The Bender Test records of children with cerebral palsy (CP) were investigated in two studies, one from India and one from Norway. Patel and Bharucha (1972) compared the Bender Test performance of 34 CP youngsters age 6 to 12 and of 80 normal pupils age 5 to 9. It was shown that imperfections on the Bender Test decreased steadily with increases in the children's ages, but that the rate of improvement is much slower for the CP children.

Grinde (1972) used four groups of subjects for her study: CP youngsters, epileptic patients, children with motor disability but no brain injury (children with polio, birth defects, etc.), and a normal control group. The CP youngsters and the birth-defect children showed about the same degree of difficulty with motor control and with guiding a pencil. Since the CP youngsters produced significantly poorer Bender Test records than the children with birth defects, Grinde concluded that the immature Bender Test scores of the CP youngsters must be related mainly to central brain dysfunction and not primarily to motor impairment.

Abnormal EEGs. Jost (1969) explored the relationship of children's Bender Test scores and EEG records. The subjects for this study were 37 youngsters of normal intelligence, age 5 to 10, who had produced below-average Bender Test protocols. Twenty-eight subjects (75%) were found to have abnormal EEGs, while 9 children (25%) had normal EEG records. It appears, therefore, that immature Bender Test scores correlate significantly with abnormal EEGs (p <.01), but not all children with poor Bender Test records necessarily have abnormal EEGs.

Van de Vegte (1965) compared Bender Test records with EEGs and medical histories of 120 emotionally disturbed hospital patients age 6 to 12. The Bender Test scores were able to discriminate significantly between subjects with and without a medical history of brain damage (t = 2.87, p <.005) and between children with normal and abnormal EEGs (t = 1.64, p <.05).

Encephalitis. Sabatino and Cramblett (1968) followed 14 children for 7 months to 2 years after their hospital admissions for encephalitis. Serious problems in visual-motor and auditory perception were found to be among the after effects of encephalitis. Nine of the 14 youngsters produced poor Bender Test records, but there was no consistency in the type of errors the children made on the Bender Test. The youngsters' poor Bender Test scores, learning difficulties, emotional liabilities, personality problems, and EEG records were all characteristic of generalized cerebral dysfunction. Thus once again we find poor Bender Test performance associated with MBD.

Muscular dystrophy. According to Marsh (1972), Duchenne's muscular dystrophy is also related to impaired visual-motor ability. Fourteen of her 21 boys with muscular dystrophy (age 6 to 13) had poor performances on the Bender Test. The Bender Test scores of the youngsters were also significantly correlated with their WISC IQ scores (p <.01).

Sickle cell trait. A study conducted by the Collaborative Child Development Program at Charity Hospital in New Orleans (Flick and Duncan, 1973) compared 42 black children with sickle cell trait with 18 control subjects. At age 7 the Bender Test performances of the children with sickle cell trait were significantly more immature (p <.03) than those of the control group. The youngsters with sickle cell trait also more often showed behavior that is usually associated with MBD, such as hyperactivity, awkwardness, short attention span, etc.

Deafness. Four recent Bender Test studies involve deaf children as subjects. Keogh et al. (1970) tested 160 children from the California School for the Deaf at Riverside. The youngsters had an age range from 8 to 17 years; each age level was evaluated separately. The subjects had an IQ mean score of 102 with an IQ range from 53 to 150. Results indicate that the Bender Test scores of deaf children, at each level, are mainly related to their IQ scores and not to the degree of hearing loss. There was also no significant difference on the Bender Test scores of children with different etiology of hearing loss (meningitis, rubella, premature birth, Rh factor, genetic, etc.). However, the Bender Test scores did discriminate significantly between the 59 youngsters who were rated as "organic" and the subjects without organic symptoms.

Edington (1971) administered the Bender Test to 55 deaf pupils from the New York School for the Deaf. All subjects had at least average IQ scores. It was found that at each age level from 5 to 10 years the Bender Test scores were within the normal range. The deaf children in this sample showed no developmental lag in visual-motor perception.

Clarke and Leslie (1971) matched three groups of deaf children (age 8 to 12) for C.A. and degree of hearing loss. Group I included youngsters with a Performance IQ score of less than 90 and more than 2 years of retardation in reading; Group II included children with a Performance IQ score of more than 90 and more than 2 years of retardation in reading; Group III was made up of pupils with a Performance IQ score of less than 90 and less than 2 years of retardation in reading. The Bender Test was able to discriminate between Group I and Group II—that is, between the children with high and low IQ scores. But no statistically significant difference was found between the Bender Test performances of the more adequate readers in Group I and the poor readers in Group III who were matched for IQ scores. The results concur with earlier findings (p. 63) that the Bender Test scores are more closely related to children's IQ scores than to reading achievement. All three groups of deaf children had below-average IQ scores and/or learning problems; it is therefore not surprising that all three groups of children had Bender Test scores that were markedly inferior to those of normal children.

Similar results were reported by Gilbert and Levee (1967). They compared the performance of 50 deaf youngsters and 50 hearing youngsters on the Bender Test and the Spiral After-Effect with an Archimedes spiral. The control group did significantly better on both measures than the deaf children. Good Bender Test scores were correlated with more aftereffect for both the deaf and the hearing youngsters.

In summary, the findings of these four studies show that the Bender Test scores of deaf children are not related to etiology or to degree of hearing loss. The Bender Test performances of deaf children with average mental ability and without serious learning problems were shown to be no different from those of youngsters who are not deaf. As with other pupils, the Bender Test scores of deaf children are most closely related to IQ scores, to school achievement, and to "organic" signs. Deaf children with below-average IQ scores and/or learning problems also produced poor Bender Test scores. The same was true for "organic" children with hearing loss.

BEHAVIOR AND MBD

Observation of children taking the Bender Test has been recommended earlier (p. 9). Such observations become absolutely essential when trying to determine if a child suffers from MBD. Without repeating in detail what was said earlier, I would like to stress again the diagnostic value of a youngster's behavior while copying the Bender Test designs. Here are some of the things to look for when watching a child: Is the youngster aware of the errors or distortions on his drawings? What is the child's attitude when approaching the task? How impulsive or deliberate is he? Is the youngster attempting to compensate for perceptual–motor problems? How much time and space does he need to complete the test? All of these aspects of behavior are significantly influenced by MBD.

However, it should also again be pointed out that there is no one-to-one relationship between any specific sign or behavior on the Bender Test and MBD; nor is it possible to predict from a single Bender Test record or test performance what the pupil's actual functioning in school or at home will be. There is, of course, no typical child with MBD. I would like to quote from the earlier chapter (Koppitz, 1963, p. 103), but substitute at this time the term MBD for brain injury: "As a group, children with [MBD] are more vulnerable than other children. They tend to mature more slowly not only in visual-motor perception but also in their attitudes and behavior. They also cannot adapt as easily to new situations and are usually less able to cope with the stresses and strains of daily life. But the specific reaction of [children with MBD] to stress will depend on many factors including [the degree of MBD], the child's mental ability, and above all the interpersonal relationships he has experienced. The Developmental Bender score can give no information about this last factor. However, a child's underlying attitudes are reflected in emotional indicators [see Chapter 10] on the Bender protocol. . . . Underlying attitudes may be expressed overtly in many different ways. The author believes that it is not possible to predict accurately [the overt behavior of a child with MBD solely] from his performance on the Bender Test." Because of this, it is always important to use the Bender Test in combination with other psychological measures and with behavior observations.

SUMMARY

Research shows that the Bender Test is a valuable aid in diagnosing MBD in elementary-school children, but only when it is used in combination with other tests and, if possible, with information concerning the youngsters' developmental, medical, and social histories, their school progress, and their behavior. A diagnosis of MBD should not be made solely on the basis of a single Bender Test record. Although the great majority of children with MBD produce poor Bender Test records, a good Bender Test protocol does not necessarily reflect an absence of MBD. Some youngsters with MBD have difficulties primarily in the areas of language and memory, while their visual-motor perception is not impaired.

Most children with MBD develop more slowly and show a lag in visual-motor integration; hence their Bender Test performances are significantly more immature than those of normal children age 5 to 10. A marked discrepancy between a youngster's IQ scores and his Bender Test scores has considerable diagnostic implications for MBD. The total Developmental Bender Test scores can better differentiate between children with and without MBD than any individual scoring item or sign; for this purpose they are as good as the Neurological Indicators on the Bender Test, if not better.

A number of recent studies have indicated that certain medical conditions and problems are associated with both poor Bender Test performance and MBD. These include low birth weight (≤ 2500 g), cerebral palsy, abnormal EEGs, encephalitis, muscular dystrophy, and sickle cell trait. Bender Test scores are not related to etiology and to degree of hearing loss in deaf children. It is furthermore not possible to determine from a Bender Test record the etiology of MBD; MBD may result from many different causes.

CHAPTER 10.
The Bender Test
and Emotional Problems

In Part VI of *The Bender Gestalt Test for Young Children* (Koppitz, 1963, pp. 123ff) I discussed the use of the Bender Test as a projective instrument and demonstrated that ten specific signs or Emotional Indicators (EIs) on the Bender Test can differentiate between children with and without emotional problems. It was further pointed out that the Emotional Indicators are not primarily related to age and maturation, as was the case with the Developmental Bender Test Scoring System, even though many children with immature visual-motor perception also reveal Emotional Indicators on their Bender Test records. Children with poor perceptual–motor integration tend to be vulnerable and prone to develop secondary emotional difficulties. But not all youngsters with poor Developmental Bender Test scores necessarily have emotional problems, nor do all children with Emotional Indicators on their Bender Test records inevitably show malfunctioning or immaturity in the visual-motor area.

Plate 19, for example, shows the immature Bender Test record of Jim, age 8½, a youngster with serious learning disabilities but with no problems in social and emotional adjustment. His Developmental Bender Test score of 6 was on the level of a 7-year-old child, he still had difficulty with the integration of parts in Figs. 4, 6, and 7. However, the Bender Test protocol revealed no Emotional Indicators. On the other hand, Steve, age 9½, had a long history of emotional and behavior problems. Steve's Bender Test record, shown on Plate 21, reflects severe emotional problems, while his Developmental Bender Test score of 1 indicates that he had no marked immaturity or problems in visual-motor perception. He was an erratic, negativistic, seriously disturbed youngster with poor language skills. He was impulsive and poorly coordinated and his attention span was short. Steve hated school and refused to do any work, even though he was able to achieve. His self-concept was extremely poor, and he was unable to get along with his peers. When he was not disrupting the class he would sit, lost in daydreams, and chew pencils.

This chapter reexamines the ten Emotional Indicators on the Bender Test and their implications in the light of recent research results. We shall also discuss a number of studies that use different signs and methods to interpret emotional adjustment of children from their Bender Test records.

EMOTIONAL INDICATORS (EIs)

Detailed descriptions, definitions, and illustrations of the ten EIs are given in the "Scoring Manual for Emotional Indicators on the Bender Test for Children" (Koppitz, 1963, pp. 132–141) and need not be repeated here. The following is just a brief summary of the definitions and implications of the ten EIs together with new findings from research.

I. Confused Order. See Plates 3, 8, 9, 10, 12, 16, 17, 20, 21, 22, 28, and 33. Bender Test designs are scattered arbitrarily on the paper without logical sequence or order. Confused Order is not unusual among 5- to 7-year-old children. It seems to be associated with a lack of planning ability and poor organization. For brighter and older children Confused Order on the Bender Test may also reflect mental confusion.

Recent research findings. Ackerman et al. (1971) found Confused Order significantly more often on the Bender Test records of 8- to 11-year-old children with learning disabilities than on the protocols of good students. In Naches' investigation (1967), Confused Order occurred more often on the Bender Test protocols of the acting-out children than on those of the control group.

II. Wavy Line in Figs. 1 and 2. See Plates 7, 8, 11, 14, 16, 17, 20, 21, 33, and 37. Two or more abrupt changes in direction of the line of dots or circles of Fig. 1 or Fig. 2. Wavy Line seems to be associated with either poor motor coordination and/or emotional instability.

Recent research findings. Wavy Line on the Bender Test was found to discriminate significantly between a group of psychiatric patients and a control group of normal children (Elliott, 1968) and between kindergarten pupils with and without emotional problems (Kai, 1972).

III. Dashes Substituted for Circles in Fig. 2. See Plates 9 and 11. At least half of all circles in Fig. 2 are replaced with dashes 1/16 in. long or longer. Substitution of Dashes for Circles has been associated with impulsivity and with a lack of interest in young children.

Recent research findings. According to Handler and McIntosh (1971) the substitution of dashes for circles or dots is associated with aggressiveness, while Brown (1965) relates it to impulsivity. Dashes in Fig. 2 were also found significantly more often on the drawings of Japanese kindergarten pupils with emotional problems (Kai, 1972).

IV. Increasing Size of Figs. 1, 2, or 3. See Plates 11, 16, and 28. Dots or circles in Figs. 1, 2, or 3 increase progressively in size until the last ones are at least three times as large as the first ones. Increasing Size on the Bender Test designs is associated with low frustration tolerance and explosiveness. The diagnostic implications of this EI increase as children get older.

Recent research findings. Increasing Size was found significantly more often on the Bender Test records of acting-out youngsters (Naches, 1967) and of kindergarten pupils with emotional problems (Kai, 1972).

V. *Large Size.* See Plates 6, 10, 11, 12, 13, 14, 21, 23, 28, and 37. The area covered by one design is twice as large as the area of the design on the Bender Test stimulus card. Large Size is associated with acting-out behavior in children.

Recent research findings. Results from Naches' study (1967) concur that Large Size on the Bender Test is related to acting-out behavior. It was also able to differentiate between psychiatric patients and a control group of normal pupils (Elliott, 1968) and between kindergarten pupils with and without emotional problems (Kai, 1972).

VI. *Small Size.* See Plates 2, 3, 7, 9, 11, 13, 15, 20, 21, 22, 29, and 35. The area covered by any one design on the Bender Test is half as large or less than the area of the design on the Bender Test stimulus card. Small Size of design tends to be related to anxiety, withdrawal, constriction, and timidity in children.

Recent research findings. Elliott (1968) and Kai (1972) showed that Small Size of Bender Test designs can differentiate significantly between psychiatric patients age 11 to 14 and control subjects, and between emotionally disturbed and well-adjusted kindergarten pupils.

VII. *Fine Line.* See Plates 4, 18, 22, 33, and 39. The pencil line is so thin that it requires effort to see the complete design. This EI is associated with timidity, shyness, and withdrawal in young children.

Recent research findings. Elliott's psychiatric patients (1968) revealed significantly more often Fine Lines on their Bender Test records than did the control group; the same was true for Kai's kindergarten pupils (1972) with emotional problems as compared to well-adjusted pupils.

VIII. *Careless Overwork or Heavily Reinforced Lines.* See Plates 8, 12, 15, 20, 21, 23, 24, 28, and 30. A complete design or part of it is redrawn with heavy, impulsive lines. When a design is erased and carefully redrawn, or if a design is corrected with deliberate lines that really improve the drawing, then this category is not scored. Careless Overwork and Heavily Reinforced Lines are associated with impulsivity, aggressiveness, and acting-out behavior in children. Plate 8 shows a Bender Test record with impulsive, careless overwork that is scored for this EI, while Plate 17 presents a Bender Test protocol with erasures and deliberate redrawing of two designs that is not scored. Careful observation and differentiation between these two methods of drawing is therefore decisive for scoring this item.

Recent research findings. Heavily Reinforced Lines were found to be associated with aggressiveness by Handler and McIntosh (1971) and with overt hostility by Brown (1965). On the other hand, erasures and careful spontaneous corrections and reworking of a design on the Bender Test were shown to be related to high intelligence and good achievement by Bravo (1972) and Keogh (1968a).

IX. *Second Attempt.* See Plates 8, 18, 21, 25, and 33. Drawing of a Bender Test design or part of it is spontaneously abandoned before or after it has been completed, and a new drawing of the design is made.

This item is only scored when two distinct drawings of one design have been made on two different locations on the paper. This EI has been associated with impulsivity and anxiety. The impulsive child gives up easily and starts over again, or starts something else rather than completing a difficult task.

Recent research findings. The aggressive children of Handler and McIntosh (1971) showed significantly more Second Attempts on their Bender Test records than did the withdrawn youngsters or the control subjects. Mogin (1966) found Second Attempt on the Bender Test to be associated with behavior difficulties in second- and third-graders, while Kai (1972) reported more Second Attempts on the Bender Test records of Japanese kindergarten pupils with emotional problems.

X.   Expansion. See Plates 4 and 6. Two or more sheets of paper are used to complete the drawings of all nine Bender Test designs. Expansion is associated with impulsivity and acting-out behavior in children. Among school-age children it seems to occur almost exclusively on the Bender Test records of emotionally disturbed retarded children.

Recent research findings. Brown (1965) and Naches (1967) concur that Expansion tends to be related to acting-out behavior. Expansion was found only once on the 109 Bender Test records of Kai's kindergarten pupils (1972). Thus it occurred too rarely to be included in a statistical analysis of the data. While Expansion occurs occasionally on the Bender Test records of American youngsters, it is entirely out of character for young Japanese children. On the other hand, Constriction on the Bender Test, which did not differentiate between American schoolchildren with and without emotional problems (Koppitz, 1963, p. 129), was shown to discriminate significantly between Japanese kindergarten pupils with and without emotional problems.

ADDITIONAL EMOTIONAL INDICATORS

At this time I would like to add two more Emotional Indicators to my list. They are *Box Around Design* and *Spontaneous Elaboration or Addition to Design.* These two EIs occur so rarely on the Bender Test of children that a controlled study and statistical treatment of the data have not been feasible. Yet I have found that when either of these signs appears on a Bender Test record it tends to have considerable clinical implications.

XI.   Box Around Design. See Plate 24. A box is drawn around one or more designs after they have been copied. This type of drawing is associated with an attempt on the part of the child to control his impulsivity. Children who exhibit this kind of drawing on the Bender Test tend to have weak inner control; they need and want outer limits and controls in order to be able to function in school and at home. The case of Frankie, age 10, illustrates this point. Frankie was a youngster who drew boxes around all nine of the Bender Test figures (Plate 24). He was a cheerful, highly individualistic, and creative boy who was also extremely immature, disorganized, and impulsive. He had a severe speech impediment and poor visual-motor integration. Since he was the youngest of 7 siblings and had been sickly as an infant, he was greatly indulged by his mother and by his older brothers. When Frankie scattered his toys and clothes and his father's tools all over the house, or when he did not do his chores, others picked up after him and did his chores for him. In school he forgot where he put his pencils and papers, he never finished his assignments, he used other children's things without permission, and he did as he pleased. But since Frankie was pleasant at all times, never got angry, and always thought of ways to amuse himself and to make things out of odds and ends, his peers and teachers just could not get mad at him for long. Both at school and at home others found it easier to cater to Frankie's whims than to make him conform to the rules others were expected to follow.

Frankie's first Bender Test record (Plate 23) drawn at age 10 years 1 month reflects his impulsivity and casual manner. There was no doubt that his visual perception was good. Frankie worked very fast without much effort or concentration. He drew the circle in Fig. A more oval than round and made a square with only three corners, the fourth one being rounded. He also placed the square somewhat apart from the circle; but then recognizing that this was not correct he scribbled between the two figures making a crude kind of connection between them. Frankie had difficulty integrating the parts of Figs. 4 and 7, but he did not bother to connect them even though he was aware of his error. Similarly, in Fig. 3 Frankie did not make the effort to draw the required number of dots; instead he just scribbled and made a continuous spiral. The same pattern was used in Fig. 5. Frankie's total Bender Test performance resembled that of an immature 5½-year-old child. His school behavior and achievement were also still on the pre-primary level. He made no progress despite low-average mental ability.

I again administered the Bender Test to Frankie when he was 10 years 9 months old. Plate 24 shows his second Bender Test record. This time Frankie again worked fast, but he put forth effort. He spontaneously drew a box around each design after he had completed it in an apparent attempt to structure himself. The drawings were immature; he still had difficulty with the integration of the parts in Figs. A, 4, and 7; and he still perseverated and had difficulty shifting directions in Fig. 6. But compared to the earlier Bender Test record on Plate 23 the second protocol shows a marked improvement in the quality of the drawings. Frankie drew neat little circles on Figs. 1, 3, and 5 and counted the dots in Figs. 1 and 3. He also attempted to correct the angles in Figs. A and 7 by drawing them over. In other words, Frankie demonstrated on his Bender Test record that he was now trying to control his impulsivity and to compensate for his poor perceptual–motor integration, but he could do this only if he had firm external structure and support. The boxes on the Bender Test record provided such structure for his drawings and enabled Frankie to function more nearly adequately.

Taking the lead from Frankie's Bender Test record, a behavior-modification program and reward system was worked out for Frankie in school that provided the kind of structure and reinforcement he needed and wanted. The results were gratifying. Within a very short time Frankie learned to hang up his coat, to finish his assignments, and to be more considerate of his peers. However, much more time was needed before Frankie began to internalize the controls and started to organize himself without external structure and reinforcement, both at home and in school.

XII. Spontaneous Elaboration or Additions to Design. See Plates 21, 25, and 26. Spontaneous changes are made on one or more Bender Test figures that turn them into objects or combine them into bizarre designs. These kinds of drawings are rare and occur almost exclusively on Bender Test records of children who are overwhelmed by fears and anxieties or who are totally preoccupied with their own thoughts. These youngsters often have a tenuous hold on reality and may confuse fact and fantasy.

Plate 25 was drawn by Danny, a disturbed, unhappy 9-year-old boy of borderline intelligence. Danny was caught up in the tensions and fights of his parents; his home and family life were rapidly deteriorating. Danny was unable to cope with the situation and sought refuge in fantasy. When the Bender Test was administered to Danny, he tried to apply himself and put forth effort. But by the time he reached Fig. 5 his emotions overwhelmed him. He turned Fig. 5 into "a choo-choo" that was to carry him away from all the turmoil at home. When asked to draw Fig. 5 over again, Danny transformed the extension on the design into "a tornado" and launched into lengthy stories of death and destruction. It required considerable urging to get Danny to complete the Bender Test. It stands to reason that Danny also had considerable difficulty concentrating in class and attending to his assignments.

Plate 26 was drawn by Seth, a bright, schizoid boy of 6 who was totally absorbed in his preoccupation with plumbing. He drew the Bender Test designs as parts of elaborate systems of pipes, pumps, and tanks. Seth was unable to concentrate on any task that was apart from his obsession with plumbing. On Plate 26, Fig. 6 is transformed into a "coil with pressure in it" that is connected to "a 150-gallon tank." Despite adequate mental ability, Seth was quite unable to function in a regular class or even in a public school. He had to be referred to a residential treatment center for children. His behavior was as atypical as his Bender Test record.

Horizontal Position of Drawing Paper. Some children turn the long axis of the drawing paper into a horizontal position instead of maintaining it in the usual vertical position when copying the Bender Test designs. Naches (1967) found that acting-out youngsters more often turned the paper into the horizontal position than withdrawn children. Ackerman et al. (1971) reported that the horizontal position of the paper did not differentiate between children with and without learning disabilities, whereas Bravo (1972) observed that an unusually large number of her intellectually superior, well-functioning pupils turned the Bender Test drawing paper into the horizontal position. It appears, therefore, that the turning of the drawing paper into a horizontal position is related to out-goingness and extraversion, but not necessarily to acting-out behavior or to emotional maladjustment. Horizontal placement of the drawing paper can evidently not qualify as a clinically valid Emotional Indicator on the Bender Test.

NUMBER OF EIs ON THE BENDER TEST RECORDS

Emotional Indicators are clinical signs that should be evaluated indi-vidually like any other clinical symptom. They may occur separately or in combination; they are not mutually exclusive. A given emotional problem can be expressed on the Bender Test in different ways. For instance, Substituting Dashes for Circles and Overwork or Heavily Reinforced Lines both signify impulsivity. A child may produce both of these signs (Plate 11) or only one of them (Plates 12 and 23) on his Bender Test record without any difference in the interpretation of the protocol. Some EIs involve opposite tendencies that may, on occasion, occur in the same youngster and that may be reflected on a single Bender Test record. Small Size of design is shown on Plate 22; Large Size of design is shown on Plate 6; Plates 12 and 21 display both small and large drawings.

As McConnell (1967) and Ackerman et al. (1971) point out, EIs lack internal consistency and cannot, therefore, be added together into a mean-ingful total EI score. It also follows that the number of EIs on a Bender Test record cannot or should not be correlated or compared with other test scores.

A single EI on a child's Bender Test protocol reflects a given attitude or trend, but it does not by itself indicate any serious emotional problem, nor does it show with certainty how this tendency will manifest itself in a school setting. Earlier studies (Koppitz, 1963, p. 130) showed that three or more EIs are necessary before one can say with some degree of con-fidence that a child has serious emotional problems and will need further evaluation. This does not mean, however, that a child with six EIs (which is rare) is twice as disturbed as a youngster with only three EIs on his Bender Test record. An interpretation of EIs should be limited to underly-ing tendencies and attitudes; one should merely develop hypotheses from the EIs that then need to be checked against other psychological data and observations.

SCHOOLCHILDREN AND EIs

The following are recent findings of studies involving EIs on the Bender Test records of school children:

Kindergarten. Kai (1970) found that kindergarten pupils with emotional problems show a significantly higher incidence of EIs on their Bender Test records than well-adjusted youngsters.

First grade. Savering (1968) showed that emotional signs on the Bender Test records of first-graders were related to teacher ratings of "work competency", including "activity level, aggressiveness, fearfulness, mood swings, stability, sociability, and surgency."

Second grade. Walker and Streff (1973) found that Bender Test performance and emotional signs were associated with teacher ratings of "self-confidence" and "self-control" for second-grade pupils.

Second and third grades. Mogin's study (1966) reveals a relationship between Emotional Indicators on the Bender Test and behavior problems.

Third grade. Fromm (1966), working with the emotional signs of Pascal and Suttell, reported significant differences between the Bender Test records of well-adjusted and poorly adjusted third-grade pupils. Handler and McIntosh (1971) discovered that emotional signs on the Bender Test discriminated between aggressive third-graders and groups of withdrawn and normal third-graders. Aggressive pupils showed more Bender Test signs of aggressiveness and fewer signs of withdrawal than either of the other two groups.

Achievement and EIs. Dibner and Korn (1969) found no significant relationship between achievement and EIs on the Bender Test records of normal schoolchildren, kindergarten through fourth grade, in a residential suburb. Similar results were reported by Ackerman et al. (1971); EIs were unable to differentiate between their third-grade boys with and without learning problems. EIs also did not correlate with reading achievement for Hammer's (1967) environmentally handicapped and middle-class first-grade pupils.

Walraven (1967) investigated the relationship between the size of the Bender Test drawings and reading achievement. The findings of his study with socially deprived children are inconclusive. A significant correlation was shown between small size of Bender Test figures and achievement on the Slosson Oral Reading Test, but not between small Bender Test designs and achievement on the Gilmore Oral Reading Test and the reading recognition scores on the Wide Range Achievement Test.

PSYCHIATRIC PATIENTS AND EIs

Acting-out behavior. Naches (1967) found significant differences in the number of EIs on the Bender Test records of a group of institutionalized acting-out children and a group of normal control subjects, matched for age, sex, and IQ scores.

Psychiatric patients versus controls. In Elliott's study (1968), a group of psychiatric patients age 11 to 14 (including both psychotic and neurotic patients) showed a significantly higher incidence of EIs and a higher Pascal and Suttell score on their Bender Test records than did a control group matched for age, sex, and IQ scores. Champion (1967) matched a group of clinic patients who were in therapy for emotional problems with a group of normal school children. The clinic patients exhibited significantly more EIs on their Bender records than did the control group. Similar results were obtained by Oliver and Kronenberger (1971) in a study using young adolescent clinic patients (age 11 to 15–11) and average pupils as subjects.

Psychotic versus neurotic patients. No significant differences were found by Elliott (1968) in the number of EIs and in the Pascal and Suttell Bender Test scores of two matched groups of psychotic and neurotic patients.

Psychiatric versus brain-damaged patients. Oliver and Kronenberger (1971) compared the Bender Test records of emotionally disturbed and brain-injured adolescent patients age 11 to 15. The Developmental Bender Test scores were able to discriminate between the two groups of subjects significantly, but there was no significant difference in the number of EIs on the Bender Test protocols. Using the emotional signs of Pascal and Suttell, Lenstrup (1968) was unable to differentiate between the Bender Test records of psychotic and the brain-damaged children who were matched for age and IQ level.

SOCIAL FACTORS, SEX, AND EIs

It has repeatedly been documented that there is a higher incidence of emotional and behavior problems among boys than among girls, and among environmentally handicapped children than among middle-class youngsters. Therefore, one would hypothesize that boys would also show more EIs on their Bender Test records than girls and that the same would be true for socially deprived youngsters as against more advantaged children.

Hammer's study (1967) offers support for both hypotheses. She found that the EIs on the Bender Test differentiated significantly between her first-grade boys and girls and between her environmentally handicapped and middle-class pupils.

EXAMINER EXPECTANCY AND EIs

The question is often raised whether or how much the examiner's expectation can influence a child's test performance. This is especially crucial when working with projective materials. For if a child's test results do reflect even in part the examiner's attitude and expectations, then the validity of the test is in doubt.

Gravitz (1969) devised an interesting study that explored the influence of examiner expectancy on Bender Test records. Ten examiners were led to expect that their subjects would produce "expansive" Bender Test records; 10 other examiners were led to believe that their subjects would draw "constricted" Bender Test designs; 10 control examiners were not given any kind of expectation regarding their subjects' Bender Test performances. Gravitz found that the expectations of an examiner did not affect the Bender Test performance of his subjects.

METHOD OF TEST ADMINISTRATION AND EIs

The results of Solomon's study (1969) indicate that the method of administering the Bender Test may influence the frequency of EIs on test protocols. Solomon gave the Bender Test to 130 second-grade pupils twice, once as a group test and once individually. More EIs were found on the group Bender Test records than on the individually obtained test protocols.

SUMMARY

Recent research results offer additional support for the clinical validity of the ten Emotional Indicators on the Bender Test that were developed earlier (Koppitz, 1963, p. 132). Two new Emotional Indicators have been added to the list: *Box Around Design* and *Spontaneous Elaboration or Addition to Design.*

Each EI should be evaluated separately for its clinical implications; the EIs cannot be added to make up a total EI score, since they lack internal consistency. A single EI on a Bender Test record merely suggests a trend or an attitude; it does not necessarily indicate any serious emotional problems. The presence of three or more EIs on a Bender Test protocol tends to reflect emotional difficulties that warrant further investigation.

A number of new studies have demonstrated that the EIs can differentiate significantly between the Bender Test records of schoolchildren (kindergarten through third grade) with and without behavior and emotional problems. The relationship between EIs and school achievement is not significant.

EIs can discriminate between groups of youngsters with psychiatric difficulties and normal control groups. However, it is not possible to make a differential diagnosis between neurotic, psychotic, and brain-damaged patients on the basis of EIs on a Bender Test record. Boys and environmentally handicapped children tend to show more EIs on their Bender Test records than do girls and middle-class pupils. The drawing of EIs on Bender Test protocols is not influenced by the examiner's expectancy.

CHAPTER 11.
Screening School Beginners with the Bender Test

As was demonstrated in the foregoing discussion, the Bender Test performance of groups of school beginners is related to their overall school functioning in the elementary grades and in middle school; but as was also pointed out, there is no one-to-one relationship between the Bender Test scores of an individual youngster and his school achievement. There is a consensus among investigators that a *good* Bender Test score is a better predictor of school progress than an average or poor Bender Test score. It appears, therefore, that the Developmental Bender Test scores by themselves are only moderately effective as screening instruments for kindergarten and first-grade pupils. This chapter demonstrates ways in which the usefulness of the Bender Test as a screening test for school beginners can be enhanced.

Let me reiterate: Anyone who administers the Bender Test and derives nothing from it but a test score is depriving himself of much valuable information. When using the Bender Test as a screening instrument, it is essential that the examiner observe the child at work (p. 6), analyze the organization and quality of the test record, and look for the Emotional Indicators (p. 84), and finally score the protocol as a developmental test of visual-motor perception.

In my 9-year follow-up study (Koppitz, 1973b) I found that many factors in addition to visual-motor perception, as measured on the Bender Test, determine long-range school achievement. Some of these other factors are also reflected on the Bender Test records. The following are two examples of how the Bender Test can be used most fully as a screening test. Plates 27 and 28 were produced by two kindergarten pupils involved in my follow-up study. Both youngsters obtained a Developmental Bender Test score of 10, or an average score for their grade level. But here ends the similarity between the two Bender Test records.

Plate 27 was drawn by Patrice, 6 years 2 months, one of the older children in her class. She was tall, mature, and well poised. She put forth much effort, and her concentration was excellent. Patrice counted the dots and circles in Figs. 1, 2, and 3, differentiated between dots and circles, attempted to draw angles when appropriate, and tried to integrate the different parts of the figures. Her drawings are well organized on the paper, and the Bender Test record shows no Emotional Indicators. Thus we find that Patrice's Bender Test performance reveals good visual perception, an awareness of numbers, good mental organization and concentration, well-developed inner control, no evidence of emotional problems, and at least average development in visual-motor perception as measured on the test score. In addition, we know that Patrice is a girl (see p. 64), that she is among the older children in her class, and that she is mature for her age. It appears, therefore, that Patrice has many positive factors working in her favor, while no negative factors are apparent. One can predict with confidence that Patrice's school progress will also be good. And, indeed, Patrice's school record revealed that she was an above-average student throughout the elementary-school grades. In the eighth grade her grade average was 87.

Plate 28 shows Edgar's Bender Test record. Edgar, age 6 years, also obtained a Bender Test score of 10, and had apparently average visual-motor perception for his grade level. But Edgar's Bender Test protocol reveals in addition much impulsivity, poor organization of the designs on the paper, and no less than four Emotional Indicators (Confused Order, Overwork in Fig. 1, Increase in Size in Fig. 1, Large Size in Fig. 2). Edgar was restless, socially immature, and small for his age. It could be predicted, therefore, that this impulsive, hyperactive, immature youngster would do less well in school than the more mature, well-poised Patrice, even though their Bender Test scores were identical. So it comes as no surprise that Edgar's achievement was somewhat below average throughout elementary school and that he always presented behavior problems. In the eighth grade his grade average was 69.

Plates 29 and 30 show two more Bender Test records of kindergarten pupils who served as subjects for the 9-year follow-up study. Both youngsters obtained Developmental Bender Test scores of 12. A score of 12 is somewhat below average for children at the end of kindergarten. The Bender Test protocol on Plate 29 was drawn by Lori, age 6 years 2 months. Lori worked very carefully, showed good motivation, and gave no indication of serious emotional or behavior difficulties. Her visual perception and her inner controls were very good. Her Bender Test score reflected above all some immaturity or lag in visual-motor integration. Lori drew circles for dots in Figs. 1, 3, and 5. She had difficulty with angles and curves, showed a tendency to rotate designs (Figs. 5 and 7), and was unable to integrate parts of Figs. A, 4, and 7. Immaturity in visual-motor perception at the end of kindergarten can easily be overcome or compensated for in time, if a child has no other serious problems. Lori was apparently one of these youngsters; she seemed to function at the average or above-average level in all areas except visual-motor integration. Her school record showed that she was an average student in the first grade and that her achievement improved as she got older and more mature. When she was in the eighth grade Lori's grade average was 80.

Plate 30 shows Greg's Bender Test record. Greg's Bender Test score of 12 was identical with Lori's, but in some respects he was less fortunate than Lori. He had many factors working against him. Since Greg's birthday was in late November, he was one of the youngest children in his class, and he was a boy (p. 61). In addition, Greg was socially, emotionally, mentally, and physically immature for his age. Perhaps the single most significant indicator of his immaturity was Greg's failure to differentiate between Figs. 1, 2, and 3 on the Bender Test. He was unable to produce any similarity to the basic configurations of Figs. 2 and 3; he also could not draw any recognizable square in Fig. Λ. In Fig. 5 Greg substituted lines for dots and distorted the Gestalt. All of these are very immature responses. The heavy overwork on the dots of Figs. 1, 2, and 3 suggests that Greg was an impulsive youngster.

Greg's immature visual-motor perception together with his age, sex, and general developmental lag added up to an overloading of negative factors that made school progress difficult. Therefore it could be predicted that Greg's achievement would most likely be below average. In fact, he did very poorly in elementary school and finally was held back; he had to repeat the seventh grade. Greg was an example of a youngster who would have profited from entering school a year later or from having an extra year at the kindergarten or primary-grade level. He was too immature to cope with a regular class at the time of school entry (Koppitz, 1971, p. 184). Instead of allowing Greg more time to mature, he had to fail for 7 years in school before finally repeating a grade. Greg's case shows that the predictive ability of the Developmental Bender Test score is greatly enhanced when a child's age, sex, behavior, and the quality of his Bender Test record are taken into account.

BENDER AND HUMAN FIGURE DRAWINGS

The screening of school beginners for potential learning difficulties is, without question, improved if the Bender Test performance is combined with the results from other tests or measures. When using the Bender Test as a group test (see Chapter 12) additional data are particularly important, since it is not possible to observe all children in a group as carefully as during individual test administration of the Bender Test. The combination of the Bender Test and Human Figure Drawings (HFDs) provides a quick and efficient group screening method. The Bender Test measures children's maturity in visual-motor perception and reflects their inner control and organization, while Human Figure Drawings are able to reveal information about the youngsters' mental ability and emotional adjustment.

In an earlier study (Koppitz, 1968, p. 177) I demonstrated how the Bender Test and Human Figure Drawings together can be used to predict first-grade achievement; 128 first-grade pupils from five different schools (ages 5–9 to 6–11) served as subjects for this study. The Bender Test and HFDs were given at the beginning of the school year; at the end of the school year the Metropolitan Achievement Test was administered. The Developmental Bender Test scores of the subjects were divided into five categories: Good, High Average, Low Average, Poor, and Very poor. The HFDs were scored for the eight Exceptional Items (knee, profile, two lips, nostrils, good proportions, arms at shoulder, four pieces of clothing) that are associated with above-average mental ability for 6-year-old children (Koppitz, 1968, pp. 29ff) and for the six Emotional Indicators (slanting

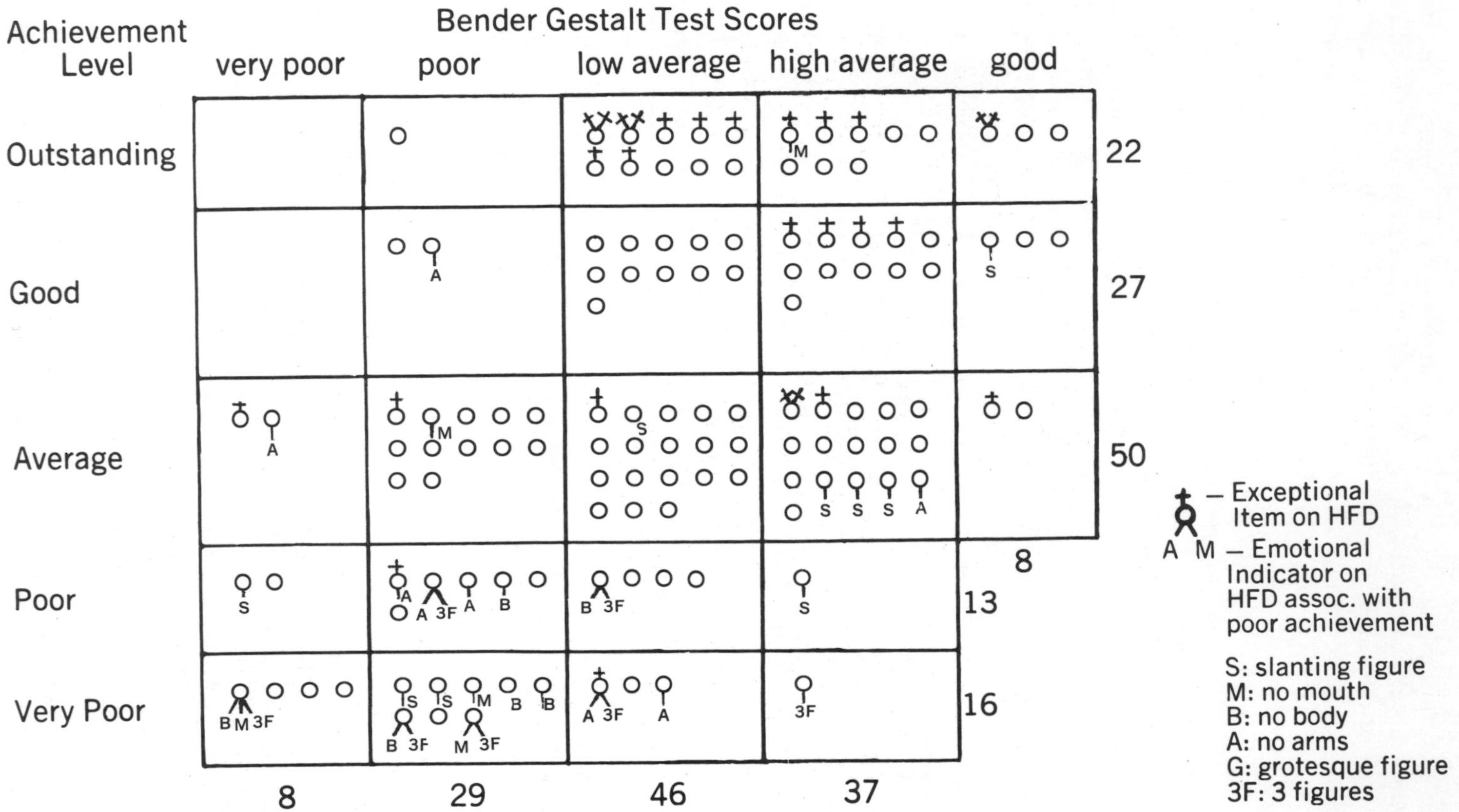

Figure 3. Achievement, HFD, and Bender Test scores for 128 first-graders. (Reproduced by permission from Koppitz EM: Psychological Evaluation of Children's Human Figure Drawings. New York, Grune & Stratton, 1968.)

96

figure, omission of mouth, omission of body, omission of arms, monster or grotesque figure, three or more figures spontaneously drawn) that tend to be related to poor school achievement in the primary grades (Koppitz, 1968, pp. 49ff). The children were then grouped according to their placement on the Metropolitan Achievement Test.

Figure 3 shows the relationship of the Bender Test and HFDs and the Metropolitan Achievement Test scores for the 128 first-graders. Figure 3 is here reproduced from *Psychological Evaluation of Children's Human Figure Drawings* (Koppitz, 1968, p. 180). According to Figure 3, 43 of the 45 pupils with High Average or Good Bender Test scores also had average or above-average achievement scores. Most of the youngsters with both Good Bender Test scores and Exceptional Items on their HFDs were above-average students. The presence of an Emotional Indicator on the HFDs tended to be related to average or below-average achievement even when the Bender Test score was High Average.

Children with Low Average Bender Test scores had average, good, or even outstanding first-grade achievement. It is important to notice that the outstanding pupils in this group tended to be bright children who revealed Exceptional Items on their HFDs, whereas half the youngsters with poor or very poor achievement in this group had emotional problems—that is, they showed one or more Emotional Indicators on their HFDs.

First-graders with Poor Bender Test scores could still obtain average achievement if they had no serious emotional problems or any other significant difficulties. Children with Poor Bender Test scores who also had emotional problems (Emotional Indicators on HFDs) were usually found to be poor students.

Results of the study show that the predictive ability of the Bender Test scores, when screening school beginners for potential learning problems and for outstanding achievement, is enhanced when the eight Exceptional Items and the six Emotional Indicators on HFDs are added. But even these measures are not sufficient, for only slightly more than one-third of the 128 first-graders in the study revealed either positive or negative signs on their HFDs. Not all bright children draw Exceptional Items on their HFDs, nor is there a one-to-one relationship between Emotional Indicators on the HFDs and serious behavior or emotional problems. It seems that verbal ability, sequencing, and recall are also extremely important for good school achievement and need to be taken into consideration (Koppitz, 1971, 1973b). None of these factors are tapped by either the Bender Test or the HFDs. Therefore an effective screening battery for school beginners should also include some form of verbal and memory test.

BENDER, HFD, AND WISC INFORMATION TEST

In another study (Koppitz, 1968, p. 179) I administered the WISC Information Test together with the Bender Test and HFDs to 133 second-graders at the beginning of the school year; 8 months later the

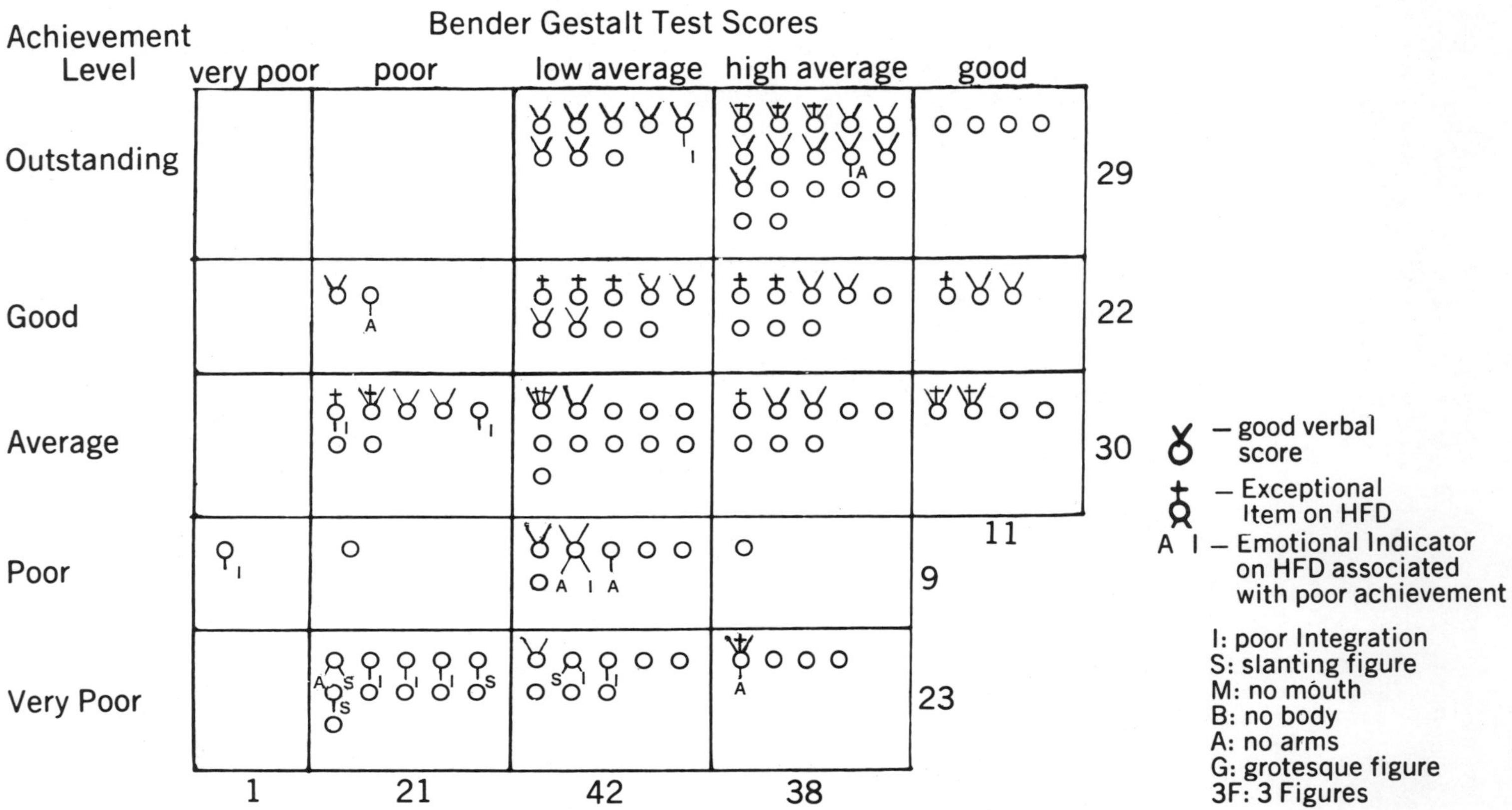

Figure 4. Achievement, HFD, Bender, and verbal scores for 113 second-graders. (Reproduced by permission from Koppitz EM: Psychological Evaluation of Children's Human Figure Drawings. New York, Grune & Stratton, 1968.)

Metropolitan Achievement Test was administered. The additional use of the WISC Information Test resulted in further marked improvement in the predictions of school achievement. Figure 4 (Koppitz, 1968, p. 182) shows that most of the second-graders with High Average or Good Bender Test scores and with average or better than average WISC Information scores (weighted score of 10 or more) and/or an Exceptional Item on the HFD were average or above-average students. Children with Low Average Bender Test scores but with good Information and/or HFD performance were also good achievers. Thus youngsters with good intelligence (Exceptional Item on HFD) and good memory for facts (high Information score) seem to be able to compensate for some immaturity or lag in visual-motor perception.

If a youngster functioned below average on two of the three tests given, then he was usually an average student. Pupils with Poor Bender Test scores who did not reveal indications of good mental ability (Exceptional Item on HFD or good scores on the WISC Information scale), while showing signs of emotional problems (Emotional Indicators on HFD), did poorly in school.

BENDER, HFD, AND VADS TESTS

More recently, I have used the Bender Test together with the HFDs and the Visual Aural Digit Span Test (VADS) (Koppitz, 1970a, 1972, 1973a, 1975) as a screening battery for school beginners. The VADS Test consists of four subtests; aural presentation of series of digits and oral recall (Aural–Oral); visual presentation of series of digits and oral recall (Visual–Oral); aurally presented series of digits and written reproduction (Aural–Written); and visually presented series of digits and written recall (Visual–Written).

These three measures—the Bender Test, HFDs, and the VADS Test—are easy and quick to administer, and the results offer a wide range of information concerning children's functioning. As was pointed out earlier, a child's achievement in the primary grades depends on the interaction or combination of many factors. The screening battery allows the examiner to make conclusions about the following: maturity in visual-motor perception (Developmental scores from Bender Test), auditory–visual and visual–auditory integration and recall (VADS Test scores), sequencing and directionality (VADS Test analysis), mental ability (HFD score), organization, inner control, attitudes (EI on Bender Test), emotional problems (Emotional Indicators on HFDs), and child's motivation and behavior (observation of child during the test administration). In addition, of course, the youngster's age, sex, and ability to write his name and numbers should be considered.

I would recommend that school psychologists using the screening battery develop normative data for the three tests for the pupils in their own school district, so that they can determine whether a given youngster

Table 12.

Interpretation of Test Scores for End-of-Kindergarten Pupils

Level of Test Scores	Bender Test Scores	Total VADS Test Scores	Number Reversals on VADS Test	Developmental* Score on HFD
Outstanding	5 or less	19 or more	0	6 or more
Good	6–7	17–18	1	5–6
Average	8–11	13–16	2–4	4–5
Poor	12–13	10–12	5	3
Very Poor	14 or more	9 or less	6–8	2 or less

*For Developmental scores on HFD see Koppitz EM: Psychological Evaluation of Children's Human Figure Drawings. New York, Grune & Stratton, 1968, pp. 26ff, 330, 331.

is typical or atypical for his particular class or group. Table 12 gives some test norms that I derived from 103 white middle-class kindergarten children at the end of the school year (June). The youngsters had an age range from 5 years 6 months to 6 years 6 months; their mean CTMM IQ score was 103, their mean Bender Test score was 9.6, and their mean VADS and HFD scores were 14.5 and 4.8, respectively.

In addition to obtaining the Developmental scores from the Bender Test, the VADS Test, and the HFDs, the children's records are checked for Emotional Indicators, for the quality of the test protocols, and for the ability to write numbers and names. I always ask each child to put his name on the completed test protocols. All the information gathered from the three test records is then recorded and summarized on a Screening Battery Summary Sheet. There is no hard and fast formula that can be applied to the use of the test scores and data. I am opposed to combining the test scores of the three tests into a single score with a cutoff point for predicting school success or failure. A meaningful prediction of a child's potential for school achievement involves a delicate balance and integration of different kinds of information and should not be based on a single test score. The use of this screening battery is simple, but it does require training and experience. In the hands of a qualified and skilled examiner the three tests together can be most helpful for pinpointing areas of strength and weakness in a child, for suggesting ways to develop individualized educational programs to meet the child's needs, and for planning the child's class placement. The results from the screening battery naturally should be discussed with the classroom teacher. Any plans for a youngster's educational program and placement should result from a combination of the teacher's recommendations and the findings of the screening battery.

The following five examples demonstrate how the screening battery can be applied with end-of-kindergarten pupils. In each case I administered the Bender Test, the VADS Test, and the HFDs individually to the youngsters in the back of the classroom. There is no reason, however, why the Bender Test and the HFDs could not also be administered as group tests. Individual administration of the three tests took approximately 12 to 15 min. per child.

Example 1. Screening Battery Summary Sheet No. 1 shows the test results for Lisa, a well-adjusted girl age 6 whose functioning was high-average or above in all areas. Her Bender Test protocol (Plate 31) with neatly drawn, well-organized designs resembles the records of 8-year-old children. The well-integrated HFD (Plate 32) reveals good details (four pieces of clothing: dress, socks, shoes, bow) and above-average mental ability. No significant Emotional Indicators are present on either the Bender Test or the HFD protocol. On the VADS Test Lisa obtained a score of 16, which is high-average; she was able to read and write numbers very well and showed no reversals. As can be seen on Plate 32, Lisa corrected numbers spontaneously when necessary and arranged them orderly along the edge of paper. She had a positive attitude while taking the tests and was relaxed; she worked carefully but easily. Lisa related readily to the examiner, was full of self-confidence, and was pleased with her accomplishments. She appeared to be socially and emotionally mature for her age. A missing front tooth also indicated that she was physically mature. There was no doubt that Lisa was ready for the first grade and that she could be expected to be an outstanding pupil.

Screening Battery Summary Sheet—Number 1

Name: Lisa   *Sex:* Female   *C.A.:* 6–0   *Time of testing:* End K (June)

Observations: Front tooth out, cheerful, small, poised, comfortable, works carefully, good motivation, pleased with self, good language.

Handedness: Right   *Writing of name:* Good

Test	Score	Level	Comments
Bender Test	4	Outstanding	Analyzes designs, counts dots, good motor control
VADS Test	16	High Average	Aural–Oral 4, Aural–Written 4 Visual–Oral 4, Visual–Written 4
Number reversals	none	Outstanding	Reads and writes numbers well
HFD	6	Outstanding	Four clothing items, well integrated, mature

Test	Emotional Indicators	Organization	Comments
Bender Test	none	Excellent	Mature, deliberate
VADS Test	—	Very Good	Neat, careful, numbers lined up at left side of paper
HFD	Short Arms	Excellent	Good social and emotional adjustment

Summary: Superior potential, bright, well integrated, above average in all areas, good social and emotional adjustment.

Predictions and recommendations: Lisa is ready for the first grade, she is likely to be an outstanding pupil.

Example 2. Screening Battery Summary Sheet No. 2 shows the test findings for Ralph, a tall, obese boy, 6 years 1 month old, who functioned below average in all areas. His Bender Test score was 16 (Plate 33); the drawings are primitve and on the level of a 4½-year-old child. Most of the designs are so distorted that they do not even resemble the figures on the Bender Test. Ralph was also quite unable to integrate the parts of the different designs into wholes. In addition, he showed as many as four Emotional Indicators on the Bender Test record, thus revealing immaturity, instability, impulsivity, and insecurity. The same features were also evident on the other two tests.

Ralph's HFD (Plate 34) shows a slanting figure with one enormous hand and fingers, while the other hand and the arms and nose are omitted.

Screening Battery Summary Sheet—Number 2

Name: Ralph   *Sex:* Male   *C.A.:* 6–1   *Time of testing:* End K (June)

Observations: Tall, obese, large head, very immature, dependent, anxious, talks and acts like 4-year-old, works hastily, careless, asks for reassurance, needs encouragement to complete tasks.

Handedness: Right   *Writing of name:* Fair

Test	Score	Level	Comments
Bender Test	16	Very Poor	Primitive, poor coordination
VADS Test	11	Poor	Aural–Oral 3, Aural–Written 2 Visual–Oral 4, Visual–Written 2
Number reversals	3	Average	Difficulty with direction, writes from R to L, reverses 2 and 7, confuses 9 and 6, unsure about 8 and 4
HFD	3	Poor	Primitive, omits arms, nose

Test	Emotional Indicators	Organization	Comments
Bender Test	Contused Order, Wavy Line, 2nd Attempt, Small Figures	Poor	Impulsive, insecure, unstable
VADS Test	—	Disorganized	Unsure about numbers, large size
HFD	Slant, Arms Omitted, Big Hand (1)	Primitive	Added house spontaneously, locked door, no windows, large smoking chimney

Summary: Very immature, insecure, dependent boy, functioning poorly in all areas, test performance suggests possible MBD.

Predictions and recommendations: Ralph is not ready for first grade; recommend placement in transitional class; will need special help with directionality, copying, work habits, organization and concentration; needs help with oral expression and sequencing, also with coordination; Ralph will need extra time in which to mature; parental cooperation is needed to encourage more independence in Ralph; if no marked improvement is noted in coming year, then referral to Developmental Evaluation Clinic is indicated; reevaluation during next school year is suggested.

He also added spontaneously on his drawing a very primitive house with a smoking chimney, a "locked door," and no windows. The addition of a house on HFDs is characteristic of very immature and/or moderately retarded youngsters. The details of the figure and the house reflect emotional problems. On the VADS Test Ralph displayed difficulties with directionality and writing. He worked alternately from right to left and from left to right. He reversed numbers 2 and 7, confused 6 and 9, and was unsure about 4 and 8. His numbers are large and arbitrarily scattered over the paper without any logic or organization.

Observation of Ralph at work showed that he was extremely immature, insecure, and dependent. He was constantly asking for reassurance and needed encouragement in order to complete tasks. The quality of his test protocols and his behavior were suggestive of MBD as well as of moderate mental retardation. It was apparent that Ralph was in no way ready to cope with a regular first grade. He needed help in just about all areas, and above all he needed more time to mature. It was recommended that Ralph be placed in a transitional or pre-first-grade class and that he be given a complete psychological evaluation during the coming year. Ralph required special help with directionality, with copying, with work habits and concentration, and with organization. It was furthermore essential to elicit the parents' cooperation in helping Ralph to develop more independent and mature behavior and attitudes.

Examples 1 and 2 are clear-cut and obvious. From the Bender Test performance alone one could predict that Lisa would be an outstanding student and that Ralph was not ready for a regular first grade and would undoubtedly fail if he did not receive some extra help with his schoolwork and class placement. Examples 3, 4, and 5 are less clear-cut, and they show how difficult it would be to make valid predictions about school achievement solely from the Bender Test records. All three youngsters functioned quite unevenly.

Example 3. Screening Battery Summary Sheet No. 3 presents the findings from Joey's test performance. Joey was young for his class, but he was tall and exhibited good concentration and attention. He was shy and quiet and worked slowly and carefully, as can be seen from his excellent Bender Test protocol (Plate 35). Although Joey was only 5 years 6 months old, his Bender Test score of 5 resembled those of 7½-year-old children. His only Emotional Indicator on the Bender Test was Small Size in Figs. A, 4, 7, and 8, suggesting some timidity and insecurity, but no serious emotional problems. If predictions concerning Joey's achievement in the first grade had to be made solely on the basis of the Bender Test, one might conclude that Joey would be an outstanding student. However, when taking the HFD and the VADS Test into account the prediction had to be modified.

Joey's HFD (Plate 36) shows marked inconsistencies. On the one hand Joey's treatment of the arms and hands is quite mature for his age; on the other hand he reveals poor integration of one arm and omission of the body. Since Joey was so young, these Emotional Indicators on the

Screening Battery Summary Sheet—Number 3

Name: Joey   *Sex:* Male   *C.A.:* 5–6   *Time of testing:* End K (June)

Observation: Tall, immature speech, *not bothered by noise or distractions*, good attention and concentration, works slowly, carefully.

Handedness: Right   *Writing of name:* OK

Test	Score	Level	Comments
Bender Test	5	Outstanding	Good spacing and differentiation of designs, no counting of dots
VADS Test	12	Poor	Aural–Oral 3, Aural–Written 3 Visual–Oral 3, Visual–Written 3
Number reversals	3	Average	Reversal of 2, 3, and 5; confuses 1 and 7, 6 and 8
HFD	4	Average	Uneven, mature arms and hands, omission of body, poor integration, as yet immature, good potential

Test	Emotional Indicators	Organization	Comments
Bender Test	Tiny Figures	Fair	Careful, constricted, effort
VADS Test	—	Good	Unsure of numbers
HFD	Body Omitted, Asymmetry of Limbs		Insecure, inconsistent

Summary: Good visual-motor perception but immature speech and language; poor auditory-visual and visual-auditory integration and recall; appears to have average ability and potential, but functions unevenly; may have poor auditory perception; is young for his class, needs time to mature.

Predictions and recommendations: Joey learns best visually; he has difficulty with aural-visual integration, sequencing and recall; appears to have average ability and potential but is still immature and young for class; needs watching; check auditory perception and hearing. Joey should be reevaluated at end of first grade.

HFD are less significant then they would be for an older child. The drawing suggests good mental potential along with immaturity and insecurity.

It was noted that Joey's speech was immature and that he suffered from an articulation problem. But more significant was Joey's score of 12 on the VADS Test. This score is poor for end-of-kindergarten pupils and is low even for his age level. Joey could read and write numbers fairly well with only a few reversals (numbers 2, 3, and 5) and with confusion between 1 and 7 and 6 and 8; but he had difficulty with sequencing, intersensory integration, and recall. Both visual–oral and aural–visual integrations were difficult for Joey. Particularly noteworthy was Joey's good attention span; the noise and confusion in the classroom while I administered the tests did not bother Joey in the least. In fact, he seemed oblivious of it. This, together with the quality of his speech and his poor oral recall, suggests the possibility that Joey suffered either from poor auditory perception or from a slight hearing loss.

Recommendations were made that Joey's hearing and auditory perception be evaluated prior to the beginning of the next schoolyear. Joey definitely had good mental potential and did not show any marked emotional problems, but there was much inconsistency. If it should be found that he indeed had poor auditory perception or a hearing impairment, then placement in a small transitional class might be in order so that he could get extra attention and help. If no serious difficulties in auditory perception or hearing were found, then Joey should be placed in a regular first grade; but even then he would need to be watched so as to prevent undue frustration and the development of secondary emotional problems. Above all, Joey needed time in which to mature and help with intersensory integration, sequencing, and recall.

Example 4. Michael was another 5½-year-old boy who was one of the youngest in his class. His test results are shown on Screening Battery Summary Sheet No. 4. In contrast to the timid Joey, Michael was outgoing and tough. He related easily to the examiner and put forth much effort; his

---

Screening Battery Summary Sheet—Number 4

Name: Michael   *Sex:* Male   *C.A.:* 5–6   *Time of testing:* End K (June)

Observation: Outgoing, at ease, puts forth effort, tongue protrudes while Michael is working; among youngest in class.

Handedness: Right   *Writing of name:* Good

Test	Score	Level	Comments
Bender Test	12	Poor	Good visual perception, immature visual-motor integration
VADS Test	14	Average	Aural–Oral 4, Aural–Written 3 Visual–Oral 4, Visual–Written 3 Good oral recall, poor written recall and writing
Number reversals	8	Very Poor	Rev. 1, 2, 3, 4, 5, 6, 7 and 9; difficulty with *directionality*
HFD	6	Outstanding	Good for age, hands with 5 fingers

Test	Emotional Indicators	Organization	Comments
Bender Test	Increase in Size	Fair	Poor planning, impulsive
VADS Test	—	Fair	Difficulty with directions
HFD	Long Arms, Big Hands	Good	Outgoing, aggressive, impulsive

Summary: Michael has average potential but is young for class; still immature visual-motor integration, even though visual perception is good; difficulty with writing and copying, reversal problems; good motivation, outgoing, aggressive tendencies; good oral recall; needs time to mature; impulsive.

Predictions and recommendations: Michael will probably be a fair student in the first grade, but will most likely improve as he gets older; he needs time to mature; Michael needs special help with visual-motor integration; he needs writing and copying exercises; he also needs structure, since he could be aggressive and impulsive. Reevaluation next year is recommended.

tongue protruded and "worked" along with him as he labored over his drawings and the writing of numbers.

Michael's Bender Test score of 13 (Plate 37) was poor, both for his age and for his class. The test protocol revealed poor coordination and poor organization and planning ability. Yet with the possible exception of Fig. 7, the configurations of all the designs were essentially correct and recognizable; but the details and the proportions were distorted. Michael also still showed a tendency to perseverate, which is common for young children. Michael's visual perception was evidently quite good; only his visual-motor integration was still immature. The Bender Test record also showed three Emotional Indicators (Confused Order, Wavy Line, and Large Size in Fig. 2) that reflect some instability and the potential for impulsive, acting-out behavior. If I had had only the Bender Test to go by, I would have predicted that Michael would have difficulty in the first grade because of his young age, his immaturity in visual-motor integration, and his impulsivity. A more complete picture emerged when Michael's HFD and VADS Test performances were also taken into account.

The long arms and huge hands on Michael's HFD (Plate 38) reflect an underlying tendency toward aggressive, acting-out behavior, but the very fact that this 5½-year-old boy drew two-dimensional arms and hands with five fingers indicates that he had average or better than average mental potential, which in turn might enable him to control the aggressiveness. Michael's VADS Test score of 14 was average for his grade level and good for his age level. He was especially good in oral recall, while the writing of numbers was difficult for him. His visual-motor integration was still quite poor, and he had problems with directionality. As can be seen on Plate 38, Michael reversed all numbers from 1 to 9 with the exception of 8, which cannot be reversed. But Michael had no difficulty writing his name, suggesting that he could write correctly once he really learned the letters and numbers.

In summary, it appears that Michael was young for his class and still had poor visual-motor coordination; but his visual perception was good, as was his motivation. He also had good mental potential and good oral recall. Michael was a sturdy, outgoing youngster with a pleasing personality. He had underlying aggressive tendencies that might result in acting-out behavior if he were unduly pressured or pushed in school before he was able to cope with the work. Michael would probably be only a fair student in the first grade. But as he got older and more mature his achievement would most likely improve. He needed a structured and supportive first-grade program where he could get special help with directionality, eye–hand coordination, and writing.

Example 5. Ann's test responses, as shown on Screening Battery Summary Sheet No. 5, range from low average to very poor. Even though Ann was 6 years 5 months old and one of the oldest children in her class, she was tiny, very immature, sweet, shy, and a bit vague. Ann looked and acted like an insecure 4½- to 5-year-old child.

Screening Battery Summary Sheet—Number 5

Name: Ann   *Sex:* Female   *C.A.:* 6–5   *Time of testing:* End K (June)

Observations: Tiny, very immature, sweet, shy, vague, immature speech, tries to please, puts forth effort, works carefully, anxious.

Handedness: Right   *Writing of name:* Fair

Test	Score	Level	Comments
Bender Test	12	Poor	Poor visual-motor integration and coordination, visual perception average
VADS Test	5	Very Poor	Aural–Oral 3, Aural–Written 0 Visual–Oral 2, Visual–Written 0
Number reversal			Difficulty reading numbers, cannot write numbers
HFD	4	Low-Average	"Boy," arms omitted

Test	Emotional Indicators	Organization	Comments
Bender Test	Wavy Line, Tiny Size, Fine Line	Fair	Shy, withdrawal, poor spacing, unstable
VADS Test			Poor oral recall, cannot read or write numbers
HFD	Arms Omitted, Tiny Figure, Heavy Shading of Body, Big Ears		Very anxious, insecure, withdrawn, emotional problems, rivalry with brother?

Summary: Ann is extremely immature although she is among the oldest in class; she has emotional problems in addition to serious lags in visual-motor integration, recall, and sequencing; she is insecure and very anxious, tries to please; limited mental ability.

Predictions and recommendations: Ann is not ready for a regular first grade; she needs a small transitional class, or, if such is not available, she would benefit from repeating kindergarten; in a regular class she is bound to fail, which would only add to her emotional problems; Ann needs emotional support and help to improve her self-confidence; parental help is essential to deal with Ann's emotional difficulties; she is still functioning on the pre-school level in all areas; rather than giving her special help in one or two areas, Ann needs a total school curriculum geared to her overall immature level of development; she needs more time to mature and should be given the opportunity to progress, without undue pressure, at her own slow rate; Ann should be reevaluated during the coming school year.

Her Bender Test (Plate 39) score of 12 was quite poor for her age level as well as for her class level. The three Emotional Indicators on Ann's Bender Test record (Wavy Line in Figs. 1 and 2, Small Size in Figs. 4 and 5, Fine Lines) reflect instability, timidity, and withdrawal. Ann was unable to complete the VADS test, since she could only read two or three numbers; the numbers she wrote (Plate 40) were unrecognizable. Even her oral recall of the aurally presented digits was quite defective. Ann had difficulty following directions, and her memory seemed to be very poor. It was difficult to determine from observation whether Ann's poor functioning in the classroom was mainly due to emotional problems, immaturity, and withdrawal, or due to limited mental ability. Test results suggest that all of these factors contributed to her poor performance. The degree of her emotional disturbance was best shown on the HFD (Plate 40). Ann's tiny drawing represents a boy; she omitted the arms, showed an unusual amount of shading on the body, and drew big empty eyes and very pronouned ears. The HFD suggests intense anxiety and insecurity. A parent–teacher conference later revealed that there was much tension in Ann's home and that her parents were in the process of separating. Furthermore, Ann was intensely jealous of her younger brother.

The various findings indicated that Ann was not only extremely immature and had modest mental ability, but that she was also overwhelmed by family problems. It was apparent that Ann would not be able to cope with the demands of a regular first grade. Recommendations were made to place Ann in an extended readiness class or in a transitional class, where she could get individual help and could work at her own level and speed. Above all, Ann needed a great deal of support and attention in order to improve her self-confidence. When it was learned that Ann would be moving during the summer to a different school district where no transitional classes were available, it was suggested that she repeat kindergarten rather than be exposed to certain failure in a regular first grade. It was hoped that Ann's emotional problems and her poor concentration would improve once her home situation stabilized. However, her mother was urged to seek professional help for Ann if changes for the better in the home situation were not evident in the near future, or if Ann's behavior did not improve.

SUMMARY

The Developmental Bender Test scores by themselves are only moderately effective as screening instruments for school beginners. There is a consensus that good Bender Test scores are better able to predict school achievement than average or poor Bender Test scores. The predictive power of the Bender Test is greatly enhanced when all aspects of the Bender Test are taken into consideration: quality of the test protocol, Developmental Bender Test scores, and Emotional Indicators, as well as the child's age, sex, and behavior while copying the designs. When used in this manner, the Bender Test can identify both outstanding and very poor pupils.

However, since school achievement also depends on many factors not reflected on a youngster's Bender Test performance, it is recommended that the Bender Test be combined with other brief tests or measurements when screening school beginners. Two quick and effective screening batteries for end-of-kindergarten and primary-grade children have been described: one involves the Bender Test, Human Figure Drawings, and the WISC Information Subtest; the other screening battery consists of the Bender Test, Human Figure Drawings, and the Visual Aural Digit Span Test.

CHAPTER 12.
The Bender Test as a Group Test*

The single most important innovation with the Bender Test in recent years has most likely been its use as a group test. As long as the Bender Test was administered only to individual youngsters, there was by necessity a limitation on the number of children to whom the test could be given and on the purposes for which it could be used. Now that group administration of the Bender Test is well established, the test is not only employed effectively as a screening instrument for groups of school children but is also a valuable tool for research with large numbers of youngsters. It is, of course, recognized that the group administration of the Bender Test inevitably forfeits some of the clinical value of the test, since the examiner cannot observe and interact with a whole group of pupils simultaneously.

Keogh and Smith (1961) were the first to publish a paper on the group technique for the Bender Gestalt Test. They explored two different methods of group administration with the Bender Test and compared these with each other and with individual administration of the test. They demonstrated convincingly that the Bender Test scores derived from the two group methods did not differ significantly from each other, nor from those obtained by the standardized method of individual Bender Test administration. During the past ten years a number of studies have been conducted that involve group administration of the Bender Test. The findings of these investigations offer support for the claims of Keogh and Smith.

PROCEDURES FOR ADMINISTERING
THE GROUP BENDER TEST

Four different techniques have been reported for the successful administration of the Bender Test to groups of school children:

1. Presentation of enlarged Bender Test cards. Keogh and Smith (1961) found that the presentation of enlarged Bender Test stimulus cards, placed in a holder at the front of the room, was most effective with school beginners. Primary-grade pupils are accustomed to looking at pictures and charts on the wall and are used to copying letters and numbers from the blackboard. Thus copying from a large card is not too dissimilar to other classroom activities. The cards Keogh and Smith used were 11 in. by 16¾ in., or roughly three times as large as the standard Bender Test cards. The designs were reproduced on the cards to scale, with the same ratio of the design size to the card size as on the regular Bender Test cards.

*This chapter was written in cooperation with the late Margaret S. Jessen, who used the Group Bender Test for many years effectively in her work as a school psychologist.

Most investigators who have administered the Bender Test to groups of pupils have followed the lead of Keogh and Smith, using the same size of enlarged cards as they did (ratio 1:3) (Bishop, 1966; Chang and Chang, 1967; Giebink and Birch, 1970; Hammer, 1967; Mlodnosky, 1972; Mogin, 1966; Singh, 1965; Vormeland, 1968; and Werner et al., 1967). Jacobs (1971), Solomon (1969), and Tiedeman (1971) enlarged the Bender Test cards four times their original size, while Jessen and Prendergast (1965) used a ratio of 1:5 for the Bender Test cards in their study.

Some of the examiners asked their subjects to copy the Bender Test designs from the large cards into special copying booklets with a separate blank page for each Bender Test figure. Other investigators gave each child one or two sheets of blank white paper, size 8½ × 11 in., and had the youngsters copy all nine designs in the standardized way onto a single sheet of paper (or more if the child so desired). Each of these methods has its obvious advantages and disadvantages. The drawing booklets assure that the child does not turn the paper and help to avoid confusion as to overlap of designs. When administering the Bender Test to a group of pupils it is impossible to note each child's moves and significant behavior. Invariably there will be a few Bender Test protocols obtained by the group method that will be confusing and difficult to score if all nine designs are drawn on the same piece of paper. On the other hand, when each design is copied on a different page of a booklet one loses the advantage of seeing how the youngster organizes the figures in a given space. The latter offers considerable insight into children's mental maturity, planning ability, impulsivity, and inner control.

The use of large Bender Test cards requires the drawing or printing of the cards, but once this has been accomplished the cards can be used over and over again without any extra equipment other than plain drawing paper and pencils. Tiedeman (1971) carried her set of cards all over the globe and used them as successfully in a modern urban classroom in this country as in a grass hut in New Guinea.

2. *Use of special Bender Test copying booklets.* In their original study Keogh and Smith (1961) experimented with the use of a special Bender Test booklet with white pages, size 8½ × 11 in., numbered at the lower outside corner. The upper one-third of each page contained a single Bender Test design reproduced exactly the same size as it appears on the standard Bender Test stimulus cards. The children were asked to copy the designs in the blank lower two-thirds of each page. All of the pupils drew the designs at the same time. When all had finished copying a given figure, they turned the page at the examiner's direction. This method of group administration is highly structured; the advantages and disadvantages as to the use of copying booklets were pointed out above. But in addition, Keogh and Smith observed that several of their kindergarten pupils got confused on the copying booklets and tried to superimpose their drawings on the printed stimulus designs. They tried to trace the figures rather than copy them. Close supervision of the children during the test administration was essential.

The use of special booklets for the group administration of the Bender Test requires the printing of special booklets, which makes it more costly than the other methods.

3. *Projection of Bender Test designs.* The second most popular method for group administration of the Bender Test with school children is the projection of individual Bender Test designs onto a screen or a wall. Three different means of projecting the figures have been described:

Opaque projector. Ruckhaber (1964) placed the standard Bender Test cards into an opaque projector and threw the images onto a screen.

Overhead projectors. Becker and Sabatino (1971), Caskey (1973), and Dibner and Korn (1969) made transparencies for each Bender Test design and projected them onto a screen or wall with the help of an overhead projector.

Slide projector. Howard (1970) and McCarthy (1971) obtained slides of the Bender Test cards and used them in a slide projector. The American Orthopsychiatric Association published not only the standard Bender Test cards (Bender, 1946) but also slides of the Bender Test designs (Bender, 1969).

All three methods of projecting Bender Test figures have the advantage that the designs can be greatly enlarged and can be seen even by a large group of pupils. One obvious disadvantage of this method of test administration is the need to darken the room, or at least to dim the lights, so that the images on the screen will be bright. This may result in poor lighting for the children who are drawing the figures. And then, of course, projection of Bender Test designs always requires the use of equipment. Fortunately, however, most schools have some type of projector available.

4. *Use of individual decks of Bender Test cards.* Another easy way to administer the Bender Test to more than one youngster at a time is to provide each child with his own set of Bender Test cards (Adams and Canter, 1969; Dibner and Korn, 1969; Dinmore, 1972). With this method the children are seated at a table or at their desks with paper and a pencil just as in the standard individual Bender Test method of administration. But instead of having the examiner show each child one stimulus card at a time, the youngsters have the whole stack of Bender Test cards in front of them. They turn the cards over at the direction of the examiner.

This particular method of Bender Test administration is especially valuable when testing a very small group of very young or immature pupils. Preferably, such groups should consist of only two or at most three children. It is quite feasible for the psychologist to observe and to monitor two or three children at the same time with this method and to take a few notes as well.

Comparison of Different Methods of Group Administration

Keogh and Smith (1961) compared the results of administering the Bender Test to kindergarten pupils by means of enlarged test cards and with the help of special Bender Test booklets; Dibner and Korn (1969) administered the Bender Test twice to kindergarten through fourth-grade pupils. The first time they projected the designs onto a wall; the second time they gave each child a separate deck of Bender Test cards to copy. Neither of these teams of investigators found any significant differences between the test scores obtained by different modes of Bender Test group administration.

Correlation Between Individual and Group Bender Test Scores

There is a consensus that no significant difference exists between individual and group Bender Test scores (Howard, 1970; Jacobs, 1971; Keogh and Smith, 1961; McCarthy, 1972; Solomon, 1969). Becker and Sabatino (1971) report a correlation of .85 between individual and group Bender Test scores for 5- to 9-year-old children. Ruckhaber (1964) obtained similar results ($r = .75$–.87) with his kindergarten pupils.

Group Size

The Bender Test has been administered as a group test to as many as 30 children at a time (Bishop, 1966; Caskey, 1973; McCarthy, 1972) and to as few as two youngsters (Dinmore, 1972). Most investigators suggest that, in addition to the psychologist, the teacher or a paraprofessional be present during group administration of the Bender Test. On occasion, when the group is very large, a third person may be helpful to assist the youngsters.

It appears that the method of test administration will determine the number of children that can effectively be tested at one time. When enlarged Bender Test cards are used the groups can include approximately 6 to 15 youngsters, according to Chang and Chang (1967), Hammer (1967), Jessen and Prendergast (1965), Keogh and Smith (1961), Solomon (1969), and Werner et al. (1967). The only investigator who reported difficulties with this method of group administration of the Bender Test was Mlodnosky (1972). Mlodnosky tested 7 hyperactive, talkative first-graders from economically deprived areas who wanted constant attention and who were unable to work independently. It seems that group administration of the Bender Test is not suitable for this particular type of youngster. For extremely immature and restless children and for pupils with serious behavior and learning problems, the individual Bender Test method is more appropriate.

The projection of Bender Test designs is especially useful when working with large groups of pupils, as was shown in the study of Becker and Sabatino (1971) and in the investigations of Caskey (1973), Howard (1970), and McCarthy (1972). These examiners gave the Bender Test to whole classes of 20 to 34 children. Individual decks of Bender Test cards have been used both with large groups of 14 to 22 pupils (Adams and Canter, 1969) and with groups of only 2 children (Dinmore, 1972).

Time Needed for Group Administration

As might be expected, the administration of the Bender Test to groups of youngsters requires somewhat more time than does the testing of a single child. Howard (1970) exposed each design for 1 min. Bishop (1966), Caskey (1973), Jacobs (1971), McCarthy (1972), Ruckhaber (1964), and Solomon (1969) all agree that group administration of the Bender Test to primary-grade pupils (kindergarten to third grade) takes about 15 to 20 min. Mlodnosky (1972) found that her immature, deprived, and hyperactive first-grade pupils needed as much as 35 min to complete the Bender Test.

APPLICATION OF THE GROUP BENDER TEST

The group Bender Test can serve a variety of different purposes. The Bender Test has been administered most often to groups of pupils (kindergarten to third grade) as a screening instrument to predict general school performance and to identify high-risk youngsters (Dibner and Korn, 1969; Hammer, 1967; Vormeland, 1968) or specifically to predict children's reading achievement (Chang and Chang, 1967; Giebink and Birch, 1970; Keogh 1965a; Mlodnosky, 1972). The relationship of group Bender Test scores and school achievement is the same as the relationship between achievement and Bender Test scores obtained from each child individually. For a detailed discussion of the relationship of Bender Test performance and school achievement see Chapter 8.

Mogin (1966) used the group Bender Test as a means of screening second- and third-graders for emotional maladjustment. Jessen and Prendergast (1965) administered the group Bender Test twice, once before and once after a period of perceptual training; the Bender Test scores were used as part of a test battery to assess the effect of perceptual training on kindergarten and first-grade pupils. Jessen also found group Bender Test results helpful for evaluating the progress of children with learning disabilities who participated in a summer program of perceptual training.

Sheffer (1970) found the group Bender Test helpful in determining the ability of educationally handicapped youngsters to copy from cards placed in front of them and above them, as compared to copying at the desk level. It is interesting to note that Bishop (1966) showed a significant correlation between the group Bender Test and the far-point copying score on the Slingerland Test (1964).

Group administration of the Bender Test facilitates research with large numbers of children. Dinmore investigated children's visual-motor perception with the group Bender Test in relation to educational settings and to the youngsters' gender. By far the most ambitious research project with the group Bender Test was Tiedeman's (1971) cross-cultural study. Tiedeman administered the Bender Test to groups of 7-year old children in 39 classrooms in 13 different countries. Even though most of these youngsters did not speak English they had no difficultly with the group Bender Test.

Jessen utilized group administration of the Bender Test on a regular basis in her capacity as school psychologist. She found it especially useful as a broad screening instrument at the end of kindergarten when teachers began to get concerned about the merits of promotion versus retention of a pupil (particularly for little boys who mature somewhat more slowly than girls of the same age and for whom many public-school programs as they are currently operating seem to be inappropriate). Jessen used large cards when administering the group Bender Test (cards four times the size of the standard cards). After the children completed the Bender Test the psychologist sorted the Bender Test protocols by means of inspection into three stacks according to the youngsters' performances: (1) average performance for 5- to 6-year-olds; (2) very immature reproductions of the Bender Test designs; (3) unusually mature copying. This rather gross procedure was followed by a consultation with the teachers who had rated the pupils' levels of maturity on the basis of their own observations. In general, Jessen found a high level of agreement between the results obtained from the group Bender Test and the teachers' estimates of the children's maturity. In the few cases where questions arose or where further investigations seemed in order, the youngsters were individually evaluated by the psychologist. The parents were then consulted, and recommendations were made for a follow-up during the summer and during the next school year, depending on the problems of the particular case.

Further testing frequently confirmed the clinical "hunches" inferred from the group Bender Test records. Jessen reported that the screening procedure with the group Bender Test more than paid off over the years. The teachers responded positively to this technique and indicated that the procedure lifted their morale at the end of the school year and often took the onus off them when a recommendation for a child was not particularly popular with the parents. In fact, according to Jessen, many teachers initiated the screening procedure for their pupils by requesting it from the psychologist.

The group Bender Test is of considerable value for the school psychologist. It is economical in terms of equipment and time and has proved to be both valid and reliable. However, it is not suggested that any diagnosis or prescription for schoolchildren be made solely on the basis of the group Bender Test. And even though the group Bender Test can be highly recommended, it should never supplant the individually administered Bender Test as a clinical instrument. The interpretation of the group Bender Test requires training and experience. With growing demands on the time of clinicians, both in and out of public-school settings, the usefulness of the group Bender Test as a forerunner of further individual study of children and as part of a test battery cannot be underestimated.

SUMMARY

Since it was first introduced in 1961, the group Bender Test has been widely accepted. Research studies have shown it to be reliable, and the test scores from the group Bender Test have been found to correlate significantly with test scores from individual Bender Test records.

The Bender Test can be successfully administered to large groups of children by projecting the designs onto a screen or wall; for medium-size groups of children (about 6 to 15) the use of enlarged Bender Test stimulus cards has been found most advantageous; the use of individual decks of Bender Test cards is especially appropriate with a very small group of immature or young children. The use of special testing booklets appears to have little advantage; extremely immature or hyperactive children tend to have difficulty with the group Bender Test, and this method of test administration is not recommended for this particular group of youngsters.

It takes approximately 15 to 20 min to administer the Bender Test to a group of school beginners. The group Bender Test can effectively be used (preferably as part of a screening battery) for the screening of kindergarten and primary-grade pupils for potential learning difficulties, as a means of assessing the effect of perceptual–motor training, as a way of evaluating children's far-point copying ability, and for research purposes, especially for cross-cultural studies.

CHAPTER 13.
Modification of Bender Test
Materials and Procedures

Psychologists have accepted the Bender Test and have used it extensively for many years. But as time passes the needs and interests of investigators and clinicians change, and this in turn results in changes in the methods and materials they employ. It is therefore not surprising that the recent Bender Test literature reports a number of modifications in Bender Test materials and procedures. Changes are inevitable and even desirable if we are to continue to learn and grow. Some of the changes with the Bender Test are extremely useful, as for instance the group administration of the Bender Test that was discussed in detail in the preceding chapter. Other changes are imaginative and helpful in gaining a better understanding of the process of visual-motor perception; a few of the modifications seem arbitrary and seem to distract rather than enhance the Bender Test's usefulness. The following is a brief account of some of the recent changes with Bender Test materials and procedures.

MODIFICATION OF BENDER TEST DRAWING PAPER

According to the standard Bender Test procedure, children copy the nine designs on a sheet of unlined white paper, size 8½ × 11 in. If the youngsters so desire they may use more than one sheet of paper. It stands to reason that the position, size, shape, texture, and quality of the paper will, in some way, influence the children's Bender Test performances. In a number of studies this influence was explored by modifying the paper on which the Bender Test designs were copied.

Weiss (1971a) studied the effect of the position of the drawing paper on the placement of the Bender Test figures by Israeli seventh-grade pupils. Half of the youngsters were given paper in the standard vertical position, while for the other half of the subjects the paper was placed in the horizontal position. Marked differences were found between the groups of students. The group that drew on vertically placed paper used more space on the paper: 87% of these children placed Fig. A in the top third of the sheet and arranged the other designs below Fig. A; 13% placed Fig. A in the middle of the sheet. The subjects who worked on horizontally placed paper used less space and arranged the designs in horizontal fashion: 59% placed Fig. A in the top third of the paper; 39% placed Fig. A in the middle of the sheet; 2% put Fig. A at the bottom of the paper.

Allen and Frank (1963) and subsequently Allen (1968) presented children with nine blank cards of exactly the same size (4 × 6 in.) as the standard Bender Test stimulus cards. The youngsters had to copy each Bender Test figure on a separate card. The investigators found that their subjects produced a higher quality of drawing on the small, separate cards than on the single piece of paper. One of the disadvantages of this procedure is, of course, that one is deprived of the opportunity to assess the children's ability to organize the nine designs in a single space.

Adams et al. conducted a series of studies with the Background Interference Procedure (BIP) method, which Canter (1963) had developed to increase the sensitivity of the Bender Test to organic brain disorders. With this method the subjects copy the Bender Test designs first on a blank sheet of paper and then again on a paper with a moderately dense background of intersecting lines. The BIP method appears to have some merit with adult organic patients. Compared with nonorganic patients, adult organic patients revealed a greater decrement in their Bender Test performance with the BIP paper than on plain paper. The findings with the BIP method for children were inconclusive.

Adams and Canter (1969) found that the BIP method was too difficult for young children. Most youngsters could not cope with it effectively before the age of 13. The BIP method failed to differentiate significantly between organic and nonorganic retarded subjects age 6 to 16 (Adams, 1970). It also failed to discriminate significantly between hyperkinetic boys and a control group (Adams et al., 1974) and between emotionally disturbed children and controls (Adams et al. 1973). However, a group of youngsters with cerebral palsy who had much difficulty with the regular Bender Test showed even more decrement with the BIP method. And finally, Hayden et al. (1970) showed that the BIP method differentiated significantly between emotionally disturbed youngsters with and without neurological impairment. The subjects for this study ranged from 7 to 13 years.

MODIFICATION OF THE BENDER TEST DESIGNS

The nine figures on the Bender Test were originally adapted by Bender from Wertheimer's designs (Bender, 1938). They were not arbitrary designs, but were specifically developed in accordance with the principles of Gestalt theory. Each design adds different dimensions and contributes something to the test. Some attempts have been made in recent years to alter the Bender Test designs in order to test specific hypotheses or to emphasize certain Gestalt functions.

Pope and Snyder (1970) modified Figs. 3, 7, and 4 of the Bender Test in an effort to explain the Gestalt theory of "good continuation."

Fuller and Laird (1963) and Fuller (1969) developed the Minnesota Percepto-Diagnostic Test to differentiate normal, primary, and organic readers. The Minnesota Percepto-Diagnostic Test (MPD) consists of six cards: three cards with Fig. A and three cards with Fig. 3 of the Bender Test. Figures A and 3 are presented in three different positions. Fuller is mainly concerned with measuring the degree of rotation of each drawing, although distortions and failure to integrate the parts of Fig. A are also given consideration.

Heinrich (1968) was interested in assessing children's "abstracting capacity." He reasoned that the drawing of concrete objects would be easier for children than the copying of abstract designs. He therefore incorporated the Bender Test designs into line drawings of actual objects. Using second- and sixth-graders as subjects, he discovered no significant difference between the youngsters' performances on the standard Bender Test copying task and their drawings of the concrete figures. In fact, the two copying scores were significantly correlated. It would appear, therefore, that abstract designs are no more difficult for average schoolchildren to copy than concrete objects.

Sabatino and Ysseldyke (1972) designed two sets of Bender Test cards with "extraneous backgrounds." On one set the standard Bender Test designs were printed on a background of diagonal lines and dots. The other set of cards showed a photographic negative of the standard Bender Test cards with the most crucial portions of the designs obliterated (that is, the figures appeared in white on black and were somewhat fragmented). Both sets of cards were able to discriminate between readers and nonreaders in a group of learning-disabled pupils age 6 to 11.

MODIFICATION OF BENDER TEST PROCEDURES

Copying methods. The standard Bender Test method requires that the child use a pencil to copy the nine designs on a piece of paper. This task is difficult for most pre-school children (Plenk and Jones, 1967; Plenk, 1968). Not only is their visual-motor perception still quite immature, but many of the youngsters also have not yet mastered the art of manipulating a regular number-2 pencil effectively. Of considerable interest, therefore, are two studies that present alternate ways of copying designs for very young children.

The first method was devised by Wise (1968), who worked with nursery-school, Headstart, kindergarten, and first-grade youngsters age 3 years 1 month to 7 years 10 months. Wise had his children copy simple designs with sticks. The stick-copying ability, just like the ability to copy with a pencil, is developmental in nature; it, too, improves with the child's increase in age, and secondarily it is related to the youngster's socioeconomic background. However, the Bender Test is too difficult for most youngsters below the age of 5, while performance on the stick-copying test can be qualitatively and quantitatively measured down to age 3. At the kindergarten level Wise's study showed a significant correlation

($r = .60; p <.01$) between the Developmental Bender Test scores and the stick-copying scores.

Wedell and Horne (1969), working with children age 5 years 3 months to 5 years 9 months, introduced a method of copying Bender Test designs with plastecine.

Matching and tracing procedures. Heinrich (1968) and Wedell and Horne (1969) compared children's visual perception, motor coordination, and visual-motor perception by means of a Multiple-Choice Bender Test method, a Tracing Bender Test method, and the standard copying method of the Bender Test. Zach and Kaufman (1972) and Allen et al. (1971) also studied visual perception by means of a Multiple-Choice Bender Test method. They compared visual perception with visual-motor performance.

The Multiple-Choice Bender Gestalt Test was designed to test visual perception. With this method the subject is shown a paper with four to seven drawings of a given Bender Test design. Only one of the drawings is correct; the other drawings show the same design in rotation or in a distorted fashion. The subject has to match the original design on the standard test card with the drawing that is exactly like it. The Multiple-Choice Bender Test method was also employed by Isaac (1973), but for a somewhat different purpose than that used by Heinrich and by Wedell and Horne. Isaac used the Bender matching technique to help "familiarize" her subjects with the Bender Test designs (see p. 25).

The Tracing Bender Test method requires that the subjects trace over the Bender Test designs with a pencil. The tracings are transferred to a blank sheet of paper underneath the test blank by means of a carbon paper. The findings of Wedell and Horne show that minor errors in matching and tracing of Bender Test designs are not related to ability to copy the same designs. Subjects who produced good Bender Test records also had good matching and tracing ability. Thus good visual-motor perception goes along with good visual perception and good motor coordination. But they found that poor performance on the standard Bender Test "does not imply impairment of all the component functions involved."

The results of Zach and Kaufman are less clear-cut. They also worked with young children—kindergarten pupils age 5 years 2 months to 6 years 1 month from low socioeconomic backgrounds. Unfortunately few actual test data are given in the study. Without more information it is difficult to fully assess the results of the investigation. Zach and Kaufman found no significant correlation between Multiple-Choice Bender Test scores and Developmental Bender Test scores. As would be expected, most of the children with good visual discrimination (that is, good Multiple-Choice Bender Test scores) also had good Developmental Bender Test scores. However, almost half the youngsters with poor performance on the Multiple-Choice task did well on the copying of the Bender Test designs, which is puzzling. However, in view of the subjects' ages and backgrounds, one might wonder if the children had difficulty in comprehending the discrimination task rather than problems in perception. For young children it is usually easier to point out differences than to find two designs that are alike. Furthermore, it is not clear whether good performance on the standard Bender Test was evaluated in relationship to that specific group of subjects or in comparison with the normative data (Koppitz, 1963, p. 33).

Heinrich's subjects were second- and sixth-grade pupils. His results showed that for the group of second-graders, with still immature visual-motor perception, the Developmental Bender Test scores were significantly related to matching, i.e., visual perception ($r = .35$; $p < .01$), as well as to tracing, i.e., motor coordination ($r = .28$; $p < .05$). The results demonstrate that both immature visual perception and immature motor coordination contribute to immature visual-motor perception. But the correlation between visual perception and motor coordination was not significant. Poor visual perception and immature or poor motor coordination do not necessarily occur in the same child or at the same time.

By the time youngsters are in the sixth grade their visual perception, motor coordination, and visual-motor perception have usually matured sufficiently so that most of them can execute the matching, tracing, and copying tasks on the Bender Test without much effort.

BENDER TEST RECALL METHOD

The Bender Test Recall method has been used for many years. In their 1963 evaluation of the Bender Gestalt Test, Tolor and Schulberg discussed no less than 17 studies dealing with the Bender Test Recall. But all of these studies involved exclusively adult subjects. When I searched the literature for my first book (Koppitz, 1963) I did not find a single study that reported on the Bender Test Recall method with children. But during the past 10 years a number of such studies have been carried out.

Bender Test Recall Procedure. Two different procedures for Bender Test Recall have been described. Becker and Sabatino (1971), Orme (1970), and Sabatino and Ysseldyke (1972) exposed each Bender Test design for 5 sec, then removed the card and had the subject draw the figure from memory. Hutton (1966), Snyder and Pope (1970), Weiss (1970), and I, in my own recent study, administered first the entire Bender Test in standard fashion; then after the subjects had copied all nine figures, they were asked to reproduce again as many of the designs as they could from memory. Snyder and Pope developed a scoring system for the Bender Test Recall and published normative data for children age 6 to 11. Unfortunately Snyder and Pope did not provide data as to the reliability and validity of their scoring system.

Standard Bender Test and Bender Test Recall. As would be expected, research results differ according to which of the two recall methods is used in a study. Becker and Sabatino reported a high correlation ($r = .78$) between standard and recall Bender Test scores of 169 elementary-school pupils. Hutton and I, on the other hand, found significant differences between the Developmental Bender Test scores and Recall scores of children, regardless of whether the recall records were scored only for the number of designs that were reproduced or for the accuracy and quality of the drawings. These findings concur with the observation of Tolor and Schulberg that the degree of accuracy in the copying of Bender Test designs is not related to the subsequent recall thereof.

Age, IQ, and Bender Test Recall. There is a consensus that the Bender Test Recall method for children resembles the standard Bender Test method in that it, too, is related to the youngster's age (Hutton, 1966; Sabatino and Becker, 1969; Sabatino and Ysseldyke, 1972; Weiss, 1970). There seems to be a low positive relationship between Bender Test Recall scores and IQ scores (Hutton, 1966).

Brain pathology and Bender Test Recall. The Bender Test Recall method is most frequently used with adult patients to help diagnose brain pathology. The results of such studies have been inconclusive. None of the studies involving children and Bender Test Recall has explored the relationship of this method and brain dysfunction. However, I tend to agree with Garron and Cheifetz (1965) that some of the basic assumptions concerning the Bender Test Recall method are unrealistic and that this procedure is not a particularly good instrument to measure or to identify brain pathology.

School achievement, emotional problems, and Bender Test Recall. Sabatino and Ysseldyke (1972) compared the Bender Test performance of 199 readers and 143 nonreaders, age 6 to 11, all of whom were of normal intelligence (WISC Full Scale IQ 90 or above). No significant differences were found between the two groups of subjects for either the Bender Test copying method or the Bender Test Recall method.

In a recent study I matched three groups of 9- and 10-year-old boys for C.A. and IQ scores. Group A ($N = 30$) consisted of emotionally disturbed patients in a residential treatment center; Group B ($N = 30$) was made up of pupils attending special public-school classes for children with learning disabilities; Group C ($N = 20$), average public-school pupils, served as control. I administered the standard Bender Test, as well as the Bender Test Recall, and the Visual Aural Digit Span Test (VADS) (Koppitz, 1972) to all 80 boys individually in school. The results reveal significant differences for the youngsters with emotional and learning problems (Groups A and B) compared to the normal control group on both the standard Bender Test and on the VADS Test (Koppitz, 1973a). However, the Bender Test Recall scores were unable to discriminate between well-functioning pupils and children with emotional and/or learning problems. This was the case both for the number of designs the children were able to recall and for the quality of the Bender Test figures reproduced from memory. School achievement, especially reading, does of course depend in part on memory and recall, but apparently not on the kind of memory measured by the Bender Test Recall method. Reading requires rather specific memory for symbol–sound association, for visual–auditory recall, and for sequencing of symbols; these functions are apparently related to the VADS Test (Koppitz, 1975) but not to the Bender Test Recall method.

Bender Test Recall method: Summary. At this point it is not clear just what the Bender Test Recall method measures and how it can contribute to a better understanding of children's mental processes, or how it can improve the diagnosis of problems in schoolchildren. Until its validity for children has been established, there seems little justification in using the Bender Test Recall method and putting forth the extra time and effort it requires. More research is needed with the Bender Test Recall method.

SUMMARY

A number of modifications of Bender Test material and procedures have been reported in the literature during the past 10 years. It was shown that position, size, and texture of the drawing paper affect children's Bender Test performances. Some investigators modified the Bender Test designs in order to test specific hypotheses about the nature of visual-motor perception.

Since most pre-school children are too immature to copy designs with a pencil, alternate copying techniques were suggested: Even young children can copy simple abstract designs with sticks or with plasticine. The results with these copying methods compare well with the results of the standard Bender Test copying method for kindergarten pupils.

The Multiple-Choice Bender Test method was developed to test visual perception, while the Bender Test Tracing method evaluates motor coordination. It was demonstrated that the Multiple-Choice Bender Test and the Tracing Bender Test are not significantly correlated, but both methods are significantly related to the standard Bender Test copying method. That is, visual perception and motor coordination are independent functions, but both are essential parts of visual-motor perception.

More research is needed to determine the validity and usefulness of the Bender Test Recall method with elementary-school children.

CHAPTER 14.
The Bender Test and Other Tests of Visual Perception and Visual-Motor Integration

There is consensus that some measure of visual perception or visual-motor integration is essential when assessing children's mental development and learning abilities. Most IQ tests include items or scales involving visual-motor perception; so do most reading-readiness tests for school beginners. A number of tests have been developed for the specific purpose of evaluating pupils' visual perception or visual-motor integration. The Bender Test is one such test; so are the Developmental Test of Visual Perception (Frostig et al., 1961; Maslow et al., 1964), the Developmental Test of Visual-Motor Integration (Beery, 1967), the Progressive Matrices (Raven, 1956), and the Visual Discrimination Test of Words (Becker, 1970).

Most examiners are partial to one particular method or test and consider it superior to others. I particularly like the Bender Test because it requires little in terms of equipment, it is easy to administer, most children enjoy it, and it provides not only developmental data but also valuable clinical information that could not be obtained from the other tests mentioned. However, I am of the opinion that the differences between the various tests are less significant than the authors of the tests and some investigators would like to believe. In order to test this hypothesis I examined all available studies that compared the Developmental Bender Test scores with the scores of the other tests mentioned above.

BENDER TEST AND FROSTIG'S DEVELOPMENTAL TEST OF VISUAL PERCEPTION

Five studies have examined the relationship between the Bender Test and the Frostig Test. Four of these used primary-grade pupils and clinic patients for subjects. They all reported significant correlations between the two sets of test scores. Becker and Sabatino (1973) tested 154 upper-middle-class kindergarten pupils with the Bender Test and the Developmental Test of Visual Perception; they obtained a correlation of .42. The study of Jessen and Prendergast (1965) showed a correlation of .39 between the Bender Test and Frostig Test scores of kindergarten and first-grade pupils; Mlodnosky (1972) tested deprived first-graders and found a correlation of .56 between the two sets of test scores. Similar results were reported ($r = .52$) by Culbertson and Gunn (1966), who used clinic patients age 7 to 12 as subjects.

In contrast to these four studies, Nielsen and Ringe (1969) found no statistically significant correlations between the Bender Test and Frostig Test scores of 20 9- and 10-year-old children with reading disabilities. The Bender Test was able to discriminate between the youngsters with and without reading problems ($p < .05$); the Frostig Test was unable to do so. The age and maturation level of the children in the Nielsen and Ringe study may account in part for the discrepancy between the results of this study and the findings of the four other investigations.

The Frostig Test consists of five subtests. Of these, Subtest V, Space Relations, seems to correlate best with the Developmental Bender Test score. Otherwise the findings are inconsistent. Becker and Sabatino reported significant correlations between all Frostig subtests and Bender Test scores with the exception of Subtest III, Form Constancy. Culbertson and Gunn found high correlations only between Bender Test scores and Frostig Subtest I, Eye–Hand Coordination, and Subtest V, Space Relations; the Bender Test scores of Mlodnosky's subjects were significantly related to Frostig Subtest III, Form Constancy, Subtest IV, Position in Space, and Subtest V, Space Relations, but not to Subtest I, Eye–Hand Coordination, and Subtest II, Figure–Ground. The inconsistencies of these findings might partially be explained by the differences in the subjects used in these studies. Further studies are needed to clarify the relationship between the Frostig subtests and Bender Test scores.

BENDER TEST AND BEERY'S DEVELOPMENTAL TEST
OF VISUAL-MOTOR INTEGRATION

Only one study explored the relationship between the Bender Test scores and the Beery Test. Krauft and Krauft (1972) selected 24 moderately retarded (IQ 50 to 80) youngsters age 6 to 12 as subjects. The correlation between the Bender Test and Beery Test scores of these slow youngsters was highly significant ($r = .82$).

Thus it appears that the Bender Test, the Frostig Test, and the Beery Test have a great deal in common (the Beery Test includes two of the Bender Test figures) and can be used more or less interchangeably, if all one desires is a single score or measure of a child's level of maturation in visual-motor perception. The Bender Test has the advantage of requiring no extra materials beyond a set of Bender Test stimulus cards. The Frostig Test and the Beery Test use specially printed, structured test booklets, and they offer programs for perceptual–motor training based on the test results. These training activities can be useful in many ways, especially for young and educationally handicapped pupils, even though there are to date no conclusive research data to show that the training procedures actually result in long-range improvements in visual-motor integration and learning.

The structures of the Beery Test and Frostig Test make them easier to administer for less experienced investigators. However, the very lack of structure on the Bender Test enables the qualified examiner to gather a wealth of clinical insights and to observe different kinds of behavior and attitudes on the part of the child; this is not possible with the other two tests. The Bender Test is, of course, a clinical test and should be used as such.

BENDER TEST AND RAVEN'S PROGRESSIVE MATRICES

The Progressive Matrices (Raven, 1956) are a test of visual perception and nonverbal reasoning. The test differs from the Bender Test in that it does not involve any motor activity. A child taking the test has merely to give a number or to point to the answer among six possible answers for each problem. Despite these differences the Bender Test and the Progressive Matrices appear to be closely related. Kerr (1972) compared the performance of 256 children, age 5 years 9 months to 9 years 4 months, on the two tests. He found that the Bender Test and the Progressive Matrices correlated significantly ($r = .69$; $p < .001$). The performances on both tests were also significantly related to the youngsters' ages and achievement levels, but not to their sex.

Stadler (1966) tested 74 first-graders from a high socioeconomic background. The Bender Test scores and the scores from the Progressive Matrices for these youngsters were also positively related ($r = .58$; $p < .01$). The results suggest that the Progressive Matrices may be of particular value in assessing perceptual integration of youngsters with fine-motor impairment, since the test does not require the ability to manipulate a pencil.

BENDER TEST AND VISUAL
DISCRIMINATION TEST OF WORDS

Becker (1970) matched 32 kindergarten pupils with "adequate spatial orientation" and 32 kindergarten pupils with "poor spatial orientation." The youngsters' spatial orientation was determined by means of the Bender Test. The Visual Discrimination Test of Words, as developed by Becker, was administered to both groups of subjects. Results indicate that the youngsters who did well on the Bender Test also tended to do well on the word-discrimination tasks, while the children who did poorly on the Bender Test also tended to have difficulty with the visual discrimination of words.

SUMMARY

Recent research findings indicate that Bender Test scores of primary-grade pupils and young clinic patients are significantly related to Frostig's Developmental Test of Visual Perception. No such relationship was shown between the two sets of test scores of 9- and 10-year-old children. Frostig's Subtest V, Space Relations, seems to correlate best with the Developmental Bender Test scores.

Bender Test scores are also significantly related to Beery's Developmental Test of Visual-Motor Integration, to Raven's Progressive Matrices, and to Becker's Visual Discrimination Test of Words. Although investigators and clinicians are usually partial to one test or the other, the differences between the findings for the various tests are usually less than is generally assumed. Each of these tests has, of course, specific advantages and disadvantages. Aside from its brevity and convenience, the Bender Test has the advantage of providing a considerable amount of clinical information in addition to measuring a youngster's level of maturation in visual-motor integration.

CHAPTER 15.
Bender Test Research
and Application 1963–1973

The marked increase in the use of the Bender Test with children during the past 10 years seems to have resulted mainly from two factors: the availability of reliable, objective scoring systems and the demonstrated validity of the Bender Test not only as a test for individual children but also as a group test. These two factors have made it possible to administer the Bender Test to large numbers of children and have broadened its range of application. Formerly the Bender Test was used primarily as a clinical instrument with individual patients. Today it still serves this function, but it is also widely used as a screening test for schoolchildren and as a research tool in controlled investigations.

A number of objective Bender Test scoring systems for use with children have been developed. Most of these are reliable and valid for the specific purposes or age levels for which they were designed. The Developmental Bender Test Scoring System has been used most frequently in research studies and appears to have the widest range of application. It was shown that the Total Developmental Bender Test score is a more meaningful measure of children's visual-motor integration than any single sign or individual scoring item on Bender Test records. In order to facilitate the scoring of Bender Test protocols, the scoring manual for the Developmental Bender Test Scoring System has been slightly modified and improved; it is presented in Appendix A.

The original normative data for the Developmental Bender Test Scoring System have been supplemented with new normative data derived from a more representative sample of youngsters age 5 through 10 years. In addition, the results from a large number of recent studies provide a wealth of data on the Bender Test performance, at each age level, of children from different socioeconomic and cultural backgrounds and for pupils at each grade level, kindergarten through sixth grade.

According to research findings, the Bender Test is primarily related to a child's age and mental ability. It is therefore essential to take the youngster's birthdate and ability into account when interpreting his Bender Test record. For 6- to 8-year-old children whose visual-motor perception has not yet fully matured, the Bender Test can serve as a brief nonverbal intelligence test. However, because of its developmental ceiling the Bender Test can only detect normal and below-normal perceptual–motor integration with older children; beyond age 8 the Bender Test can no longer effectively discriminate between youngsters of average and above-average mental ability.

Traditionally the Bender Test has been used as a clinical instrument to identify neurological impairment or brain injury. Recent research shows that with few exceptions the Bender Test can reveal the presence of brain dysfunction in children, but it is difficult to tell anything about the etiology of such brain dysfunction solely from a Bender Test record. Thus it is not possible to determine from a Bender Test protocol whether a youngster shows immaturity or malfunction in visual-motor perception as a result of a developmental lag or whether this is due to a genetic flaw or is the consequence of severe early deprivation or of brain trauma that resulted in a brain lesion. Additional information about the child's development and background and results from other tests are needed for a differential diagnosis.

A number of investigations offer support for the validity of the Emotional Indicators on the Bender Test for differentiating between children with psychiatric problems and well-adjusted children. But the Emotional Indicators by themselves are unable to discriminate between neurotic, psychotic, and brain-injured children. Once again we find that the Bender Test is most effective as part of a diagnostic battery or in combination with additional information. Two new Emotional Indicators have been added to the original list of ten such signs. They are *Box Around Design* and *Spontaneous Elaboration or Addition to Design.* These particular signs occur only rarely, but when they do appear on Bender Test protocols they have considerable clinical significance.

The Bender Test has been used most often during the past 10 years with elementary-school children. The Bender Test can differentiate groups of well-functioning pupils from groups of poor students; yet this does not imply a one-to-one relationship between the Bender Test performance and school achievement for each individual pupil. Generally the Bender Test can predict a youngster's overall school functioning reasonably well, and more specifically it is related to arithmetic and to writing. Contrary to a widely held assumption, the Bender Test is not closely related to reading. In addition to visual perception, reading involves visual–oral association, the discrimination, sequencing, and blending of sounds, and oral recall. None of these latter factors is reflected on a child's Bender Test performance.

Most pupils with learning disabilities reveal a significant discrepancy between their Bender Test scores and their IQ scores; even learning-disabled youngsters with good mental ability tend to show marked developmental lag or malfunction in visual-motor integration. Their rates of improvement on the Bender Test have been shown to be related to their rates of progress in school achievement.

Today there is much concern with the early identification and prevention of learning problems. The Bender Test has frequently been used as a screening instrument at the end of kindergarten or at the beginning of the first grade to help identify high-risk children. Research findings indicate that the Bender Test alone is only moderately effective as a screening instrument, but together with brief measures of the youngsters' emotional adjustment, verbal ability, and memory, both the group Bender Test and the individual Bender Test are most useful in identifying pupils who may need further evaluation and special consideration. It has been demonstrated how the Bender Test can be combined with the Visual Aural Digit Span test and Human Figure Drawings to form a short, easy-to-administer, and effective screening battery for school beginners.

Four different techniques for administering the Bender Test to groups of pupils have been described. The selection of a group Bender Test method should depend on the number of youngsters to be tested at a given time. Group Bender Test records are scored and interpreted in the same manner as individual Bender Test protocols, although some of the clinical information obtained with the individual Bender Test is inevitably lost in the group administration.

A number of interesting modifications of the Bender Test materials and procedures have been devised during the past decade. However, the standard Bender Test, as developed by Bender in 1938, is still the most frequently used form of the test, and it continues to be one of the most versatile and useful psychological tests available. The popularity of the Bender Test has spread in recent years beyond the United States to other countries on this continent and abroad.

PLATES

Plate	Name	Age	Mental Ability	Comments	Page References
1	Alison	9–8	Above Av.	well functioning	3, 54, 74
2	Chris	5–0	Above Av.	kindergarten	14, 85
3	Angelo	5–0	Below Av.	kindergarten	14, 84, 85
4	Ricki	7–11	Mod. Ret.	ED, impulsive	15, 55, 85, 86
5	Brian	7–3	Av.	poor integration	15
6	Terry	6–8	Low Av.	LD, ED, impulsive	85, 86, 89
7	David	8–0	Av.	rotation of paper	7, 22, 84, 85
8	John	10–9	Av.	LD, ED, concretistic	3, 23, 84, 95
9	Glenn	9–6	Low Av.	perceptual problem	3, 24, 84, 85
10	Glenn	10–2	Low Av.	perceptual problem	24, 84, 85
11	Rocco	7–0	Mod. Ret.	impulsive, moody	54, 55, 68, 84, 85, 89
12	Rocco	9–10	Mod. Ret.	impulsive, moody	54, 55, 68, 85
13	Rocco	12–2	Mod. Ret.	impulsive, moody	54, 55, 68, 85
14	Sharon	10–11	Mod. Ret.	poor coordination	3, 62, 74, 84, 85
15	Susano	10–1	Av.	LD, non-reader	62, 85
16	Kevin	7–11	Av.	LD, immature	7, 68, 69, 84
17	Kevin	9–5	Av.	LD, immature	68, 69, 84, 85
18	Kevin	12–4	Av.	LD, good progress	68, 69, 85
19	Jim	8–6	Low Av.	LD, non-reader	4, 72, 83
20	Tom	8–6	Low Av.	LD, non-reader	72, 84, 85
21	Steve	9–11	Av.	LD, emot. problem	83, 84, 85, 88, 89
22	Billy	8–6	Mod. Ret.	brain-tumor	74, 84, 85, 89
23	Frankie	10–1	Low Av.	LD, disorganized	85, 87, 89
24	Frankie	10–9	Low Av.	LD, impulsive	85, 86, 87
25	Danny	9–10	Mod. Ret.	emot. disturbed	85, 88
26	Seth	6–7	High Av.	schizoid	88
27	Patrice	6–2	Above Av.	kindergarten	93
28	Edgar	6–0	Low Av.	kindergarten	20, 84, 85, 93, 94
29	Lori	6–2	Above Av.	kindergarten	20, 85, 94
30	Greg	5–7	Below Av.	kindergarten	85, 94
31	Lisa	6–0	Above Av.	kindergarten	74, 101
32	Lisa	6–0	Above Av.	kindergarten	101
33	Ralph	6–1	Below Av.	kindergarten	84, 85, 102
34	Ralph	6–1	Below Av.	kindergarten	102
35	Joey	5–6	Good vis.-mot.	poor language	85, 103
36	Joey	5–6	Good vis.-mot.	poor language	103
37	Michael	5–6	Poor vis.-mot.	good potential	84, 85, 106
38	Michael	5–6	Poor vis.-mot.	good potentional	106
39	Ann	6–5	Below Av.	kindergarten	85, 107
40	Ann	6–5	Below Av.	kindergarten	107, 108

Plates are here reduced photographically 45 percent from 8½ in. × 11 in. originals.

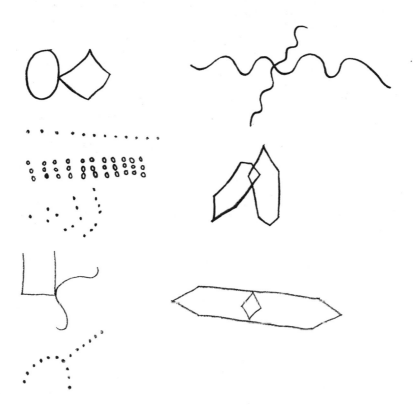

Developmental Score

0

Emotional Indicators
none

Plate 1.   Alison, C.A. 9–8.

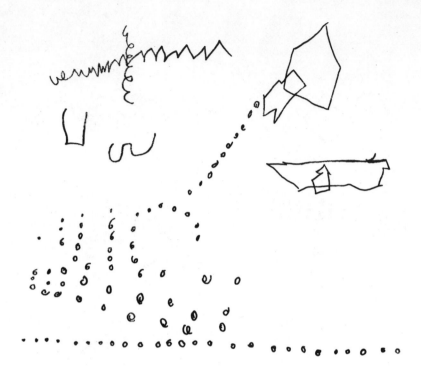

Developmental Score
3
4
6
10
14
15
18a
20
21a
21b
<u>24</u>

11

Emotional Indicators
   I.   Confused Order
 VI.   Small Size (A, 4)

Plate 2.   Chris, C.A. 5–0.

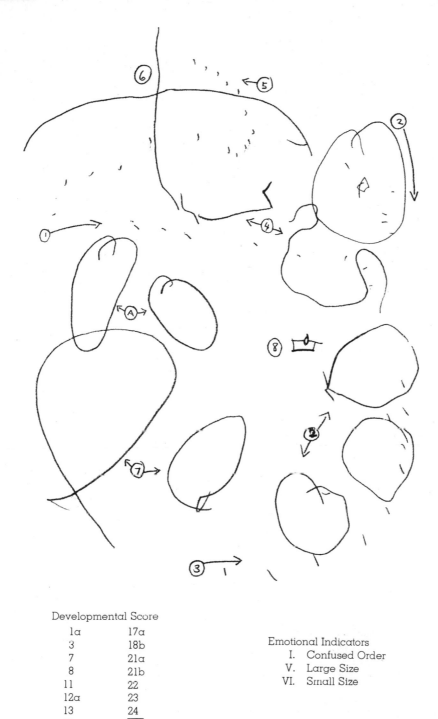

Developmental Score

1a	17a
3	18b
7	21a
8	21b
11	22
12a	23
13	24
14	16
16	

Emotional Indicators
  I. Confused Order
  V. Large Size
  VI. Small Size

Plate 3.   Angelo, 5–0.

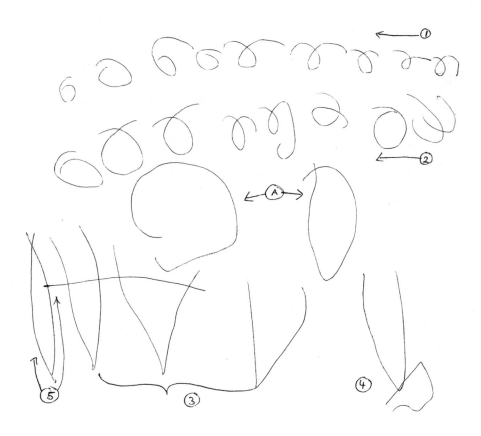

Emotional Indicators
- I.   Confused Order
- V.   Large Size
- VII. Fine Line
- X   Expansion

Developmental Score

1a	17b
1b	18a
2	19
3	20
4	21a
8	21b
12a	22
12b	23
13	24
14	25
17a	21

Plate 4 (Side 1).   Ricki, 7–11.

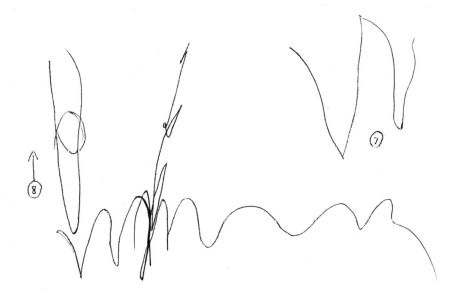

Plate 4 (Side 2).   Ricki, 7–11.

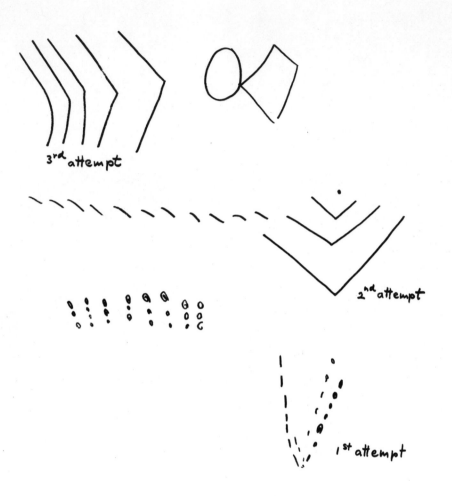

Plate 5. Brian, 7–3.

Emotional Indicators
V. Large Size
X. Expansion

Plate 6. Terry, C.A. 6–8.

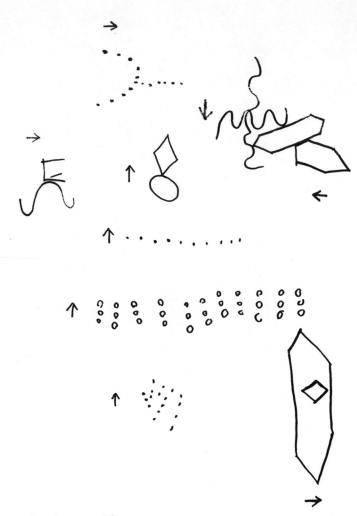

Developmental Score
         2
        13
        23
       ———
         3

Emotional Indicators
    II.   Wavy Line
    VI.   Small Size (A)

Plate 7.   David, C.A. 8–0.

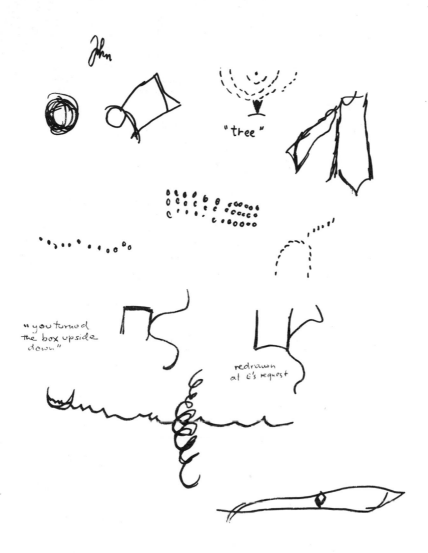

John

"tree"

"you turned
the box upside
down."

redrawn
at E's request

Emotional Indicators
  I.   Confused Order
  II. Wavy Line
  VIII. Overwork
  IX. 2nd Attempt

Developmental Score
       1b
       11
       12a
       18a
       20
       21a
       21b
       23
       24
       ──
       9

Plate 8. John, C.A. 10–9.

Developmental Score
2
5
7
11
13
16
18a
20
21b
24
___
10

Emotional Indicators
I.   Confused Order
III.   Dashes (2)
VI.   Small Size (A, 7)
VIII. Overwork (4, 5)

Plate 9. Glenn, C.A. 9–6.

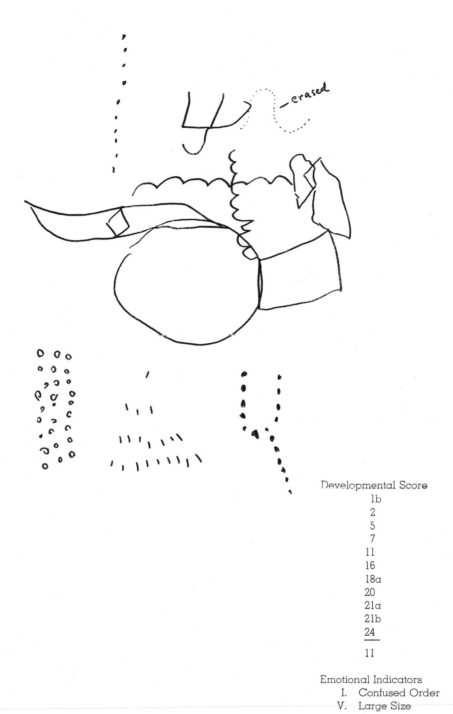

erased

Developmental Score
1b
2
5
7
11
16
18a
20
21a
21b
24
___
11

Emotional Indicators
I. Confused Order
V. Large Size

Plate 10. Glenn, C.A. 10–2.

Developmental Score
1a
1b
6
8
12a
13
14
17a
18a
20
21b
22
24
___

Emotional Indicators
II.   Wavy Line
III. Dashes (2)
IV.   Increase in Size (2)
V.   Large Size (2)
VI.   Small Size (4, 5, 6, 7)   13

Plate 11.   Rocco, C.A. 7–0.

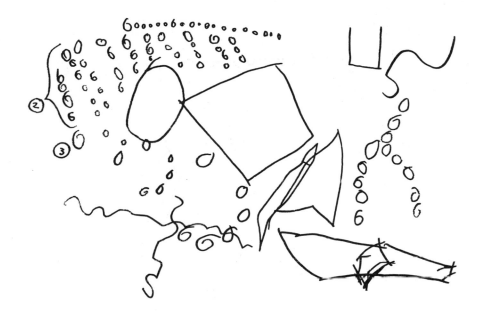

Developmental Score
      1b
      4
      6
      8
      10
      14
      15
      18a
      20
      21a
      21b
      22   Emotional Indicators
      24   I. Confused Order
    ─────   V. Large Size
      13   VIII. Overwork

Plate 12.   Rocco, C.A. 9–10.

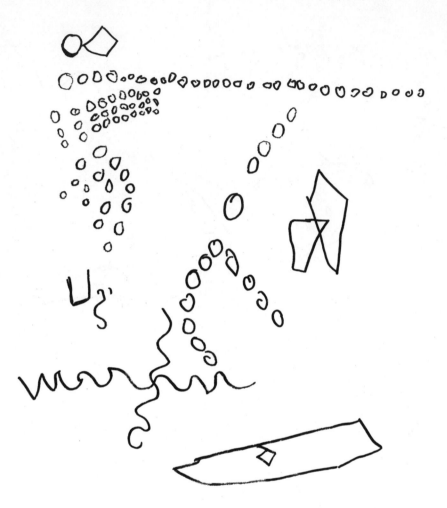

Emotional Indicators
    V.   Large Size (5)
   VI.   Small Size (A, 4)

Developmental Score
4
6
10
13
14
15
18a
20
21b
<u>24</u>

10

Plate 13.   Rocco, C.A. 12–2.

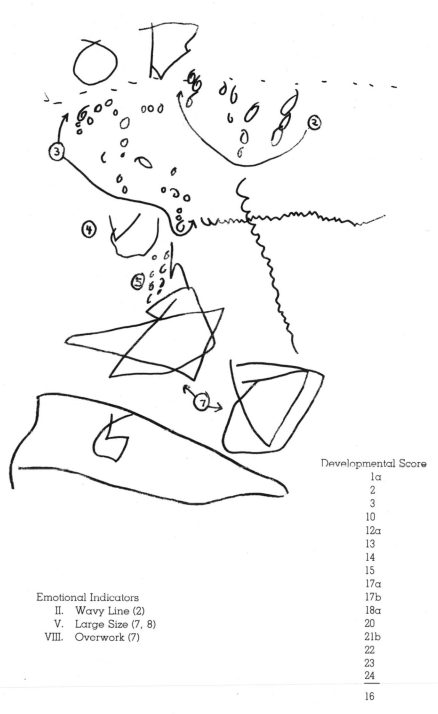

Developmental Score
1a
2
3
10
12a
13
14
15
17a
17b
18a
20
21b
22
23
24

16

Emotional Indicators
   II.   Wavy Line (2)
   V.   Large Size (7, 8)
VIII.   Overwork (7)

Plate 14.   Sharon, C.A. 10–11.

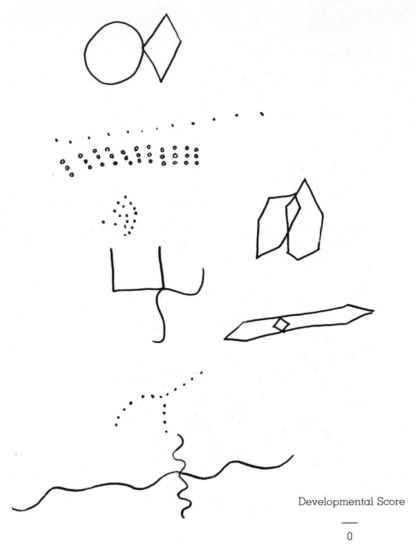

Developmental Score

———

0

Emotional Indicators
VI.   Small Size (3)

Plate 15.   Susano, C.A. 10–1.

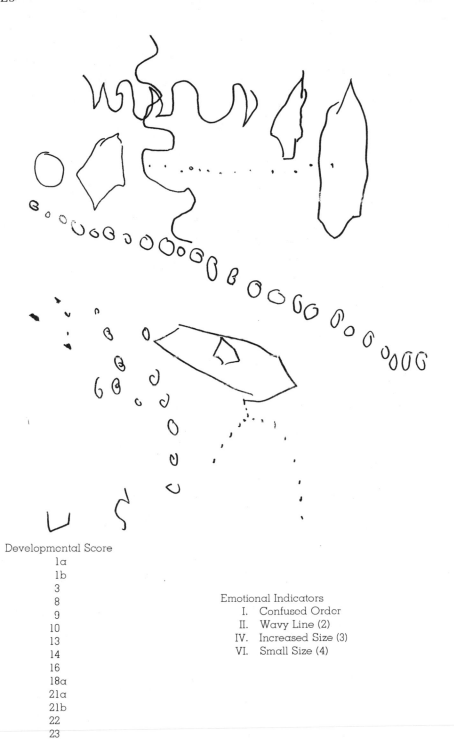

Developmental Score
1a
1b
3
8
9
10
13
14
16
18a
21a
21b
22
23
24
———
15

Emotional Indicators
I.   Confused Order
II. Wavy Line (2)
IV. Increased Size (3)
VI. Small Size (4)

Plate 16.   Kevin, C.A. 7–11.

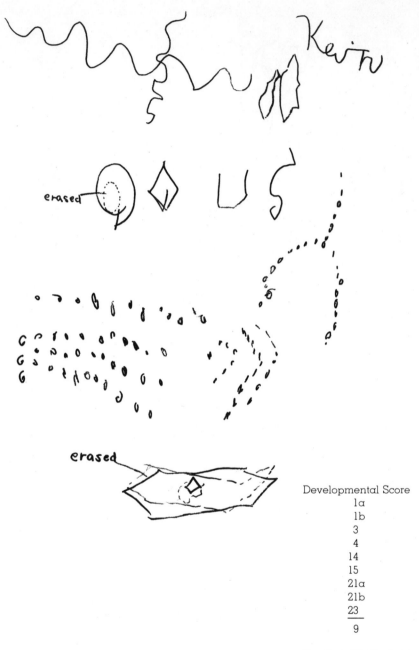

Developmental Score
1a
1b
3
4
14
15
21a
21b
23
―――
9

Emotional Indicators
I.   Confused Order
II. Wavy Line
VI. Small Size

Plate 17. Kevin, C.A. 9–5.

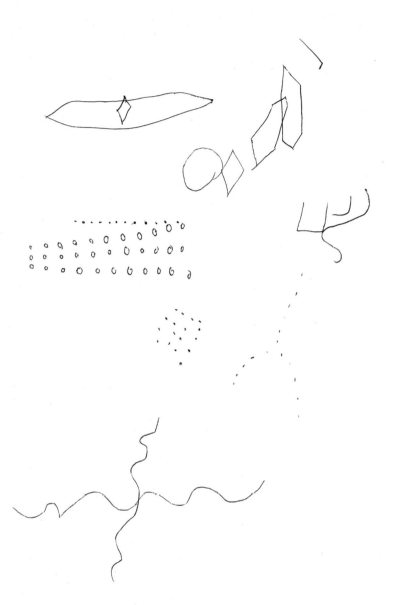

Developmental Score
1b
$$\frac{24}{2}$$

Emotional Indicators
VII.   Fine Line
IX.   2nd Attempt

Plate 18.   Kevin, C.A. 12-4.

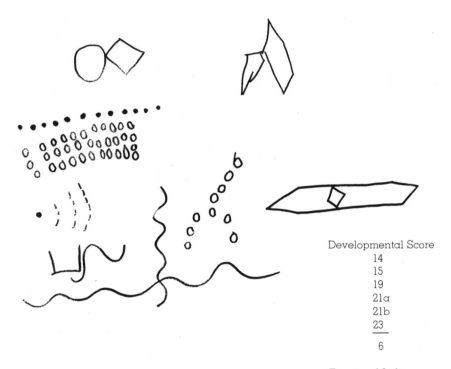

Developmental Score
14
15
19
21a
21b
23
———
6

Emotional Indicators
none

Plate 19. Jim, C.A. 8–6.

Developmental Score
4
10
15
18a
20
<u>24</u>
6

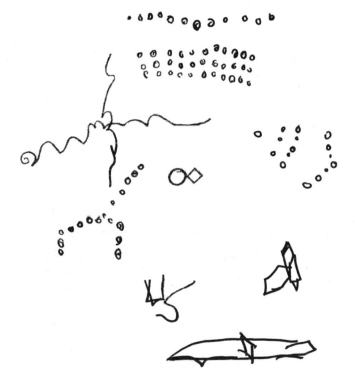

Emotional Indicators
  I.   Confused Order
 II.   Wavy Line
 VI.   Small Size (A, 4, 7)
VIII. Overwork

Plate 20.   Tom, C.A. 8–6.

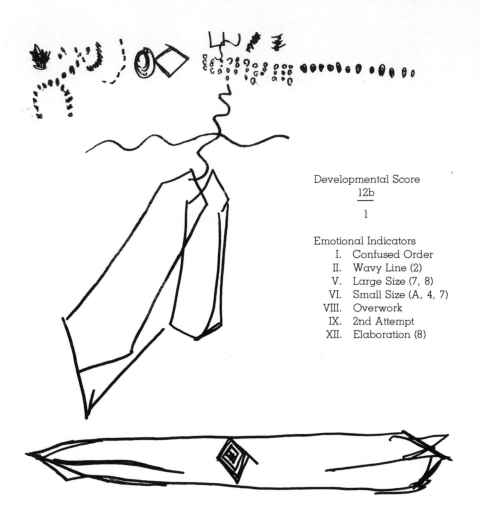

Developmental Score
$$\frac{12b}{1}$$

Emotional Indicators
    I.   Confused Order
   II.   Wavy Line (2)
   V.   Large Size (7, 8)
  VI.   Small Size (A, 4, 7)
VIII.   Overwork
  IX.   2nd Attempt
  XII.   Elaboration (8)

Plate 21. Steve, C.A. 9–11.

Developmental Score
            1a
            2
            7
            13
            14
            17b
            18a
            20
            21a
            21b
            23
            24
            ──
            12

Emotional Indicators
    I.   Confused Order
    VI. Small Size
    VII. Fine Line

Plate 22.   Billy, C.A. 8–6.

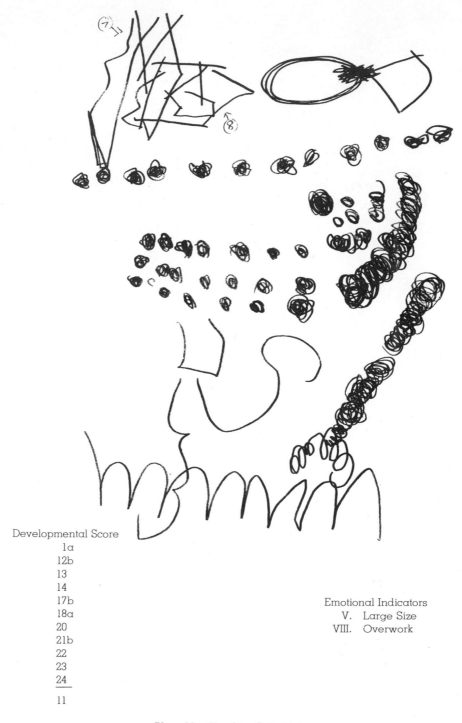

Developmental Score
1a
12b
13
14
17b
18a
20
21b
22
23
24
___
11

Emotional Indicators
V.   Large Size
VIII.   Overwork

Plate 23.   Frankie, C.A. 10–1.

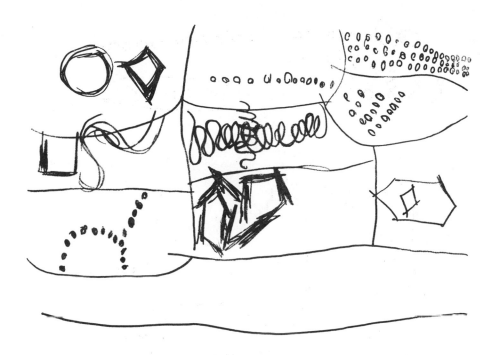

Developmental Score
3
4
9
10
14
18a
20
21b
22
23
___
10

Emotional Indicators
VIII.   Overwork
XI.   Boxes

Plate 24.   Frankie, C.A. 10–9.

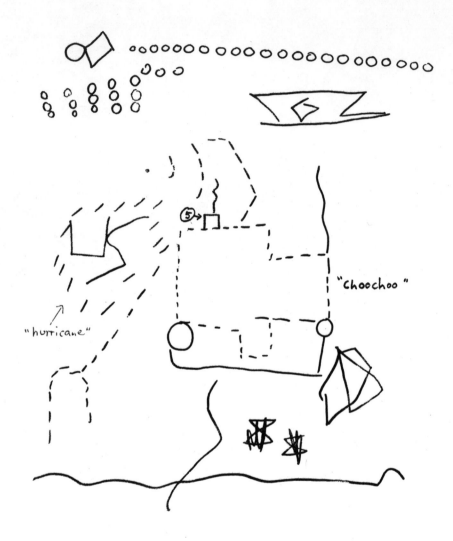

"hurricane"

"choochoo"

	Developmental Score
	1b
	4
	6
	14
Emotional Indicators	17a
VI. Small Size (A)	18b
IX. 2nd Attempt (7)	19
XII. Elaboration	21b
	23
	24
	10

Plate 25.   Danny, C.A. 9–10.

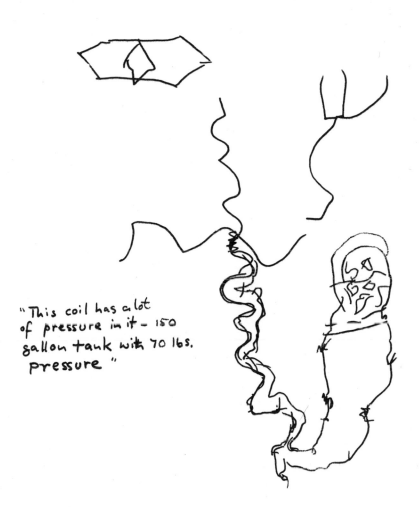

"This coil has a lot
of pressure in it – 150
gallon tank with 70 lbs.
pressure"

Plate 26. Seth, C.A. 6–7.

Developmental Score
1a
6
9
13
14
18a
20
21b
23
24
―――
10

Emotional Indicators
none

Plate 27.   Patrice, C.A. 6–2.

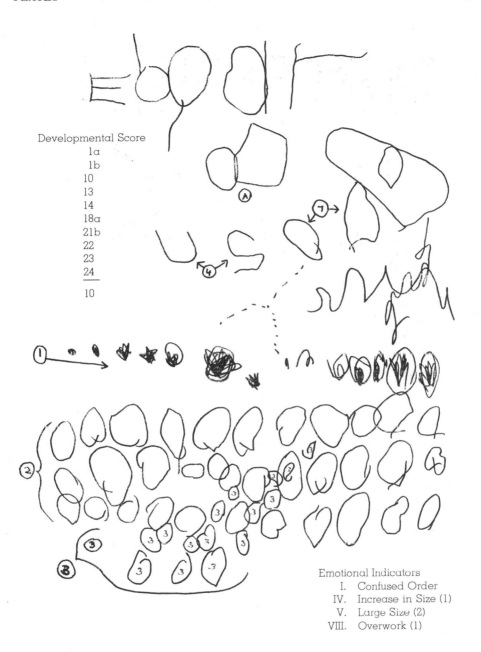

Developmental Score
1a
1b
10
13
14
18a
21b
22
23
24
___
10

Emotional Indicators
   I.   Confused Order
 IV.   Increase in Size (1)
  V.   Large Size (2)
VIII.   Overwork (1)

Plate 28. Edgar, C.A. 6–0.

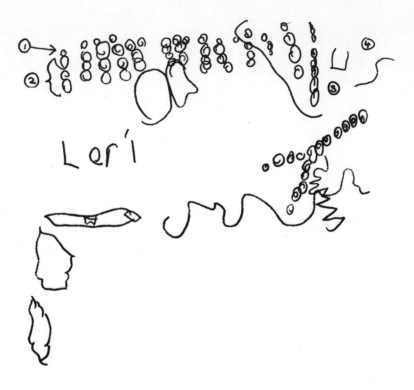

Developmental Score
1a
4
10
14
15
16
18a
20
21b
22
23
24
―――
12

Emotional Indicators
  I. Confused Order
 VI. Small Size (4)

Plate 29. Lori, C.A. 6–2.

Developmental Score
1a
3
8
12a
13
14
17a
17b
18a
20
21b
24
───
12

Emotional Indicators
II.   Wavy Line
VIII. Overwork

Plate 30.   Greg, C.A. 5–7.

Lisa

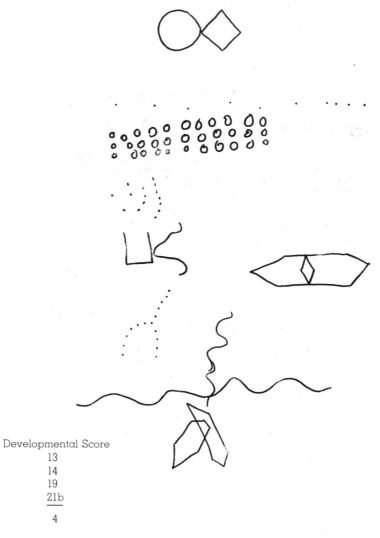

Developmental Score
       13
       14
       19
       21b
       ___
        4

Emotional Indicators
   none

Plate 31.   Lisa, C.A. 6–0.

123456789

532

526

4937

46813

426

262

9178

2976

Lisa

Plate 32.   Lisa, C.A. 6–0.

Developmental Score

1a	18b
1b	21a
3	21b
6	22
8	23
13	24
14	25
16	___
17a	16

Emotional Indicators
I.   Confused Order
II. Wavy Line
VII. Fine Line
IX. 2nd Attempt (8)

Plate 33.   Ralph, C.A. 6–1.

Plate 34.   Ralph, C.A. 6–1.

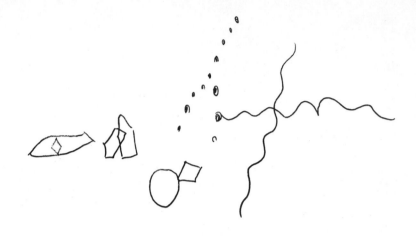

Developmental Score
1b
6
10
21b
24
—
5

Emotional Indicators
    I.   Confused Order
  VI. Small Size

Plate 35.   Joey, C.A. 5–0.

1 2 3 4 5 6 7 8 9
7 6 5 4 3 2 1
2
3

4 5 6
9 7 7 8
7 6 5 4   Joey

Plate 36. Joey, C.A. 5–6.

Developmental Score
    1b
    6
    7
    10
    13
    15
    18a
    20
    21a
    21b
    23
    24
    ——
    12

Emotional Indicators
  I. Confused Order
  II. Wavy Line
  V. Large Size (2)

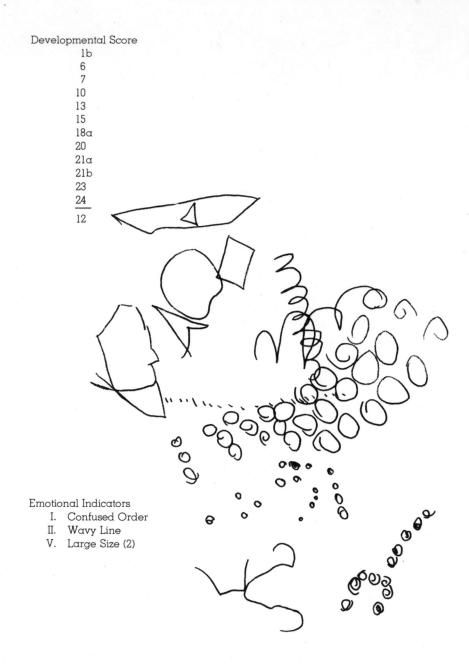

Plate 37.   Michael, C.A. 5–6.

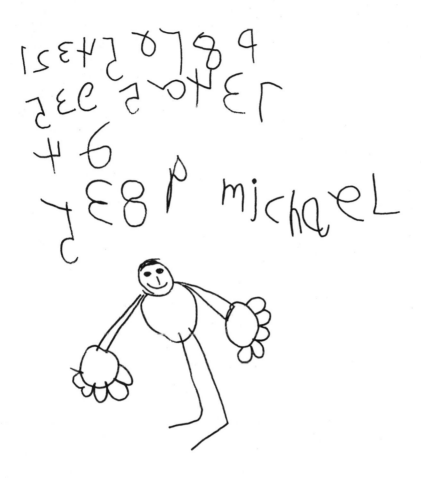

Plate 38. Michael, C.A. 5–6.

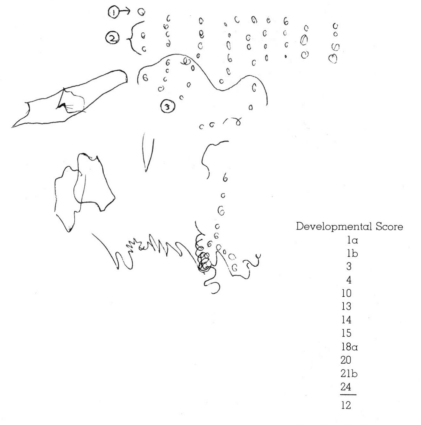

Developmental Score
1a
1b
3
4
10
13
14
15
18a
20
21b
24
___
12

Emotional Indicators
II.   Wavy Line (2)
VI.   Small Size (4)
VII.   Fine Line

Plate 39.   Ann, C.A. 6–5.

Ahn

Plate 40.   Ann, C.A. 6–5.

APPENDIX A
Revised Scoring Manual
for the Developmental Bender
Test Scoring System

    The Revised Scoring Manual for the Developmental Bender Test Scoring System includes the same 30 scoring items that appeared in the Scoring Manual of *The Bender Gestalt Test for Young Children* (Koppitz, 1963, pp. 16–21). The Revised Scoring Manual does not invalidate or change the earlier scoring manual; it merely clarifies and sharpens some of the definitions and descriptions of the scoring items so as to make the scoring of Bender Test records easier and avoid confusion and errors.

    Once again it should be emphasized: "Only clearcut deviations are scored. In case of doubt an item is not scored. Since the Scoring System is designed for young children with as yet immature fine motor control, minor deviations are ignored" (Koppitz, 1963, p. 15). The use of a protractor and a ruler greatly facilitates the scoring of several items. When scoring a Bender Test protocol it is essential to check each of the 30 scoring items as being either present or absent. The sum of all scoring items present on a given Bender Test record equals the total Developmental Bender Test score.

Figures are here reduced photographically by 20 percent from original drawings.

Definition and Examples
of Scoring Items

FIGURE A

Distortion

1a. Distortion of shape: Circle or square or both are excessively mis-shapen (see Plates 3, 4, 11, 14, 16, 17, 22, 23, 27, 28, 29, 30).
Examples: Longest dimension of circle or square is twice as long as the shortest dimension

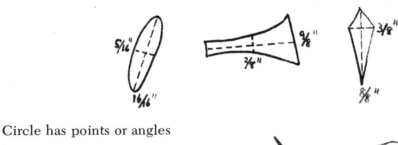

Circle has points or angles

Square has "ears," extra or missing angles

Two sides of a corner of the square are more than ⅛ in. apart at point of junction with circle

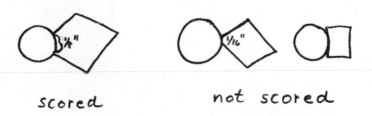

scored   not scored

1b. Disproportion between size of circle and square: area of one is at least twice as large as area of the other (see Plates 4, 8, 10, 11, 12, 16, 17, 18, 25, 28, 33, 35).
Examples:

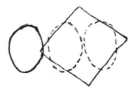

2. *Rotation*
Rotation of total figure or part of it by 45° or more (see Plates 7, 9, 10, 14, 22).
Examples: Rotation of total figure

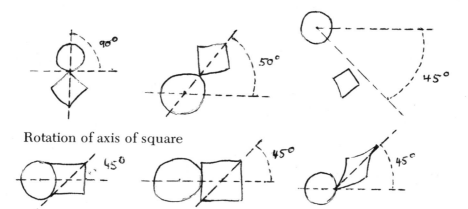

Rotation of axis of square

3. *Integration*
Failure to join circle and square, circle and adjacent corner of square more than ⅛ in. apart; this applies also to overlap (see Plates 2, 3, 4, 14, 16, 17, 24, 30, 33, 39).
Examples:

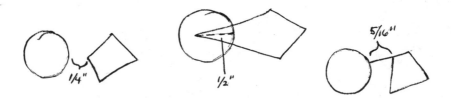

Figure 1

4. *Distortion*

    Five or more dots converted into circles. Circle is defined as an open
    space surrounded totally or almost completely by a line (see Plates 2,
    4, 12, 13, 17, 20, 24, 25, 29, 39).

    Examples: Scored

    Enlarged dots or partially filled circles, dashes, and curves are not
    scored; in case of doubt do not score.

    Examples: Not scored

5. *Rotation*

    Rotation of figure by 45° or more (see Plates 9, 10).

    Examples:

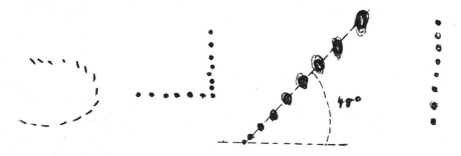

6. *Perseveration*

    More than 15 dots in a row (see Plates 2, 11, 12, 13, 25, 27, 33, 35, 37).

    Example:

Figure 2

7. *Rotation*
   Middle row of circles rotated by 45° or more (see Plates 3, 9, 10, 22, 37).
   Examples.

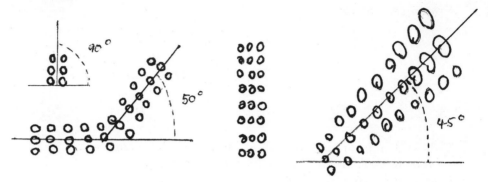

8. *Integration*
   One or two rows of circles omitted; row of dots in Fig. 1 used as third row for Fig. 2; four or more circles in the majority of columns; row of circles added. Substitution of dots or dashes for circles is *not* scored (see Plates 3, 4, 11, 12, 16, 30, 33).
   Examples: Scored

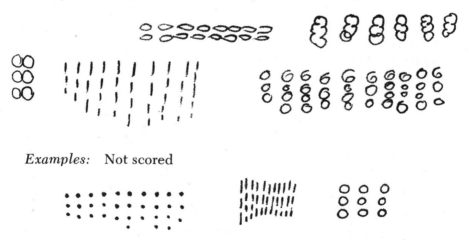

   Examples: Not scored

9. *Perseveration*
   More than 14 columns of circles in a row (see Plates 16, 24, 27).
   Example:

Figure 3

10. *Distortion*

    Five or more dots converted into circles. Circle is defined as an open space surrounded entirely or almost completely by a line; enlarged dots or partially filled circles, dashes, and curves are *not* scored. In case of doubt do not score (see Plates 2, 12, 13, 14, 16, 20, 24, 28, 29, 35, 37).
    Examples: See Fig. 1, scoring item number 4

11. *Rotation*

    Rotation of long axis of design by 45° or more (see Plates 3, 5, 8, 9, 10).
    Examples:

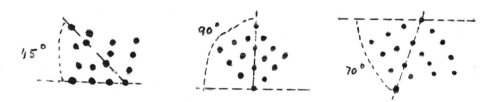

Integration

12a. Shape of design lost; failure to increase the number of dots on each succeeding row; shape not recognizable or reversed; conglomeration of dots; single row of dots; do *not* score incorrect number of dots or extra or missing row of dots (see Plates 3, 4, 5, 8, 11, 14, 30).
    Examples: Scored

Examples: Not scored

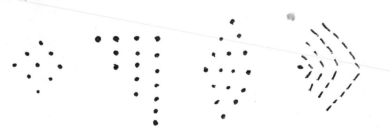

12b. Continuous line, either instead of or in addition to rows of dots (see
      Plates 4, 5, 21, 23).
      Examples:

Figure 4

13. *Rotation*
    Rotation of whole figure or part of it by 45° or more (see Plates 3, 4, 7, 9, 11, 13, 14, 22, 23, 27, 28, 39).
    Examples: Rotation or reversal of whole figure

    Examples: Rotation of open box

    Examples: Rotation of curve

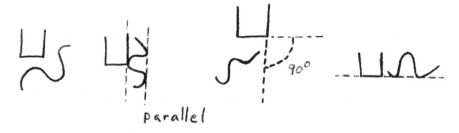

14. *Integration*
    Curve and adjacent corner of box more than ⅛ in. apart; this applies also to overlap; curve adheres to one whole side of box (see Plates 2, 3, 4, 11, 12, 13, 14, 16, 19, 22, 25, 27).
    Examples:

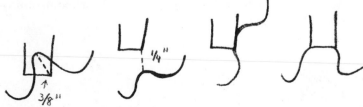

Figure 5

15. *Distortion*

Five or more dots converted into circles. Circle is defined as an open space surrounded totally or almost entirely by a line (see Plates 2, 6, 12, 13, 14, 17, 19, 20, 29, 37, 39).

Examples: See Fig. 1, scoring item number 4

16. *Rotation*

Rotation of whole figure or part of it by 45° or more (see Plates 3, 9, 10, 16, 29, 33).

Examples: Rotation of whole figure

Examples: Extension rotated, points toward left or down; extension placed 10 or more degrees to left of midpoint of arch.

Integration

17a. Shape of design lost; conglomeration of dots; straight line or circle of dots instead of arch; extension cuts through arch; do *not* score square or angle instead or arch (see Plates 3, 4, 11, 13, 25, 30, 33).

Examples:

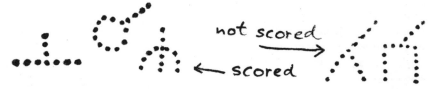

17b. Continuous line instead of dots either on arch or extension or both (see Plates 4, 14, 22, 23, 30).

Examples:

Figure 6

Distortion

18a. Distortion of shape; three or more distinct angles or points instead of
curves; in case of doubt do *not* score (see Plates 2, 6, 8, 9, 10, 11, 12,
13, 14, 16, 20, 22).
Examples:

18b. Straight lines; less than two complete sinusoidal curves or no curves
at all in one or both lines (see Plates 3, 25, 33).
Examples:

19. *Integration*
Two lines crossing not at all or at extreme end of one or both lines or
less than one complete sinusoidal curve from end of line; two inter-
woven lines (see Plates 4, 19, 25, 31).
Examples:

20. *Perseveration*
Six or more complete sinusoidal curves in either direction (see Plates
2, 8, 9, 10, 12, 13, 14, 20, 22, 23, 24, 27).
Example:

sinusoidal
curve

Figure 7

Distortion

21a. Disproportion between size of two hexagons; area of one must be at least twice as large as area of other (see Plates 2, 3, 8, 10, 12, 16, 17, 19, 22, 33, 37).
Examples:

21b. Hexagons excessively misshapen; extra or missing angle on one or both hexagons; "ears" or curves for angles (see Plates 2, 3, 6, 8, 9, 10, 11, 12, 13, 14, 16, 17, 19, 22).
Examples:

22. *Rotation*
Rotation of whole figure or part of it (see Plates 3, 6, 11, 12, 14, 16, 23, 24, 28, 29, 33).
Examples: Rotation or reversal of whole figure

Examples: Two hexagons parallel instead of at an angle; angle between hexagons 90° or more.

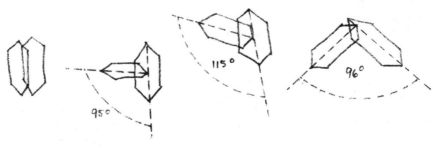

23. *Integration*

Hexagons do not overlap or overlap excessively; one hexagon pene-
trates through other one (see Plates 3, 6, 7, 8, 14, 16, 17, 19, 22, 23,
24, 25).

Examples:

Figure 8

24. *Distortion*
     Distortion of shape; hexagon and/or diamond excessively misshapen;
     extra or missing angles; diamond omitted (see Plates 2, 3, 8, 9, 10, 11,
     12, 13, 14, 16, 18, 20, 22, 23).
     Examples:

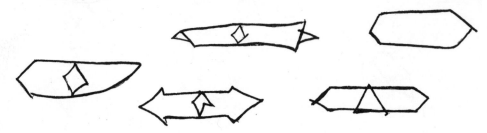

25. *Rotation*
     Rotation of figure by 45° or more; turning of paper in order to make
     most economical use of space and drawing figure in rotated position
     in relation to the other figures is *not* scored, but procedure should be
     noted on the protocol (see Plates 4, 33).
     Examples:

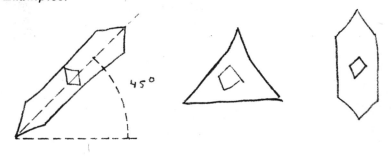

APPENDIX B

Table 13.

Normative Data for Developmental Bender Test Scoring System
*Distribution of Bender Test Mean Scores
and Standard Deviations.*

Age Group	1964 Normative Sample*			1974 Normative Sample†		
	N	Mean	SD	N	Mean	SD
5–0 to 5–5	81	13.2	3.8	47	13.1	3.3
5–6 to 5–6	128	10.2	3.8	130	9.7	3.4
6–0 to 6–5	155	8.0	3.8	175	8.6	3.3
6–6 to 6–11	180	6.4	3.8	60	7.2	3.5
7–0 to 7–5	156	5.1	3.6	61	5.8	3.3
7–6 to 7–11	110	4.2	3.4	47	4.6	2.8
8–0 to 8–5	62	3.4	3.1	53	4.2	2.5
8–6 to 8–11	60	2.7	2.8	60	3.0	2.5
9–0 to 9–5	65	2.2	2.5	78	2.8	2.2
9–6 to 9–11	49	1.8	2.2	47	2.3	2.1
10–0 to 10–5	27	1.5	1.8	76	1.9	1.9
10–6 to 10–11	31	1.2	1.5	68	1.8	1.8
11–0 to 11–11				73	1.4	1.4

*N = 1104, socio-economic cross section; 98% white, 2% non-white.

†N = 975, socio-economic cross section; 86% white, 8.5% black, 1% oriental, and 4.5% Mexican-American and Puerto Rican.

APPENDIX C

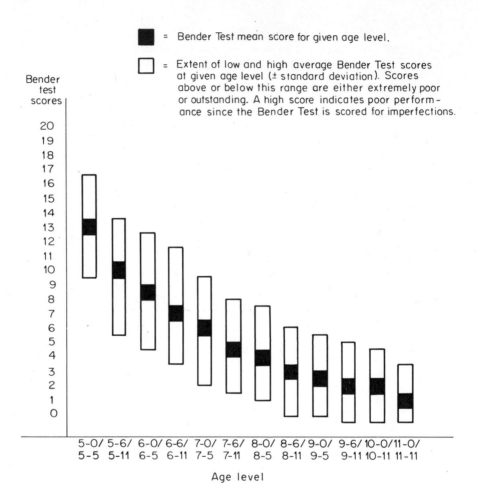

Figure 5. Distribution of Bender Test mean scores and standard deviations. The normative data presented here were derived from the 1974 normative sample, N = 975.

APPENDIX D

Normative Data for Developmental Bender Test Scoring System.
Individual Bender Test Scores and Age Equivalents

Bender Test Score	Age Equivalent	Bender Test Score	Age Equivalent
21	< 4–0	10	5–6 to 5–8
20	4–0	9	5–9 to 5–11
19	4–1	8	6–0 to 6–5
18	4–2 to 4–3	7	6–6 to 6–11
17	4–4 to 4–5	6	7–0 to 7–5
16	4–6 to 4–7	5	7–6 to 7–11
15	4–8 to 4–9	4	8–0 to 8–5
14	4–10 to 4–11	3	8–6 to 8–11
13	5–0 to 5–1	2	9–0 to 9–11
12	5–2 to 5–3	1	10–0 to 10–11
11	5 4 to 5–5	0	11–0 to 11–11

APPENDIX E

Table 15.

Normative Data for Developmental Bender Test Scoring System
*Percentile Scores**

Percentile	Age Level												
	5-0/ 5-5	5-6/ 5-11	6-0/ 6-5	6-6/ 6-11	7-0/ 7-5	7-6/ 7-11	8-0/ 8-5	8-6/ 8-11	9-0/ 9-5	9-6/ 9-11	10-0/ 10-5	10-6/ 10-11	11-0/ 11-11
95	7	4	2	2	1	0	0	0	0	0	0	0	0
90	9	5	3	3	2	1	1	0	0	0	0	0	0
80	10	7	5	4	3	2	2	1	1	1	0	0	0
75	11	8	6	4	3	2	2	1	1	1	0	0	0
70	11	8	6	5	4	3	2	1	1	1	0	0	0
60	12	9	7	6	5	4	3	2	2	1	1	1	1
50	13	10	8	7	6	5	4	3	2	2	1	1	1
40	14	11	9	8	7	6	5	3	3	3	2	2	2
30	15	12	11	9	8	7	6	5	4	3	3	3	2
25	16	12	11	10	8	7	6	5	5	3	3	3	2
20	16	13	12	11	9	8	7	6	5	4	4	3	3
10	19	15	14	13	12	9	8	7	6	6	5	4	3
5	21	16	15	14	13	10	9	8	8	7	6	5	4

*Percentile scores were derived from the 1974 normative sample, N = 975.

REFERENCES

Ackerman PT, Peters JE, Dykman RA: Children with specific learning disabilities: Bender Gestalt Test findings and other signs. J Learning Disabilities 4:437–446, 1971

Adams J, Canter A: Performance characteristics of school children on the BIP Bender Test. J Consult Psychol 33:508, 1969

Adams J: Canter Background Interference Procedure applied to the diagnosis of brain damage in mentally retarded children. Am J Ment Defic 75:57–64, 1970

Adams J, Lieb JJ: Canter, BIP and Draw-A-Person test performance of Negro and Caucasian children. Psychology in the Schools 10:299–304, 1973

Adams J, Hayden B, Canter A: The relationship between the Canter Background Interference Procedure and the hyperkinetic behavior syndrome. J Learning Disabilities 7:110–115, 1974

Adams J, Kenny TJ, Canter A: The efficacy of the Canter Background Interference Procedure in identifying children with cerebral dysfunction. J Consult Clin Psychol 40:489, 1973

Allen RM, Frank GH: Experimental variation of the mode of reproduction of the Bender Gestalt stimuli. J Clin Psychol 19:212–214, 1963

Allen RM: Experimental variation of the mode of reproduction of the Bender Gestalt stimuli by mental retardates. J Clin Psychol 24:199–202, 1968

Allen RM, Adamo C, Alker LN, Levine MN: A study of recognition and reproduction of Bender Gestalt figures by children of average and below intelligence. J Genet Psychol 119:75–78, 1971

Ames LB: Children with perceptual problems may also lag developmentally. J Learning Disabilities 2:205–208, 1969

Baer DJ, Gale RH: Intelligence and Bender Gestalt Test performance of institutionalized and noninstitutionalized school children. J Genet Psychol 111:119–124, 1967

Becker JT: Spatial orientation and visual discrimination. Percept Mot Skills 31:943–946, 1970

Becker JT, Sabatino DA: Reliability of individual tests on perception administered utilizing group techniques. J Clin Psychol 27:86–88, 1971

Becker JT, Sabatino DA: Frostig revisited. J Learning Disabilities 6:180–184, 1973

Beery KE: Developmental Test of Visual-Motor-Integration. Chicago, Follett Educational Corp, 1967

Bender L: A Visual Motor Gestalt Test and Its Clinical Use. Research Monograph No 3. New York, American Orthopsychiatric Association, 1938

Bender L: Bender Motor Gestalt Test: Cards and Manual of Instructions. New York, American Orthopsychiatric Association, 1946

Bender L: On the proper use of the Bender Gestalt Test. Percept Mot Skills 20:189–190, 1965

Bender L: Visual motor Gestalt function in six and seven year old normal and schizophrenic children, in Jervis GA, Zubin J (eds): Psychopathology of Mental Development. New York, Grune & Stratton, 1967

Bender L: Bender Motor Gestalt Test: Set of Nine 35 mm Slides of Test Cards. New York, American Orthopsychiatric Association, 1969

Bender L: Use of the Visual Motor Gestalt Test in the diagnosis of learning disabilities. J Special Educ 4:29–39, 1970

Billingslea FY: The Bender Gestalt: A review and perspective. Psychol Bull 60:233–251, 1963

Bishop S: The validity of the Slingerland Screening Test for identifying children with specific language disabilities for a sample of second grade children. MA thesis, California State University at San Jose, 1966

Black FW: Reversal and rotation errors by normal and retarded readers. Percept Mot Skills 36:895–898, 1973

Bravo L: A study of the secondary emotional effects of underlying neurological handicap in sectors of the Mexican school population. Paper presented to the California Association of School Psychologists, San Francisco, March 1971

Bravo L: The conservation, stimulation, and development of superior mental ability. Paper presented to the California Association of School Psychologists, 1972

Bravo VL: Psychological tests in the diagnosis of infantile minimal cerebral dysfunction. Revista Latinoamericana de Psicologia 5:131–141, 1973

Brenner MW, Gillman S, Zangwill OC, Farrell M: Visuo-motor disability in school children. Br Med J 4:259–262, 1967

Brown F: The Bender Gestalt and acting out, in Abt LE (ed): Acting Out, Theoretical and Clinical Aspects. New York, Grune & Stratton, 1965, pp 320–332

Cabrini M: Bender Gestalt Test as a measure of reading readiness. MA thesis, St. John College, Cleveland, 1968

Canter A: A background interference procedure for graphomotor tests in the study of deficit. Percept Mot Skills 16:914, 1963

Caskey WE: A comparison of a group Bender Visual Motor Gestalt Test with the individual Visual Motor Gestalt Test with kindergarten children and the relationship of the two Bender Tests with IQ. PhD dissertation, Kent State University, 1973

Cellura AR, Butterfield EC: Intelligence, the Bender Gestalt Test and reading achievement. Am J Ment Defic 71:60–63, 1966

Cerbus G, Oziel IJ: Correlation of the Bender Gestalt and WISC for Negro children. Percept Mot Skills 32:276, 1971

Champion DW: A comparison of the Human Figure Drawing, Bender Visual Motor Gestalt, and a behavior rating scale in identifying children with emotional disturbance. MA thesis, San Jose State College, 1967

Chang TM, Chang VA: Relation of visual-motor skills and reading achievement in primary-grade pupils of superior ability. Percept Mot Skills 24:51–53, 1967

Choynowski M: Curve-fitting as a method of statistical correction of developmental norms, shown on the example of the Bender-Koppitz Test. J Clin Psychol 26:135–141, 1970

Clarke BR, Leslie PT: Visual-motor skills and reading ability of deaf children. Percept Mot Skills 33:263–268, 1971

Condell J: The Bender Gestalt Test with mentally retarded children using the Koppitz revised scoring system. J Clin Psychol 19:430–431, 1963

Connor JP: Bender Gestalt Test performance as a predictor of differential reading performance. J School Psychology 7:41–44, 1969

Culbertson FM, Gunn RC: Comparison of the Bender Gestalt Test and Frostig Test in several clinic groups of children. J Clin Psychol 22:439, 1966

Dibner AS, Korn EJ: Group administration of the Bender Gestalt Test to predict early school performance. J Clin Psychol 25:265–268, 1969

Dierks D, Cushna B: Sex differences in the Bender Gestalt performance of children. Percept Mot Skills 28:19–22, 1969

Dinmore GC: Developmental Bender Gestalt performance as a function of educational setting and sex of young Negro children. PhD dissertation, University of Pennsylvania, 1972

Doubros SG, Mascarenhas J: Relations among Wechsler Full Scale scores, organicity-sensitive subtest scores and Bender-Gestalt error scores. Percept Mot Skills 29:719–722, 1969

Dykman RA, Peters JE, Ackerman PT: Experimental approaches to the study of minimal brain dysfunction: A follow-up study. Ann NY Acad Sci 205:93–108, 1973

Edington G: The use of the Bender-Gestalt in the personality assessment of deaf teenage girls. Thesis, New York University, 1971

Egeland B, Rice J, Penny S: Inter-scorer reliability on the Bender Gestalt Test and the revised Visual Retention Test. Am J Ment Defic 72:96–99, 1967

Elliott JA: A validation study of the Koppitz and Pascal and Suttell systems with eleven through fourteen year old children. Thesis, University of Michigan, 1968

Fiedler MF, Schmidt EP: Sex differences in Bender-Gestalt drawings of seven-year old children. Percept Mot Skills 29:753–754, 1969

Fischer CT: Contextual approach to assessment. Community Mental Health J 9:38–45, 1973

Fisher S: Learning disabilities in children: Sibling studies IV. Two tests of perceptual-motor function: The Draw-a-Person and the Bender-Gestalt. Bull Orton Soc 18:55–61, 1967

Flick GL, Duncan C: Perceptual-motor dysfunction in children with sickle cell trait. Percept Mot Skills 36:234, 1973

Flint FS: A validation and developmental study of some interpretations of the Bender Gestalt Test. PhD dissertation, New York University, 1966

Friedman J, Strochak RD, Gitlin S, Gottsagen ML: Koppitz' Bender scoring system and brain injury in children. J Clin Psychol 23:179–182, 1967

Fromm DM: A study of some factors in the Bender Gestalt reproductions of well adjusted and poorly adjusted boys with particular emphasis upon the interpretive processes. PhD dissertation, University of Oklahoma, 1966

Frostig M, Lefever W, Whittlesey J: A Developmental Test of Visual Perception for evaluating normal and neurological children. Percept Mot Skills 12:383–394, 1961

Fuller GB, Laird JT: The Minnesota Percepto-Diagnostic Test (MPD). J Clin Psychol vol 19, Monograph Supplement No 16, 1963

Fuller GB: The Minnesota Percepto-Diagnostic Test (revised). J Clin Psychol vol 25, Monograph Supplement No 28, 1969

Furr KD: Standard scores for the Koppitz Developmental Scoring System. J Clin Psychol 26:78–79, 1970

Garron DC, Cheifetz DI: Comment on Bender Gestalt discernment of organic pathology. Psychol Bull 63:197–200, 1965

Giebink JW, Birch R: The Bender Gestalt Test as an ineffective predictor of reading achievement. J Clin Psychol 26:484–485, 1970

Gilbert JG, Levee RF: Performances of deaf and normally hearing children on the Bender Gestalt and the Archimedes spiral test. Percept Mot Skills 24:1059–1066, 1967

Goff AF: An empirical study of reliability and concurrent validity for the Koppitz scoring system of the Bender Gestalt Test with primary school children. PhD dissertation, Southern Illinois University, 1968

Goff AF, Parker A: Reliability of the Koppitz scoring system for the Bender Gestalt Test. J Clin Psychol 25:407–409, 1969

Gravitz HL: Examiner expectancy effects in psychological assessment: The Bender Visual Motor Gestalt Test. PhD dissertation, University of Tennessee, 1969

Greene R, Clark FK: Predicting reading readiness with the Bender Gestalt Test in minority students. Personal communication, 1973

Grinde T: Barn med hjerneskader og vanførhet livssituasjon og personlighetstreek. Nordisk Psykologi 24:128–135, 1972

Hain JD: A scoring method for identifying brain damage. J Consult Psychol 28:34–40, 1964

Hammer GT: The group Bender Gestalt Test as a predictor of academic potential in first grade with attention of environmental effects. PhD dissertation, University of California at Los Angeles, 1967

Handler L, McIntosh J: Predicting aggression and withdrawal in children with the Draw-a-Person and Bender Gestalt. J Personality Assessment 35:331–337, 1971

Hanvick L: A note on rotation in the Bender Gestalt Test as predictors of EEG abnormalities in children. J Clin Psychol 9:399, 1953

Hartlage LC, Lucas DG: Scaled score transformations of Bender Gestalt expectancy levels for young children. Psychology in the Schools 8:76–78, 1971

Hartman RK: An investigation of the incremental validity of human figure drawings in the diagnosis of learning disabilities. J School Psychology 10:9–16, 1972

Hayden BS, Talmadge M, Hall M, Schiff D: Diagnosing minimal brain damage in children: A comparison of two scoring systems. Merrill-Palmer Quarterly of Behavior and Development 16:278–285, 1970

Heinrich MJ: Sources of visual-motor dysfunctions associated with some cases of reading disorder. PhD dissertation, Cornell University, 1968

Henderson NB, Butler BV, Gaffeney B: Effectiveness of the WISC and Bender Gestalt test in predicting arithmetic and reading achievement for white and nonwhite children. J Clin Psychol 25:268–271, 1969

Hoffman SD: The Bender Gestalt Test: A crosscultural test? PhD dissertation, University of Oklahoma, 1966

Holroyd J: Crossvalidation of the Quast and Koppitz Bender-Gestalt signs of cerebral dysfunctioning. J Clin Psychol 22:200, 1966

Holroyd RG: On the translation of Koppitz' normative data into standard scores: A response to Furr. J Clin Psychol 27:88, 1971

Howard J: The group Bender Gestalt Test as a screening procedure for the identification of children with lag in visual perceptual development. J School Psychology 8:64–65, 1970

Hunter EJ, Johnson LC: Developmental and psychological differences between readers and nonreaders. J Learning Disabilities 4:572–577, 1971

Hutt M, Briskin GJ: The Clinical Use of the Revised Bender Gestalt Test. New York, Grune & Stratton, 1960

Hutton JB: Bender recall of children as related to age and intelligence. Percept Mot Skills 23:34, 1966

Isaac B: Perceptual-motor development of first graders related to class, race, IQ, visual discrimination and motivation. EdD dissertation, Rutgers University, 1971

Isaac B: Perceptual-motor development of first graders related to class, race, intelligence, visual discrimination and motivation. J School Psychology 11:47–55, 1973

Jacobs JC: Group administration of the Bender Gestalt Test. Psychology in the Schools 8:345–346, 1971

Jastak JF, Bijou SW, Jastak SR: Wide Range Achievement Test (rev ed). Wilmington, Guidance Associates, 1965

Jessen M, Prendergast L: An investigation of the effects of early perceptual training in Kindergarten and first grade on reading success. Paper presented to the California Association of Education Research, 1965

Jost KC: Validity of the Koppitz Developmental Bender Scoring system in the prediction of EEG abnormality in young children. Personal communication, 1969

Kagan J, Klein RE: Cross-cultural perspectives on early development. Am Psychol 28:947–961, 1973

Kai T: The correlation between the Emotional Indicators (EI) of the Bender Gestalt Test and the emotional problems in younger children. Memoirs of the Faculty of Education, Kumamoto University, 18, section 2, 1970

Kai T: An examination of Koppitz Bender Gestalt Test (II): The correlation between each item of Emotional Indicators (EI) and the emotional problems in younger children. Memoirs of the Faculty of Education, Kumamoto University, 20, section 2, 1972

Kaspar JC, Lampel AK: Interrater reliability for scoring the Bender Gestalt using the Koppitz method. Percept Mot Skills 34:765–766, 1972

Kawaguchi M: A developmental study of the Bender Gestalt Test. Jap J Educ Psychol 18:58, 1970

Keim RP: Visual-motor training, readiness, and intelligence of kindergarten children. J Learning Disabilities 3:256–259, 1970

Kelly TJ, Amble BR: IQ and perceptual motor scores as predictors of achievement among retarded children. J School Psychology 8:99–102, 1970

Keogh B, Smith: Group techniques and proposed scoring system for the Bender Gestalt Test with children. J Clin Psychol 17:172–175, 1961

Keogh BK: The Bender Gestalt as a predictive and diagnostic test of reading performance. J Consult Psychol 29:83–84, 1965a

Keogh BK: School achievement associated with successful performance on the Bender Gestalt Test. J School Psychology 3:37–40, 1965b

Keogh BK, Smith CE: Visuo-motor ability for school prediction: A seven year study. Percept Mot Skills 25:101–110, 1967

Keogh BK: The Bender Gestalt with children: Research implications. Paper presented at the APA convention, San Francisco, 1968a

Keogh BK: The copying ability of young children. New Research in Education 11:43–47, 1968b

Keogh BK, Smith CE: Changes in copying ability of young children. Percept Mot Skills 26: 773–774, 1968

Keogh BK, Smith CE: Early identification of educationally high potential and high risk children. Paper presented at the APA convention, Washington, 1969

Keogh BK, Vormeland O: Performance of Norwegian children on the Bender Gestalt and Draw-a-Person tests. Scand J Educ 14:105–111, 1970

Keogh BK, Vernon M, Smith CE: Deafness and visual-motor function. J Special Education 4:41–47, 1970

Kerr AS: Determinants of performance of the Bender Gestalt Test and Raven's Progressive Matrices (1947) Test. J Learning Disabilities 5:219–221, 1972

Klatskin EH, McNamara NE, Shaffer D, Pincus J: Minimal organicity in children of normal intelligence: Correspondence between psychological test results and neurological findings. J Learning Disabilities 5:213–218, 1972

Koppitz EM: The Bender Gestalt Test for Young Children. New York, Grune & Stratton, 1963

Koppitz EM: Use of the Bender Gestalt Test in elementary school. Skolepsykologi 2:193–200, 1965

Koppitz EM: Psychological Evaluation of Children's Human Figure Drawings. New York, Grune & Stratton, 1968

Koppitz EM: The Visual Aural Digit Span Test with elementary school children. J Clin Psychol 26:349–353, 1970a

Koppitz EM: Brain damage, reading disability and the Bender Gestalt Test. J Learning Disabilities 3:429–433, 1970b

Koppitz EM: Children with Learning Disabilities: A Five Year Follow-up Study. New York, Grune & Stratton, 1971

Koppitz EM: The Visual Aural Digit Span Test: Experimental Edition. Mount Kisco, NY, Koppitz, 1972

Koppitz EM: Visual Aural Digit Span Test performance of boys with emotional and learning problems. J Clin Psychol 29:463–466, 1973a

Koppitz EM: Bender Gestalt Test performance and school achievement: A nine year study. Psychology in the Schools 10:280–284, 1973b

Koppitz EM: Bender Gestalt Test, Visual Aural Digit Span Test and reading achievement. J Learning Disabilities 1975 (in press)

Krauft VR, Krauft CC: Structured vs. unstructured visual-motor tests for educable retarded children. Percept Mot Skills 34:691–694, 1972

Lambert NM: An evaluation of scoring categories applicable to children's performance on the Bender Visual Motor Gestalt Test. Psychology in the Schools 7:275–287, 1970

Lambert NM: An item analysis and validity investigation of Bender Visual Motor Gestalt Test score items. Psychology in the Schools 8:78–85, 1971

Landmark M, Grinde T: Children's Bender drawings from 1938 to 1962. Copenhagen, Monograph, Nord Psykol, 1964

Lenstrup M: A comparative study of psychotic and brain-injured children. Copenhagen, Ejnar Munsksgaards Forlag, 1968

Lubin B, Wallis RR, Paine C: Patterns of psychological test usage in the United States: 1935–1969. Professional Psychology 2:70–74, 1971

Maloney MP, Ward MP: Bender Gestalt performance of "organic" and "functional" mentally retarded subjects. Percept Mot Skills 31:860, 1970

Marmorale A, Brown F: Mental health intervention in the primary grades. Monograph No 7, Community Mental Health J, 1974

Marsh GG: Impaired visual-motor ability of children with Duchenne muscular distrophy. Percept Mot Skills 35:504–506, 1972

Maslow P, Frostig M, Lefever D, Whittlesley J: The Marianne Frostig Developmental Test of Visual Perception, 1963 standardization. Percept Mot Skills 19:463–499, 1964

McCarthy DP: The feasibility of a group Bender Gestalt Test for preschool and primary school-aged children. EdD dissertation, University of Northern Colorado, 1972

McConnell OL: Koppitz' Bender-Gestalt scores in relation to organic and emotional problems in children. J Clin Psychol 23:370–374, 1967

McNamara JR, Porterfield CL, Miller LE: The relationship of the Wechsler Preschool and Primary Scale of Intelligence with the colored Progressive Matrices (1956) and Bender Gestalt Test. J Clin Psychol 25:65–68, 1969

McQuarrie CW: A perceptual testing and training guide for kindergarten teachers. Winterhaven, Fla, Lions Research Foundation, 1967

Miller LC, Loewenfeld R, Lindner R, Turner J: Reliability of Koppitz' scoring system for the Bender Gestalt. J Clin Psychol 19:2111, 1963

Mlodnosky LB: The Bender Gestalt and the Frostig as predictors of first-grade reading achievement among economically deprived children. Psychology in the Schools 9:25–30, 1972

Moeller CE: Preferences for orientation and figure rotation by young children in copying and recall. PhD dissertation, George Washington University, 1972

Mogin LS: Administration and objective scoring of the Bender Gestalt Test in group screening of primary grade children for emotional maladjustment. PhD dissertation. Rutgers State University, 1966

Morgenstern M, McIvor W: The relationship between Bender Gestalt performance and achievement among retardates. Training School Bulletin 70:84–87, 1973

Moseley D: Performance of deprived children on the Bender Gestalt Test. PhD dissertation, South Central Region Education Lab, University of Oklahoma, 1969

Murphy GM: Visual-motor coordination and perception at the beginning of first grade. Personal communication, 1964

Naches AM: The Bender Gestalt Test and acting our behavior in children. EdD dissertation, Colorado State College, 1967

Newcomer P, Hammill D: Visual perception of motor impaired children: Implications for assessment. Except Child 39:335–337, 1973

Nielsen HH, Ringe K: Visuo-perceptive and visuo-motor performance of children with reading disabilities. Scand J Psychol 10:225–231, 1969

Norfleet MA: The Bender Gestalt as a group screening instrument for first grade reading potential. J Learning Disabilities 6:384–388, 1973

Oberstein R: Bender, IQ, and reading tests. MA thesis, Brightwaters, NY, 1968

Obrzut JE, Taylor HD, Thweatt RC: Re-examination of Koppitz' Developmental Bender Scoring System. Percept Mot Skills 34:279–282, 1972

Oliver RA, Kronenberger EJ: Testing the applicability of Koppitz' Bender Gestalt scores to brain-damaged, emotionally disturbed and normal adolescents. Psychology in the Schools 8:250–253, 1971

Orme JE: A practical guide to estimate intelligence, attainments and intellectual deficit. Acta Psychol 32:145–161, 1970

Pascal G, Suttell B: The Bender Gestalt Test. New York, Grune & Stratton, 1951

Patel S, Bharucha EP: The Bender Gestalt Test as a measure of perceptual and visuo-motor defects in cerebral palsied children. Dev Med Child Neurol 14:156–160, 1972

Plenk AM, Jones J: An examination of the Bender Gestalt performance of three and four year olds and its relationship to Koppitz scoring system. J Clin Psychol 23:367–370, 1967

Plenk AM: Development of a scoring system for the Bender Gestalt Test for children of preschool age. PhD dissertation, University of Utah, 1968

Pope P, Snyder RT: Modification of selected Bender Designs and interpretation of the first graders' visual-perceptual maturation with implications for Gestalt theory. Percept Mot Skills 30:263–267, 1970

Quast W: The Bender Gestalt: A clinical study of children's records. J Consult Psychol 25:405–408, 1961

Raven JC: The Coloured Progressive Matrices (Revised order 1956). London, H.K. Lewis, 1965

Rice JA: Feasibility of perceptual-motor training for Headstart children: An empirical test. Percept Mot Skills 34:909–910, 1972

Rimmer A, Weiss AA: A model of conceptual development for the Bender Gestalt Test. Isr Ann Psychiatry 10:188–196, 1972

Rock I: The perception of disoriented figures. Sci Am 230:78–85, 1974

Routh DK, Roberts RD: Minimal brain dysfunction in children: Failure to find evidence for a behavioral syndrome. Psychol Rep 31:307–314, 1972

Ruckhaber CJ: A technique for group administration of the Bender Gestalt Test. Psychology in the Schools 1:53–56, 1964

Ryckman DB, Rentfrow R, Fargo G, McCartin R: Reliabilities of three tests of form-copying. Percept Mot Skills 34:917–918, 1972

Sabatino DA, Cramblett HG: Behavioral sequelae of California Encephalitis Virus infection in children. Dev Med Child Neurol 10:331–333, 1968

Sabatino DA, Becker JT: Relations among five basic tests of behavior. Percept Mot Skills 29: 487–490, 1969

Sabatino DA, Ysseldyke JE: Effect of extraneous "background" on visual-perceptual performance of readers and non-readers. Percept Mot Skills 35:323–328, 1972

Satz P, Rardin D, Ross J: An evaluation of a theory of specific developmental dyslexia. Child Dev 42:2009–2021, 1971

Savering FR: Children's Bender Gestalt Drawings in relation to maturity and behavior ratings. MA thesis, Southern Connecticut State College, 1968

Schlange H, Stein B, von Boetticher I, Taneli S: Göttinger Formreproduktions-Test (G-F-T) zur Diagnose der Hirnschädigung im Kindesalter. Göttingen, Verlag für Psychologie, 1972

Schoolcraft DR: The effectiveness of the Bender Gestalt Test for children and the knowledge of letter names in the prediction of reading achievement with first grade children in a rural area. PhD dissertation, University of Georgia, 1972

Seifert JG: The relationship between visual-motor perception and the speed of eye movements by selected boys. PhD dissertation, Kent State University, 1967

Shaw MC, Cruickshank WM: The use of the Bender Gestalt Test with epileptic children. J Clin Psychol 12:192–193, 1956

Sheffer P: The group Bender Gestalt Test to determine near and far perception and transfer in children. Personal communication, 1970

Silberberg N, Feldt L: Intellectual and perceptual correlates of reading difficulties. J School Psychology 6:237–245, 1968

Singh B: The Bender-Gestalt Test as a group test. Ontario J Educ Res 8:35–45, 1965

Skore ML: The use of the Bender Gestalt in assessing latent intellectual ability of culturally disadvantaged children. PhD dissertation, Wayne State University, 1968

Slingerland BH: Teacher's manual to accompany scoring technique for identifying children with specific language disabilities. Cambridge, Mass, Educators' Publishing Service, 1964

Smith CE, Keogh BK: Developmental changes on the Bender Gestalt Test. Percept Mot Skills 17:465–466, 1963

Smith DC, Martin RA: Use of learning cues with the Bender Visual Motor Gestalt Test in screening children for neurological impairment. J Consult Psychol 31:205–209, 1967

Snyder RT, Freud SL: Reading readiness and its relation to maturational unreadiness as measured by the spiral after-effect and other visual-perceptual techniques. Percept Mot Skills 25:841–854, 1967

Snyder RT, Kalil J: Item analysis, inter-examiner reliability and scoring problems for Koppitz scoring on the Bender Gestalt for six-year olds. Percept Mot Skills 27:1351–1358, 1968

Snyder RT, Pope P: The Bender Gestalt Visual Memory Technique for children. Original norms and scoring procedure. Paper presented at the National Convention of the National Association of School Psychologists, 1970

Solomon SJ: A comparison of performance on group and individual administrations of the Bender Visual Motor Gestalt Test using the Koppitz scoring system. MA thesis, California State University at San Jose, 1969

Sonoda T: The Bender Gestalt Test for young children. A review of the verification studies made on Koppitz' scoring system. Kumamoto Shodai Ronshu 27:1–24, 1968

Sonoda T: A study of the Bender Gestalt Test by Koppitz scoring system to the Japanese children. Kumamoto Tandai Ronshu 42:1–6, 1971

Sonoda T: A study of the development of visual-motor perception. Kumamoto Shodai Ronshu 37:1–9, 1973

Stadler A: Visual perception and first grade reading achievement. MA thesis, San Jose State University, 1966

Stavrianos BK: Can projective test measures aid in the detection and differential diagnosis of reading deficits? J Projective Techniq Person Asses 35:80–91, 1971

Sternlicht M, Pustel G, Siegel L: Comparisons of organic and cultural familial retardates on two visual-motor tasks. Am J Ment Defic 72:887–889, 1968

Taylor HD, Thweatt RC: Cross-cultural developmental performance of Navajo Children on the Bender Gestalt Test. Percept Mot Skills 35:307–309, 1972

Thweatt RC: Prediction of school learning disability through the use of the Bender Gestalt Test: A validation study of Koppitz' scoring technique. J Clin Psychol 19:216–217, 1963

Thweatt RC, Obrzut JE, Taylor HD: The development and validation of a soft-sign scoring system for the Bender Gestalt. Psychology in the Schools 9:170–174, 1972

Tiedeman R: A comparison of seven-year olds around the world. Lecture, San Jose State College, June 1971

Tolor A: The graphomotor techniques. J Project Techniq Person Assess 32:222–228, 1968

Tolor A, Schulberg H: An evaluation of the Bender Gestalt Test. Springfield, Ill, Charles C Thomas, 1963

Van de Vegte HG: Bender and EEG of emotionally disturbed children. Personal communication, 1965

Von de Voort L, Senf GM: Audiovisual integration in retarded readers. J Learning Disabilities 6:170–179, 1973

Vega M, Powell A: The effects of practice on Bender Gestalt performance of culturally disadvantaged children. Florida J Educ Research 12:45–49, 1970

Vormeland O: The Bender Gestalt Test as a group test with young school children. Scand J Educ Research 12:21–38, 1968

Wagner EE, Murray A: Bender-Gestalts of organic children: Accuracy of clinical judgment. J Project Techniq Person Assess 33:240–242, 1969

Walker RN, Streff J: A perceptual program for classroom teachers: Some results. Genet Psychol Monog, May 1973

Walraven MP: Perceptual relationships: Personality–reading. PhD dissertation, University of Oklahoma, 1966

Wedell K, Horne IE: Some aspects of perceptuo-motor disability in five and a half year old children. Br J Educ Psychol 39:174–182, 1969

Weiss AA: Directionality in four Bender-Gestalt figures. Percept Mot Skills 29:59–62, 1969

Weiss AA: Reproduction from memory and frequency of recall of Bender-Gestalt figures in non-clinical subjects of different ages. Isr Ann Psychiatry 8:143–145, 1970

Weiss AA: The influence of sheet positions on placements of Bender-Gestalt figures. Isr Ann Psychiatry 9:63–67, 1971a

Weiss AA: Directionality in four Bender-Gestalt figures II. Percept Mot Skills 32:412–414, 1971b

Weiss AA: Incidence of rotations of Bender-Gestalt figures in three age groups of normal Israeli school children. Percept Mot Skills 32:691–694, 1971c

Werner EE, Simonian K, Smith RS: Reading achievement, language functioning and perceptual-motor development of ten and eleven year olds. Percept Mot Skills 25:409–420, 1967

Wertheimer W: Studies in the theory of Gestalt Psychology. Psychol Forsch vol 4, 1923

Wewetzer KH: Das hirngeschädigte Kind. Stuttgart, G Thieme Verlag, 1959

Wiener G, Rider VR, Oppel WC, Fischer LK, Harper PA: Correlates of low birth weight: Psychological status at six to seven years of age. Pediatrics 35:434–444, 1965

Wiener G, Rider VR, Oppel WC, Harper PA: Correlates of low birth weight: Psychological status at eight to ten years of age. Pediatr Res 2:110–118, 1968

Wiener G: The Bender Gestalt Test as a predictor of minimal neurological deficit in children eight to ten years of age. J Nerv Ment Dis 143:275–280, 1966

Wile DB: Age and pathology differences in Bender-Gestalt performance. PhD dissertation, University of California, Berkeley, 1965

Wise JH: Stick copying of designs by preschool and young school-age children. Percept Mot Skills 27:1159–1168, 1968

Zach L, Kaufman J: The effect of verbal learning on visual motor performance. J Learning Disabilities 2:218–222, 1969

Zach L, Kaufman J: How adequate is the concept of perceptual deficit for education? J Learning Disabilities 5:351–356, 1972

Index

c
d
e
8 f
9 g
0 h
1 i
8 2 j